A New Narrative for Psychology

Explorations in Narrative Psychology

Mark Freeman
Series Editor

Books in the Series

Speaking of Violence
Sara Cobb

Narrative Imagination and Everyday Life
Molly Andrews

Narratives of Positive Aging: Seaside Stories
Amia Lieblich

Beyond the Archive: Memory, Narrative, and the Autobiographical Process
Jens Brockmeier

The Narrative Complexity of Ordinary Life: Tales from the Coffee Shop
William L. Randall

Rethinking Thought: Inside the Minds of Creative Scientists and Artists
Laura Otis

Life and Narrative: The Risks and Responsibilities of Storying Experience
Edited by Brian Schiff, Sylvie Patron, and A. Elizabeth McKim

Not in My Family: German Memory and Responsibility After the Holocaust
Roger Frie

A New Narrative for Psychology
Brian Schiff

A New Narrative
for Psychology

Brian Schiff

OXFORD
UNIVERSITY PRESS

OXFORD
UNIVERSITY PRESS

Oxford University Press is a department of the University of Oxford. It furthers
the University's objective of excellence in research, scholarship, and education
by publishing worldwide. Oxford is a registered trade mark of Oxford University
Press in the UK and certain other countries.

Published in the United States of America by Oxford University Press
198 Madison Avenue, New York, NY 10016, United States of America.

© Oxford University Press 2017

Library of Congress Cataloging-in-Publication Data
Names: Schiff, Brian, author.
Title: A new narrative for psychology / Brian Schiff.
Description: New York, NY : Oxford University Press, [2017] |
Series: Explorations in narrative psychology | Includes bibliographical references.
Identifiers: LCCN 2016056183 | ISBN 9780199332182 (hardcover : alk. paper)
Subjects: LCSH: Psychology—Research. | Narrative inquiry (Research method)
Classification: LCC BF76.5.S295 2017 | DDC 150.72—dc23
LC record available at https://lccn.loc.gov/2016056183

9 8 7 6 5 4 3 2 1

Printed by Sheridan Books, Inc., United States of America

To Mathilde, Ella, Max, and Annabelle, for all your love and for our shared hopes for the future.

CONTENTS

ACKNOWLEDGMENTS

Although, in many ways, I have always been a psychologist, I have always had a feeling that the psychology that I studied was inadequate to get at the problems that really bothered me—about the mystery of my life and the puzzling lives of others. I know that many of us feel the same way.

This book is primarily addressed to the next generation of psychologists, those interested in the discipline casually or as a career, who wish to know something more, or something more deeply, about persons and why we live the lives that we do, and to those who, optimistically and idealistically, want to understand others and begin the process of change and renewal that the discipline and this world so desperately need. I sincerely hope that this work will be the starting point in your reflections.

I am infinitely indebted to my colleagues who read through various drafts of this manuscript and generously gave me their insights and critiques: Jens Brockmeier, Matti Hyvärinen, Jim Lamiell, Hanna Meretoja, Bill Randall, Brent Slife, Brett Smith, and the members of the Personological Society. But I would like to most especially thank my series editor and friend, Mark Freeman, who read through the entire manuscript and told me, frankly, how to make it better. Mark, I hope that I did the argument justice.

I would like to acknowledge the support of the Cherrick Center for the Study of Zionism, the Yishuv and the State of Israel, and the Harry S. Truman Research Institute for the Advancement of Peace, who funded my research on Palestinian students at the Hebrew University of Jerusalem that is featured in this book.

I want to thank the administration at the American University of Paris for believing in this project and believing in me—thank you, Celeste Schenk, Valerie Gille, Neil Gordon, and Scott Springer.

I would also like to thank Abby Gross, Courtney McCarroll and the staff at Oxford University Press for your hard work and commitment to this book.

Thank you to my friends and colleagues who have been conversation partners over the years and have helped along my thinking: Zvi Bekerman, Brian de Vries, Phil Hammack, Bill Hirst, Ruthellen Josselson, Sharon Kangisser-Cohen, Gary Kenyon, Christin Köber, Michele Koven, Nadia Masarweh, Ruth Mayo, Beth McKim, Thomas Michael, Chaim Noy, Sylvie Patron, Deborah Schiffrin, and Anneke Sools.

Thanks to my supportive colleagues at the American University of Paris (George Allyn, Jens Brockmeier, Kersten Carlson, Kathleen Chevalier, Seta Kazandjian, Sharman Levinson, Lissa Lincoln, Paschale McCarthy, Maria Medved, Claudia Roda, and Charles Talcott), Saint Martin's University (Russell Hollander, Jeanette Munn, David Price, and Rona Ruben), and Wellesley College (Jonathan Cheek, Tracy Gleason, Julie Norem, and Paul Wink).

I would like to thank my wonderful students from the American University of Paris, Saint Martin's University, and Wellesley College, who have helped me in this journey, each in their own way, and have been a critical voice and source of inspiration. I would especially like to thank Fanie Collardeau, Carolina Porto, Emilie Quenensse, Mathilde Toulemonde, and Acadia Webber who contributed to the interview projects discussed in this book. To all of my students, I hope that you have learned as much from me as I have learned from you.

I am indebted to my teachers, Elliot Mishler, Peter Novick, Jimmy Reeves, Rick Shweder, and Tom Trabasso. I would especially like to acknowledge Amia Lieblich and Bert Cohler (1938–2012). Amia's guidance, wisdom, and attentive ear have been a constant source of support and strength over many years. Bert's thoughts, voice, and presence resound throughout this text.

Finally, to my wonderful and loving family (Norman and Nettie, Meyer and Rose, Judy and Howard, Larry and Sandra, Caroline and Francis, Mark, Scott, Gwen, and Sasha, Maryse, Renée, Louis, Caroline, Lucie, and Maya), thank you for sharing your lives and love with me.

I have been working on many of the ideas in *A New Narrative for Psychology* over a number of years. Although the work is substantially rethought and revised, some of the arguments are based upon my previous writing, including the following: Schiff, B. (2013). Fractured narratives: Psychology's fragmented narrative psychology. In M. Hyvärinen, M., Hatavara & L. C. Hydén (Eds.), *The travelling concepts of narrative* (pp. 245–264). Amsterdam: John Benjamins; Schiff, B. (2012). The function of narrative: Toward a narrative psychology of meaning. *Narrative Works: Issues, Investigations & Interventions,* 2(1), 34–47; Schiff, B., Toulemonde, M. & Porto, C. (2012). Identity in the first person plural: Muslim-Jewish couples in France. In R. Josselson & M. Haraway (Eds.), *Navigating multiple identities: Race, gender, culture, nationality, and roles* (pp. 167–186). New York: Oxford University Press; Schiff, B. (2006). The promise (and challenge) of an innovative narrative psychology. *Narrative Inquiry, 16*(1), 19–27. I am very grateful that I have had the opportunity to formulate these ideas into a comprehensive argument and to present them to a large readership.

PART I

Introduction

What's the Problem?

Is there a problem? It depends on who you talk to. For most insiders, there isn't a problem. Contemporary psychology is doing just fine. The discipline is progressing toward ever more accurate and powerful models of human thought and action. For others, the problem is that psychology is outdated and obsolete—about to be replaced by a version of evolutionary psychology or brain science.

For others still, the problem is that our methods are inexact and need to be fine-tuned. Indeed, psychology recently witnessed a major controversy over the reproducibility of psychological research. Published in *Science*, the controversy centered on the Open Science Collaboration's (2015) finding that a mere 39 out of 100 experimental and correlational studies published in top-tiered journals (*Psychological Science, Journal of Personality*, and *Journal of Experimental Psychology: Learning, Memory, and Cognition*) could be replicated. More than half of the research studies published in the most competitive and highly vetted journals did not demonstrate consistent results when the same design and procedures were repeated.

One way of interpreting the Open Science Collaboration's results is that scientific psychology needs additional checks and balances in order to ensure the quality of published research and to allow increased visibility and collaboration in the scientific enterprise at all stages of the research process. Nosek, the lead researcher from the Open Science Collaboration, and colleagues (2015) argue that journals should encourage replication and should require the posting of data, code, and research materials to public access archives, as well as pre-registration of analysis plans.

However, psychology's problems are much more deeply seated and enduring than the reliability controversy imagines. Although the controversy should shake our faith in the power of psychology to produce repeatable and generalizable results, it also distracts us from the far more troublesome crisis of interpreting quantitative research, which remains far from view and discussion. Even if psychologists manage to produce more rigorous and replicable research, we will continue to misinterpret our data and to avoid the most fundamental and pressing problems of psychology.

Psychologists need to ask some tough questions about the entire research enterprise. What are the limits of our preferred methods for understanding the dynamics of human psychology? What can we learn about the fundamental questions that should drive the study of human psychology? Are there better ways to understand human beings?

For those observing closely, psychology's real crisis is not due to the Open Science Collaboration's findings—as disastrous as the results certainly are. Rather, the crisis is much more basic, structural, and trenchant. Psychological research and theory are in danger of being irrelevant to the understanding of persons and everyday experience. Psychology misses what is essential and interesting to know about human beings. In a world that is so in need of innovative strategies for understanding others, psychology has little to offer. This is the problem.

The solution is not improving the rigor of the status quo, as Nosek et al. (2015) suggest, or better technology. The real problem is, essentially, a conceptual one, which requires new ways of thinking about and studying human beings. As Wittgenstein (1953/1958) warned at the end of his *Philosophical Investigations*,

> The confusion and barrenness of psychology is not to be explained by calling it a "young science." . . . For in psychology there are experimental methods and *conceptual confusion.* . . . The existence of experimental methods makes us think we have the means of solving the problems which trouble us; though problem and method pass one another by. (p. 232)

In my estimation, Wittgenstein's words were prescient of the current state of psychology and are still largely correct. We are still a "young science" and are still misled into thinking that an experimental method is the "means of solving the problems which trouble us." Our task must be to get beyond conceptual confusion and to bring together method and problem into a more certain relationship. We must not continue to let "problem and method pass one another by."

It is odd, but despite massive growth over the past century, psychology is still very far away from knowing what it is. Psychology appears to be constantly in the throes of a disciplinary identity crisis. It lacks a common vision, language, tools, and goals. Instead, psychologists are a group of loosely affiliated researchers, consultants, thinkers, teachers, and clinicians who agree that they are "psychologists" and that they all are, on some level, concerned with "things psychological." This hardly constitutes a satisfying answer to fundamental questions that continue to plague us: What is psychology? What is the purpose of psychology? What kinds of questions should psychologists endeavor to answer? What should be our central goals and aspirations? What do psychologists hope to know, reveal, describe?

Within the discipline there is a surging interest in unity as a goal for contemporary psychology (Sternberg, 2005). Those in favor of unity argue that psychology will never become a true science, like the natural sciences, if psychologists cannot agree on a basic theoretical approach, core concepts, and shared problems (Staats, 2004, 2005). Although the conversation on a unified psychology now has a substantial literature, it is interesting to note that there are persistent differences of opinion on what constitutes "unity" or what a "unified psychology" should look like (Yanchar & Slife, 1997). Or, even, if unity is a worthy goal to pursue. For better or for worse, there is little agreement on the necessity or shape of theoretical unity in psychology.

In the absence of shared goals, problems, or theory, psychology is unified by one factor: method. In large measure, psychologists agree on how psychological questions should be studied. As Danziger (1997) suggests, the study of the psychological variable is what truly unites contemporary psychology as a discipline. Psychology is the study of variables. And the variable is the major product of psychological research.

The point is easy enough to prove. Flip through the pages of any mainstream journal that publishes psychological research and one will invariably find psychological variables (and lots of them). Historically, psychology has opted for methodological over theoretical unity. Psychology is devoid of common theories about the nature of human nature, or even a common understanding of its elemental questions, but abundant in all kinds of variables, strategies to measure them, and analytic tools to submit variables to statistical testing.

Although there are benefits to sharing a common method of study, the study of psychological variables also carries with it a heavy price. Variable approaches are not value neutral. Every method introduces prejudice into our observations. Furthermore, not all research questions that psychologists should investigate can be effectively studied using variable-centered approaches. But researchers are obliged to pour their research into the variable mold in order to participate in the discussion at the center of the discipline. In order to be a research psychologist, one cannot opt out of the system. If you break out of the variable mold, it is virtually impossible to publish in psychology's most prestigious journals—which has direct consequences for jobs and promotions. Because of this, researchers are compelled to use methods of study inappropriate to their research question or to relegate critical research questions to the fringes of the discipline (Mishler, 1999). Furthermore, as I will argue, this reliance on variable-centered methods seriously compromises our ability to understand persons and to describe the true nature of psychological processes.

I argue for an alternative vision of a unified psychology. My conception of unity is not the same old vision—unity through methods of study. Not surprisingly, a narrative perspective plays a central role in this vision. A narrative perspective dramatically increases the range of possible questions that psychologists can address and provides necessary insights into human thought, action, and interpretation. But, it also offers a new understanding of psychology itself and what the discipline can become. Indeed, this book can be read as a strong argument for why psychology needs a narrative perspective as a central force in scientific psychology. In my view, narrative has the potential to enhance what we can currently glean using existing perspectives by grounding research in the life experience of actual persons and how they interpret themselves, others, and the world.

THE NARRATIVE IN (AND OF) PSYCHOLOGY

Two poles frame the argument of this book: narrative and psychology. The book is about both. It is concerned with the big questions about the nature, practice, and direction of the discipline of psychology. But it is also about narrative and what the concept of narrative can do to transform our understanding of human beings.

I approach the subject from a critical perspective. I offer readers a clear contrast between the current version of psychology and a new one, a narrative perspective, which places interpretation and meaning making at the center of our theoretical and analytic deliberations on human beings.

Although I imagine that many of my readers are already conversant in the vocabulary of the narrative turn, I consciously reach out to students and researchers who are curious about how the close study of narrative can deepen their understanding of persons and psychological processes. I am also interested in presenting the rationale for narrative psychology to psychologists and researchers who are unfamiliar with this approach or who may be, *a priori*, unfriendly to narrative. I hope to reintroduce narrative psychology as viable and necessary to the advancement of contemporary psychological science. In fact, I will argue that a narrative perspective is essential for understanding the complexity of human experience in a way that is true to the reality of our lives.

For those beginning to study narrative psychology, this book is an excellent first text. However, readers familiar with narrative will find this book useful in several respects. It is not a textbook. I have a rhetorical agenda for narrative psychology, which, I hope, reorients our notions of what narrative is, what it can do, and what role it should play in the psychological understanding of lives.

The overriding impetus of this book is to catalyze disciplinary change in the direction of an energetic and influential narrative perspective at the center of the conversation in contemporary psychology. It is my strong belief that this historical moment, the beginning of the twenty-first century, represents a unique window of opportunity for disciplinary change and renewal. There are several indications that mainstream psychology is becoming more open to qualitative and narrative research. In 2015, the British Psychological Society's section Qualitative Methods in Psychology celebrated its tenth anniversary. In 2014, the American Psychological Association (APA) changed the name of Division 5 from "Evaluation, Measurement & Statistics" to "Quantitative and Qualitative Psychology." In 2013, the APA journal *Qualitative Psychology* began publication. In addition, there are growing opportunities for publications and scholarly convocation.

In Chapters 1 and 2 of this book, I provide a clear argument for the weaknesses inherent in contemporary psychological research and the need to develop an alternative psychology—a narrative one to supplant the dominant variable-centered model. As I argue, the current configuration of psychological research and theory is unable to address those problems that are most essential and fundamental to human psychology. My strongest argument is that variable-centered methods are unable to observe the dynamics of psychological processes as they unfold in persons' reflections and the concrete situations that they find themselves in. These are essential arguments in establishing the necessity for new strategies. These chapters answer the following questions: What is missing from contemporary accounts? What is flawed and needs to be repaired?

I do not believe that we can go about *business as usual* under the illusion that contemporary psychology is bringing us any closer to a more accurate, complete, or useful understanding of those very problems central to the psychology of humans. These chapters not only serve a critical purpose, but also provide arguments for researchers in psychology, and the social sciences at large, who are just beginning their work in narrative to understand and clearly explain the motivation for their work. Why turn to narrative? Why narrative psychology? Why narrative psychology now?

In Part II (Chapters 3 through 5), I reformulate the concept of narrative psychology as the study of interpretive actions. These chapters are more than an introduction. I go beyond current practice in narrative psychology to describe a new interpretive model of understanding human lives. I am offering not only a new path for psychology, but a new path for narrative psychology. In this light, I reframe narrative psychology as an interpretive, hermeneutic, practice. I describe, explicate, and apply a theory for understanding interpretive actions.

In Part III (Chapters 6 through 9), I discuss the theory and practice of narrative analysis, provide a model for thinking about research arguments in psychology and discuss sound practices for narrative research. I also address narrative's status as psychological science and reorient the relationship between narrative and mainstream psychology. In the Conclusion, "Unity in Psychology?," I argue that a narrative perspective can work synthetically to develop more realistic and richly developed understandings of psychology.

The style of the book is clear and direct. I discuss the extensive problems that contemporary psychology leaves unaddressed because of its exclusive reliance on variable-centered methods. I also describe how close attention to persons in context could help psychologists to address some of the fundamental problems of human psychology.

In a sense, I view a narrative perspective as the remedy for the inability of contemporary psychology to study meaning in human lives. This is my own proposition for what the study of narrative in psychology could entail. Although the book takes a strong position, these pages are an opening to a dialogue about the future of psychology and the potential of a narrative perspective to make an impact on a world in desperate need of knowledge, perspective, and understanding of human beings.

CHAPTER 1
Out of Context

Those unfamiliar with psychology often think that the discipline studies persons—but, really, it doesn't. Academic psychology has amazingly little to say about persons (Mishler, 1996). The center of gravity is elsewhere. Psychology is the study of theoretical constructs called variables. Not much has changed since Carlson (1971) perceptively asked, "Where is the person in personality research?" However, the problem is not just one for personality psychologists. It is engrained in the system as a whole. In psychology, persons are most notable for their absence.

Historian of psychology Kurt Danziger (1997) traces the origins of the psychological variable to the behaviorist experimental tradition. Danziger argues that the behaviorist Charles Tolman significantly expanded the notion of variables beyond the skeletal concepts of stimulus and response to include a whole new set of "intervening variables" that included "any hypothetical intra-individual event, force, disposition, process, state, ability, etc. that is assigned a causal role in behavior" (p. 167). It is interesting to consider the use of variables as a behaviorist innovation. Variables do not require researchers to consider the subjective experience of persons. Rather, they function perfectly well—in some ways better—by avoiding a consideration of internal attributes such as meaning, subjectivity, or agency. Traces of the behaviorist disdain of mental processes remain intact in variable-centered approaches.

Although the historical origins of psychological variables are found in behaviorism, personality psychology extended the use of variables as a part of normal scientific practice to general psychology. Danziger (1997) points to Henry Murray's collaborative volume *Explorations in Personality*, published in 1938, as one of the seminal texts responsible for institutionalizing variables in psychological research. Danziger writes that "Henry Murray was perhaps the last person one would have expected to encourage the use of such terminology" (p. 174). But, in order to assemble and evaluate competing theoretical approaches to personality, Murray and his colleagues chose a common metric, that of the psychological variable. "Whatever [the contributor's] theoretical and ideological differences they agreed that in practice the things they were trying to investigate had to be treated as variables" (Danziger, 1997, p. 175). Theoretical disputes between different perspectives were negotiated (perhaps *silenced* is a better word) by an agreement to focus on data fashioned and analyzed in the same manner.

The pact to ignore theoretical unity in favor of methodological unity continues to the present day. The consequences of this agreement have far-reaching effects on every aspect of mainstream psychology.

WHAT'S VARIABLE

Essentially, variables are abstract ideas, developed by researchers, in order to study aspects of human beings and the social world. It is important to underline that variables are derived from the researcher's interpretation of others and bear the mark of the researcher's perspective. Certainly, researchers can claim to have some insight into their own psychological experiences; they are not complete outsiders. But participants must respond and measure up to what the researcher proposes. Although psychological research attempts to write the interpretive and subjective stance of the researcher out of the scientific process, in fact, subjectivity is deeply embedded, from the very first steps, in the definition of our variables.

From the perspective of quantitative psychology, one of the appealing features of variables is that an amazing variety of ideas can be put into a comparable metric. Variables can be constructed to measure biological states, body types, behaviors, opinions, life events, family structure, cultural setting, economic status, internal dispositions such as personalities or motivations, and much much more. The possibilities for devising new variables appear to have no limits; their proliferation is staggering.

Another appealing feature is the systematic and consistent manner in which variables can be measured. Variables may begin as vague notions, but they are assessed by a set of specific rules or procedures; this is what researchers call an *operational definition*. In constructing operational definitions, a theoretical concept is put into concrete form so that it can be consistently, reliably, measured in groups of persons.

Operational definitions are thought to be repeatable. Once the definition is given enough detail and richness, the same operation can be hypothetically completed by researchers separated by time and culture in a way that is, theoretically, consistent with previous assessments. For example, one can measure individual differences in the construct of *shyness* by giving people a set of written questions on which to rate themselves. In theory, each time that we measure shyness, the same procedure should yield consistent results. Of course, we could come up with other operational definitions of shyness, such as the amount of time spent alone, lack of interaction in a social situation, peer rating of shyness, and so on.

The stock and trade of psychologists is formulating variables, measuring them, and seeing how they relate to each other statistically. If you want to know what psychologists really do, this is it. The practice of psychological research is the creation and definition of variables, and then the discovery of regularities that describe a single variable or connections between variables within a sample.

In the variable mold, subjectivity is treated as a mental substance that can be assessed by precise tools. Theoretically, just like persons everywhere, we all have more or less of these substances. It is as if the person were the vessel for a plethora of substances, like vapors or liquids, that are concealed inside them. We all have more or less shyness, motivation, self-esteem, or prejudice.

Not only are these mental substances discoverable in all persons, but psychologists also seek to understand how they operate in persons *in general*. Psychological research does not concern how shyness functions inside me, or any particular person, but how it functions in persons *on average*. Psychological research and theory are abstract, are focused on the level of the variable, and seek to describe and compare these substances in people in general. This is what really interests psychologists: the extent to which variables relate to other variables, and how *generalizable* these relationships are.

Many years ago, Gordon Allport (1962) observed that psychology is preoccupied with the general and disdains the particular. Allport wrote that psychologists "pursue our acquaintance with Bill long enough to derive some hypothesis, and then spring like a gazelle into the realm of abstraction, drawing from Bill a 'testable proposition' but carrying with us no coordinated knowledge of him as a structural unit" (p. 406). Psychologists are not interested in describing how and why Bill remembers witnessing war as a child, or the stories about how he became a doctor and what they mean to him as a person and a member of various social groups. This would be a distraction to what we really want to know about "memory processes" and "decision-making rules." The assumption is that these substances can be pulled outside of the life experience of the person. I will argue that they cannot.

Psychology searches for the universal laws of human nature that are true about all persons, regardless of who they are, how, when, or where they lived, or any fact that might set them apart from others. The goal is to develop "covering laws," causal or probabilistic, to explain how, given similar conditions, we can expect similar results (Hempel, 1962). Our attention turns immediately away from the particularities of the person and how he or she makes sense of the world to describing the nature of abstract processes. Psychologists leap to abstraction uncomfortably fast.

I am not denying, nor would Allport, the possible significance of these abstractions, their utility, or their potential commonality. It is often helpful to talk about persons using the language of abstract mental attributes, motivations, feelings, meanings, or dispositions. This language is part of our folk psychology and we do it all the time. Also, our subjective world does share properties with the subjectivity of those around us. It would be a radical position to assume that there are no psychological universals (Shweder, 2003). These are some of the strengths of variable-centered research. But this is far from the whole story.

The greatest weakness of variable-centered research is its enormous success, prevailing over all alternative methods of studying psychology and leading to the over-application of variable-centered methods to every question that psychologists might conceivably study. There are instances in which a variable-centered approach is the most appropriate tool to use, for example, if we are interested in surveying percentages of people who feel a certain way or have lived through a particular experience, or if we need an assessment that an intervention is, on the whole, effective. But this approach is also very limited—to describe the dynamic process of how human psychology functions, we need to move beyond abstract variables and to alternate models of theory and research.

Indeed, the abstract quality of variable-centered research makes it empty. When these abstractions are taken out of the context of the person who is acting, feeling, or thinking, psychologists make a series of logical errors.

One of the main consequences of shifting our attention from persons to variables is that researchers misinterpret actions, thoughts, and feelings as abstract and decontextualized facts—but they aren't. Actions and thoughts are things that persons do. They are embodied and have meaning within the context of a particular person's life experience and social world. By moving to the abstract, variable-centered thinking deprives psycho logical processes of their authentic context. Variable-centered research abstracts psychological processes out of the context of the person and, therefore, distorts what the process means.

Psychological processes don't exist, except as part of the experience or action of a particular person on a certain occasion. Persons feel, think, and act. These are experiences that have context and meaning. Emotions, thoughts, and actions don't float in the air or walk down the street. They aren't capable of a relation or dialogue in a human sense. However, this is exactly how we talk about psychological processes in their variable form. We speak about well-being and shyness as if they can be spoken about apart from a person who is happy or shy, and as if these variables can enter into "relationships" with other variables.

It is an amazing fact that in the pages of psychology's most prominent journals, one finds that virtually no persons, other than the authors, are present. No names are mentioned. And although research participants are still often White American college students taking their first course in psychology, these abstractions are intended to apply to all human beings at all times. Theoretically, psychologists aspire to identify the common, generalizable, and universal elements of human thinking and action. In my opinion, this is a problematic stance for a science that is concerned with such intimate subjects such as thought, feeling, and action.

As Henrich, Heine, and Norenzayan (2010) argue, researchers study "Western, Educated, Industrialized, Rich, and Democratic (WEIRD) societies" (p. 1) in order to draw universally applicable conclusions; however, as their research review shows, WEIRD societies are clear outliers on a variety of measures. But the solution is not, as Henrich, Heine, and Norenzayan (2010) argue, to make our methods more rigorous so that we can be more confident that our research generalizes universally. They write: "our aim . . . is to inspire efforts to place knowledge of such universal features of psychology on a firmer footing by empirically addressing, rather than *a priori* dismissing or ignoring, questions of population variability" (p. 3). The problem cuts much deeper than questions of population and sampling. It is a question of our global orientation to psychological research.

In contrast to Henrich, Heine, and Norenzayan (2010), I argue that we need to put psychology back into context. In other words, we must begin to understand psychological processes as part of the life experience of persons who dwell in bodies, who are engaged in social relationships, and who are immersed in cultural worlds in historical time. Variable-centered thinking, even extending our research to non-WEIRD societies, takes the process out of context. And, moving to the abstract, we lose the phenomenon. We lose sight of the context that made the process possible and imbued it with meaning. Persons think, persons act, and persons feel within a particular social and historical horizon. But variables don't. They don't do anything, but we imbue them with agency.

Psychological processes have an even more specific connotation. They can be thought of as something that we "have" or something that we "do" (Cantor, 1990). Some psychological phenomena are described as dispositional characteristics that are more or less stable traits. Others are described as action-oriented thinking processes, which are active in time and context. For example, cognitive personality psychologists speak about defensive pessimism (Norem, 2001), personal projects (Little, 2000), and life tasks (Cantor, Norem, Niedenthal, Langston, & Brower, 1987), which involve a consideration of how psychological processes unfold in time and context. Although the cognitive approach has the virtue of a more complex and realistic account of how psychological processes function, both kinds of variables are problematic in their treatment of experience.

Syntactically, "having" is a kind of adjective and "doing" is verbal. In most languages, both verbs and adjectives require or imply a pronoun to form a complete sentence. It is "I," "you," "she," "Bill," "they," or "we" who is these things, or who carried out these actions, felt these emotions, and considered these thoughts. Without a pronoun, it is not clear to whom the adjectives and verbs apply.

In the same way that a sentence requires a subject, it is most appropriate to interpret psychological processes here at the level of the person. By placing the process in the context of the person and their social world, we are able to more fully understand the nature of the process and the function that it serves in the life and world of this person. Of course, this syntactic argument is not definitive proof of the need for a subject. But, in talking about psychological processes, it is even more critical. "Who" is inscribed in experience itself.

Of course, the notion of the person carries heavy conceptual baggage from various realms: religious, legal, philosophical. I am also using *person* differently from how personality psychologists currently employ the term as a vessel for traits, states, and motives. By *person*, I mean the fact that intentions, thoughts, emotions, and desires are embodied in a specific experiencing subject.

In *Being and Time*, Heidegger (1926/1962) begins from the premise that persons are always situated in some discrete place and time. Often, we are so caught up in the world, wrapped up in the flow of activity, that we don't recognize that we are experiencing something. But when we stop and distance ourselves from the pressing activities of the everyday, we notice it. Heidegger uses the somewhat cryptic expression of "Dasein" to denote human being, agent, subjective center, or person. But, literally, "Dasein" means something like "existence" or, in Heidegger's hands, "to be there" or "the there of being" (Haugeland, 2013). The "there" in Dasein should be understood as spatial but also temporal. Experience is always discovered in some concrete time and place. It is my experience and it has the quality of being located in a particular "there."

Harré (1983) distinguishes between the self and the person, arguing that the person is the primary structure, of experience and awareness, located in space and time. It is a physical location. I am here now. For Harré, persons are found everywhere that you go; experience has a physical location, it is embodied. But of course people do not universally have the same self or the same views on what it means to be a person. Although persons, defined as the location of experience in time and space, may be universal, for Harré, the self is not. The self is imbued with diverse meanings that depend on the local world. Persons are the center of experience, action, and interpretation, but the sculpted cultural self comes from being a person in a particular here and now.

Finally, Geertz argues that the way in which Westerners conceive of the self as a "bounded, unique, more or less integrated motivational and cognitive system" (1984, p. 126) is almost certainly an artifact of Western culture. However, he continues, "some sort of concept of this kind, one feels reasonably safe in saying, exists in recognizable form among all social groups" (p. 126). In other words, although there is wide variation in the kinds of selves that we find across the globe, we find persons everywhere.

The person is the central context for experiencing and interpreting the world. Persons have psychological experiences. Even if these processes are themselves constructed by, and constituted in, our interaction with others and the social world (Vygotsky, 1978), even if we are never truly alone in our thoughts but always are seeing the world and the past in reference to some particular group (Halbwachs, 1980), and even if I am thinking with cultural tools, I am still the one who is thinking. Experience always has a "who" attached to it (Wertsch, 1991). Someone has to be doing the thinking, acting, or feeling. This is exactly the opposite assumption of variable-centered approaches that effectively sever persons from their experience.

Abstraction from the person and from experience is a second possible step. Based on adequate observation, we may theorize about how psychological processes work in common ways in people at large. We can say, people think like this. But, this is a very large step and there is a long distance between the deliberate work of meticulous observation on concrete experience and an abstraction large enough to cover human nature. At best, we might be able to characterize the small group of persons that we have studied. Even this move is difficult and requires substantial justification. It also requires understanding how the process functions in persons, one by one.

When we take a psychological process out of context and turn it into an abstract variable, we have manufactured two interpretive anomalies: (1) without an understanding of how the process functions in the person, we do not really understand the process itself; and (2) we miss the person and how they understand their life. Even in personality psychology, the specialization that should be closest to the study of personhood, persons are most remarkable because of their absence.

STABILITY OR CHANGE—OR WHAT?

In order to understand how persons elude study, it is instructive to look at how personality is conceptualized and researched. The stability of personality over time is one of the central problems of the "having" side of personality psychology. Is personality stable, or does it change over the life course? A consideration of this problem helps to illustrate some of the deep and structural weaknesses of variable-centered approaches applied to the study of psychological processes.

Personality psychologists have been discussing the question of stability for a long time. Even William James (1890) argued that the establishment of professional and intellectual habits in our twenties and thirties were inescapable and had a profound effect on our character. As James is often quoted, "in most of us, by the age of thirty, the character has set like plaster, and will never soften again" (p. 121). Jung (1930/1960) voiced a contrary point of view; he believed that mid-life was a time of change, reversing previously held beliefs and ways of thinking and acting.

But is there really an answer to this question? As I will argue, the question is too abstract to be really answerable. It implies an understanding of persons that is inaccurate, placing personality out of the context of actual lives and the meanings that persons give to their experience.

How do researchers go about answering such a question? And, what conclusions do they draw? Employing different operational definitions of variables and different analytic strategies, personality is viewed as both stable and changing. This is the finding argued in the literature: it's both. But what can that possibly mean?

For example, Haan, Milsap, and Hartka's (1986) descriptive study of longitudinal personality change and stability on 118 persons over a 50-year period, from the ages of 5–7 to 55–62 years old, used an observer-rated California Q-sort. On the basis of a factor analysis, they grouped the 100-item Q-sort into six clusters: self-confident/victimized; assertive/submissive; cognitively committed; outgoing/aloof; dependable; and warm/hostile. They found that, on the whole, there are strong correlations between adjacent developmental periods, but that over longer periods of time these correlations become very weak. In other words, when we correlate scores from the same person over time, persons tend to hold their own position relative to the group, which is called *rank order stability*, at least over short periods of development. At the same time, Haan et al. also found mean level changes in most personality clusters over time, even after age 30.

In a meta-analytic review of the literature on personality development, Caspi, Roberts, and Shiner (2005) argue that when compared with others, persons hold their position on the major dimensions of personality over long periods of development. In other words, compared to other persons, we become neither more nor less extraverted or agreeable, or one of the other Big Five factors that is argued to constitute the compendium of essential traits of human personality (McCrae & Costa, 2008). In Caspi et al.'s (2005) research, persons stay the same in relation to others. This trend appears to begin in adolescence, but becomes even more apparent in middle and late adulthood. Although there are significant continuities in rank order stability, average personality scores fluctuate over the course of adulthood. Once again, as in Haan et al.'s (1986) study, there are changes in the mean ratings of the group over time. For example, according to Roberts and Mroczek (2008), the mean score on agreeableness goes up over adulthood.

However, others, such as Ardelt (2000), argue that the issue of stability or change is "far from being settled." Reviewing her meta-analytic findings, she writes,

> The analyses indicate that personality can change over the course of a person's life, particularly if age at first measurement is low or over 50, if the retest interval is large, if individual personality aspects rather than the overall personality are considered, and if personality aspects other than the big five NEO traits are assessed. (p. 400)

In other words, the more that we get into the details, the more vast generalizations about personality change or stability break down. For instance, when considering "overall personality" or using instruments such as the Big Five, more stability is evident. Stability decreases in other measures that tap into more idiosyncratic aspects of personality.

So, as Block and Robbins (1993) ask, "What then can be concluded about 'consistency' and 'change?'" (p. 921). This is a difficult question. But, overall, when personality is studied as an abstract variable, the answer is both "change" and "consistency." With some dissenters, the most common finding is that when considered as an abstract variable, persons tend to maintain continuity over time relative to others in the same group, or at least change is slow, while the group mean for some variables changes. Such a finding does not necessarily argue that something is wrong with the analyses. There are possible conditions under which one can see personality *at the group level* as both changing and stable.

Block and Robbins (1993) continue, and answer their own question:

> Like almost any psychological attribute, self-esteem changes in some ways and is continuous in other ways throughout the life course. However, it is too easy to resort to the homily that there is continuity amidst change and change amidst continuity. To go beyond this trivially true, blandly wise response to a simplistically posed question regarding consistency versus change, it is necessary to approach the problem in deeper, more differentiated ways. What is needed is further study of the ways in which individuals maintain continuity or change at different periods of their life and the concomitants, consequences, and antecedents of these continuities and changes. (p. 921)

I agree wholeheartedly with this statement; we do need to move beyond the "blandly wise response" to say something more useful about persons. The route that I suggest begins from an in-depth consideration of how persons interpret their life experience. This is a different tack from the one that Block (1971/2014; Block and Robbins, 1993) and others following Block, such as Magnusson (1999), call a "person-centered" versus a "variable-centered" approach. Please note that, for Block and Magnusson, "person-centered" is, exactly, what I have been calling *variable-centered*. It is quantitative, deals with abstract variables, but does so in order to study *intra*-individual continuity and change. This move is surely an improvement over statistical analyses that emphasize overall group averages, but we are still dealing with vast abstractions and still far away from grappling with how and why aspects of personality are expressed and how and why they change over time in the lives of real persons.

The challenge is to go even deeper, to go even more descriptive, and to go even closer to how persons understand themselves and their world.

In order to get back into context, we need to move beyond abstractions and study the concrete. Even a "person-centered" method, such as Block and Magnusson advocate, is not able to study the way that interpretation shapes and recasts personality development over the life course.

How do we answer the question of personality change? What do the results tell us? How do we get back from such abstract results, to persons? In fact, the results tell us nothing about persons. We never do get back to persons.

We might ask, how does this research apply to me? At 40-something, I am pretty conscientious. Does that mean that I can expect to be even more so? Because the correlation is not a perfect one, it cannot serve as evidence for claims about any individual (Lamiell, 2003). There is an average trend, but the trend does not allow us to predict individual cases. Does that mean that persons at particular points in the life cycle will have different personalities? Once again, one needs to take into account the size of the effect in the group, as well as individual variability. The differences are not that large. They are incremental, but statistically significant. They are also averages—certain people change, but others remain the same. But we don't know anything about how change and stability work as processes in people's lives. What are the interpretive, social, and cultural dimensions that influence personality development? Do the results tell us anything useful about how persons experience the world? Or about how they make sense of their personality?

One could generate hundreds of interesting questions about personality across adulthood that variable-centered research will not be able to approach. It could be argued that these are not the right kinds of questions—but they are. They are exactly the kinds of questions that psychologists need to ask. Shouldn't psychology be able to talk about experience and how persons make meaning of the past, present, and future? Shouldn't it be directly relevant to our lives?

The trenchant problem is our adherence to the standard craft of personality research for answering questions about persons and their experiences. The research is highly quantified. The local immediate experience of a single human being is not thought to be suitable for scientific investigation. Indeed, mainstream psychology is predominantly concerned with uncovering "generalizable" laws that guide human thought and conduct. In other words, we want to know the general principles that guide psychology everywhere; our results should apply to people that we did not study on all corners of the globe. This is one of the reasons that psychologists cling to statistical methods of analysis: to estimate whether or not we are likely to find the same results in the general population.

But, as Runyan (1982) argues, psychology is so concerned with generalizing that it fails miserably in the effort to particularize. Variable-centered methods possess very real limits on how we can understand and describe others. Placing our emphasis on averages and variables, we ignore the particular. We can talk a lot about what happens to the average individual, but when it comes to talking about you, me, or the person in front of us, there is precious little to say. We can say that on average, these processes are connected in the population. But this is of little value for studying the real world, or confronting real-world problems in which there are no imaginary average individuals but only actual ones. How does our research speak to the lives of the people whom we meet and those who ask for help? How does research inform our advice to resolve social conflict? We can refer to our findings that talk about averages and tendencies. When psychologists say, "People who are such and such tend to also think such and such," we should also ask, "but what about me or her?"

We can speak about averages, but when we move to talking about the particular, our language is impoverished. There is nothing to say. Rather than saying something about the real world, contemporary psychology opts to say nothing in particular, about anyone, and therefore avoids saying anything meaningful beyond the purely demographic (Lamiell, 2013).

Psychological processes have distinct meanings and functions for different persons in different situations. A useful way to think about this problem is to take any abstraction of a psychological process, such as shyness, and to analyze the function and meaning of the variable for different persons in various contexts. Although there is a sense in which we can abstract the same common psychological principle across time and history, being shy has various concrete enactments for each person. Marie is aware that she is shy and uses it as an explanation for why she avoids talking in class. Mark isn't shy with his family, but has problems voicing his point of view at work, and subsequently shyness means that he is kept from advancing to the top ranks of his company.

In actual practice, the function of shyness is even more complex because it exists within a host of other motives, preoccupations, situations, relationships, moods, historical practices, cultural systems of meaning, and so on. Shyness isn't just shyness, nor is any other psychological variable. A person experiences and enacts shyness in a particular here and now. Psychological processes mean nothing unless we understand the following: *Who* is thinking, acting, and experiencing? *When and where?* In what social, historical, and cultural horizon? The process needs to be contextualized as part of the person's life and world.

Perhaps we should say that persons both change and remain the same, but in all kinds of different and contradictory ways that are difficult to investigate and describe. Life is messy. And the answer would depend on the person. This is exactly the point. To understand whether or not personality changes over time, we need to ask how personality changes in this person's life. How and why? Beyond a thick and richly descriptive account of persons in all their complexity, the answer is vacuous.

When we begin to examine such a problem, we find that the answer looks more like a work of fiction, a short story or novel, rather than a mathematical formula; natural and social forces impinge on the protagonist's life, but how and why the protagonist changes (or doesn't) also depend on the interpretations and choices that they make and how they tell their story. Provocative as it is to suggest, at the moment, literature might be a keener observer of real-life psychological processes than the discipline of psychology.

In a chapter aptly titled "Missing Persons," Mishler (1996) argues that a consideration of personal trajectories is critical to understanding developmental processes. Developmental psychology relies on group averages in order to interpret developmental changes over time. But this reliance on mean scores across groups of persons conceals the fact that development is idiosyncratic, accented by advances and setbacks to particular goals. By focusing on group means, developmentalists miss a complex understanding of personal pathways that characterize actual developmental processes as diverse as reading skills or identity formation. Mishler writes that in a variable-centered approach

> [v]ariables "do" all the work: they are the focus of measurement and statistical analysis, and the key terms in our statements of causal relationships. . . . In this way, individuals are stripped of agency; they "endure" but they have no initiative, they are sites with measurable attributes but do not "participate" in or actively produce the events of interest. (p. 79)

A perspective on human development that focuses on the person or case, Mishler continues, "are designed for this task of restoring agency to individuals in our research and our theories. They grant them unity and coherence through time, respecting them as subjects with both histories and intentions" (p. 80).

Perhaps a better answer to the question of whether personality changes over time is that "personality" neither changes nor remains the same. Personality variables don't do anything. As other things found in the world, like stones or buildings, they just are. Rather, persons, imbued with agency and effected by history, change or remain the same. Reducing persons to variables does violence to our understanding of human beings and their capacity to interpret life and make sense of themselves.

Variable-centered approaches attempt to split apart persons into their component parts in order to focus on one aspect of human lives in isolation of everything else. In so doing, we take psychological phenomena out of their proper context. And we have effectively dismantled the object that we sought to study. The process vanishes before our very eyes. We have created an artful abstraction, but interpreting what it means for understanding persons or lives over time is unclear. Something substantial is missing from the account.

If psychology's mission is to understand human meaning making—and I think that it should be—then we need to do more than describe fragments of persons, torn from their proper context. Psychology misses what it means to be a living and breathing human being, engaged in the world, making sense of experience, telling stories, and reflecting on the past. Instead, we focus our energy on the description of psychological variables. We are more concerned with describing the variable, and submitting it to statistical analysis, than listening to how persons make sense of themselves and the world. But it is the person who acts and thinks, and it is only in the context of the person's life and world that the process, which the variable is trying to represent, makes sense.

The component parts of men and women are not much help in interpreting the reality of a human life. Indeed, we are missing what is fundamental to psychology. We are missing a rich and complex theoretical and empirical description of persons in context. We need an account of what persons actually say and do, an account of how persons make sense of self, others, and the world. The task we have before us is to reassemble a psychology of meaning, to create a vision of the person in conversation with the social and cultural world.

CHAPTER 2
Out of the Head

A second problem emerges when examining how variables are typically used in psychological research. In most cases, psychologists are interested not only in the distribution of a single variable, but also in the association between variables. The problem is that associations between variables, which are based on group averages, are misinterpreted as individual psychological processes. In fact, statistical analysis of variables gives the impression that we have observed the actual relationship between variables when in fact we have not.

HANGING TOGETHER

In psychology, the association between variables can be conceptualized in two broad metaphors: experimental and correlational. On the one hand, we can think of the relationship between variables as experiments in which researchers assess whether or not an experimental manipulation produces a change in an outcome variable. In the experimental paradigm, if we have sufficiently controlled for alternative explanations, changes in the outcome variable indicate a statistical relationship between the manipulation and the outcome variable. On the other hand, we can conceptualize the relationship between variables as correlations, measuring the extent to which two variables are associated or, as I have heard many times over, how they hang together.

Both experimental and correlational designs begin with an operational definition of the variables to be measured. They follow the rules that I outlined in the previous chapter. Observations are made on the basis of these operational definitions, variables are calculated, and then researchers use one or more statistical procedure(s) in order to detect consistent relationships across groups of individuals. Both experimental and correlational methods are probabilistic (Cronbach, 1957). If the variables of interest co-occur in a stable fashion and the magnitude of the relationship is sufficient, as determined by statistical analysis, then it can be argued that a "statistically significant" relationship was observed.

Obviously, research in psychology is infinitely more complex than this description. Researchers employ a variety of research designs and analytic techniques. The current fashion is toward ever more complicated analytic techniques such as structural equation modeling, which appears to be the *sine qua non* of being published in the most prestigious journals. Although these statistical tools are frequently used and published, many psychologists, including researchers, have difficulty reading and interpreting the results—often misreading what the statistical analyses actually mean (Gigerenzer, 2004). Many skip from the introduction to the discussion section without bothering to decipher the methods or results. We just take it for granted that the researchers knew what they were doing, or that the editor was able to "catch" any "faults" in the methods used.

Although the field is becoming more sophisticated in the range of statistical procedures, for our purposes, experimental and correlational approaches are sufficient for understanding the crisis in contemporary psychology. The main problem isn't that the statistics are faulty, or even that the analyses are not competently executed. The problem is much more basic. The conclusions that we draw from these analyses are *not warranted* from our observations. We ask these methods to explain more than they can, and then we use our own uninterpreted biases and experiences to fill in the details that elude our analysis.

A FATAL PROBLEM

In his investigation of William Stern's psychology, Lamiell (2003) traces the evolution of psychological thinking from Wundtian experimentalism to contemporary methodological practices. Lamiell argues that there is no direct line from Wundt's foundational experimental work to the present. Wundt employed a single-subject experimental design, intent on discovering the subjective properties of psychological experience that would be "common to all." He studied single individuals and then tried to apply these results to other individuals.

However, Lamiell makes a critical distinction between the Wundtian brand of experimentalism that seeks to discover what is common to all and contemporary methods that seek to explain the average or general aspects of human nature by aggregating results across a large number of persons and correlating this data.

Averages work just fine when describing distributions across populations. But what is epistemologically problematic is to treat these averages as if they represent the actual processes, happening inside persons, in the dynamic interaction between persons or with cultural tools. Lamiell calls this error the Thorndike maneuver, "which entails an acceptance of the view that the aggregate statistical findings issuing from studies of variables marking differences between individuals provide scientific warrant for knowledge claims concerning the behavior/psychological functioning of individuals" (2003, p. 184). In other words, in direct contradiction with contemporary practice, researchers cannot equate group averages derived from statistical regularities with individual subjective experience. But we do. This is the standard practice in psychology; we do it *all* the time.

Of course, as Lamiell (2003) recounts, there are certain conditions in which this claim is theoretically true. When the correlation between variables is perfect, the same relationship found in the aggregate should be the same one found in the individual. But practically, this state of affairs is never true. Correlations in psychology hover closer to 0 than to 1. Lamiell writes:

> There are conceivable, albeit highly restrictive, and rarely, if ever, realized empirical circumstances under which knowledge of what holds true for an aggregate of individuals is at once and perforce knowledge of what holds true in general for the individuals within that aggregate. The problem is that contemporary "nomotheticism" requires for its metaphysical and epistemological coherence the assumption that this is always true, in other words, that whatever is true in the aggregate is inevitably at least a partial "window" onto individual level phenomenon. Without this assumption, "nomotheticism" cannot possibly work as an approach to understanding individuals except under conditions never realized empirically. It happens, however, that this critical assumption is false, and therein lies the fatal problem. (p. 191)

If the implications of this simple fact were ever realized, the blow to psychology would be enormous. How can we continue our research knowing that the assumed relationship between aggregate statistics and individual psychological states does not apply except under conditions that are *never* empirically realized? The problem is, as Lamiell emphasizes, *fatal*.

However, contemporary psychology proceeds *as if* findings that account for averages between people actually apply to what happens inside the person. The practice is so entrenched that it is difficult for psychologists to recognize and then verify that this is indeed the underlying logic in the overwhelming majority of psychological research. Averages and individuals are confused.

Contemporary psychology uses statistical relationships in order to study associations between psychological variables. But, in statistical analysis, we are not actually observing how two variables connect with each other. We are not able to observe exactly how they interact and the effect that they have on one another. To do so, we would need to shift from the level of averages to the level of the person. What we are able to observe is the extent to which variables co-occur or co-vary across a group of people—how they hang together. If we are only able to assess how processes co-vary, we have not observed how the variables interact. But we consider that we have observed this relationship, and write about it, *as if* we have.

Certainly, this is a point that Lamiell would agree with. But, in fact, I am going one step beyond Lamiell in my criticism. Even if the relationship is a perfect one—in the language of correlation coefficients, Pearson's σ = 1—psychologists would still fail to do their job connecting together aspects of the same person's experience. Even in the case of σ = 1, statistical analysis has not observed the process that is being inferred. If in fact there is a connection between the variables, it is essential from the perspective of science to observe the meaningful associations that implicate them in a relationship, or, at the very least, to establish the signs that reveal this relationship. What binds these abstract variables together? How does the association actually work?

Two things that go together are not, therefore, related. Some other logical operator must be in place in order to establish the relationship between them. Televisions and DVD players are highly correlated in a statistical sense. They show up in living rooms and offices all over the world. But does one produce or affect the other? Do they commune? Both are just kind of there. Other forces are at work in bringing together these two objects. The objects don't have agency, but the people who want to watch movies do. Science demands that we go beyond just merely being there together.

This is a logical error and a gloss over the data analysis, which, if properly understood, seriously undermines the legitimacy of statistical methods as a means of exploring the structure and dynamics of internal mental life and how persons interpret and act in the world. To go beyond the fact that two psychological variables appear together, researchers need ways of demonstrating a connection, that they bring about or produce one another or that they have an even more complex relationship. I would argue that it entails rewriting the narrative of contemporary psychology in order to explore the central aspects of human meaning making.

PERSONALITY WITHOUT PROCESS

As an example, one can turn to countless articles in the literature that demonstrate this logical error. But I will turn to a well-executed research study by Klohnen, Vandewater, and Young (1996) that investigates the relationship between ego-resiliency and psychological and physical functioning in adulthood. Analyzing data from two longitudinal studies, one of women from Radcliffe College and the other of women from Mills College, Klohnen et al. (1996) argue that ego-resiliency "is an important personality resource that might enable individuals to competently and adaptively negotiate their lives under changing conditions, such as those of the midlife transition" (p. 432).

There is a lot to be praised in Klohnen et al.'s (1996) work. Longitudinal studies are quite rare in personality research. Even more unusual are studies that include comparable data from more than one longitudinal set. Klohnen et al. (1996) also use two different operational definitions of ego-resiliency; they measure ego-resiliency with observer based and self-report measures. This kind of multi-method design is also rare. Furthermore, the conceptual basis for the research is compelling. Perhaps a characteristic of personality, such as ego-resiliency, can account for why some people age well and others do not. In other words, I have picked an excellent piece of research to critique; in fact, this is the reason that I picked it. I want to reemphasize that the problems that I raise are shared by the discipline as a whole and are not unique to this particular study.

Klohnen et al.'s (1996) correlational data demonstrate a robust relationship between ego-resiliency and various forms of psychological functioning. What makes the study noteworthy is that the relationship between ego-resiliency and psychological functioning is found across operational definitions; both self-report and observer measures of ego-resiliency are correlated with psychological functioning; and across samples, both the Radcliffe and the Mills College samples show the same pattern over time. Ego-resiliency at age 43 is correlated with psychological and physical health in later life. For example, in the Mills sample, both measures of ego-resiliency are correlated with life satisfaction at age 52; the observer-rated measure of ego-resiliency correlated with life satisfaction at $\sigma = .27$ ($p < .01$) and the self-reported measure at $\sigma = .37$ ($p < .01$). In the Radcliffe sample, observer-based measures of ego-resiliency were correlated with life satisfaction at age 48 ($\sigma = .34$, $p < .01$). Similar patterns were found when correlating ego-resiliency at age 43 with other measures of positive functioning at ages 48 and 53, such as relationship satisfaction, work, physical health, and body image. These findings led Klohnen et al. to support their notion that

> [d]epending on personal resources—specifically levels of ER [ego-resiliency]—individuals bring to the developmental tasks of middle age, their experience of this period is likely to differ in important ways: Individuals going into this period with high levels of ER are more likely to experience this time of life as an opportunity for change and growth, whereas more ego-brittle individuals are more likely to experience this period as a time of stagnation and decline. (p. 440)

The grounds of my critique are not based upon the specific conclusions of Klohnen et al's research, but on the form of argument that they are making from their evidence. Their research shows a structural problem in working from the conceptualization of the problem to conclusions that are ubiquitous in psychological research.

What connects ego-resiliency with positive functioning? On average, they go together. They seem to be tapping into the fact that these variables hang together. But the problem is, what do these relationships tell us? As Lamiell (2003) cautions, statistical analyses derived from group averages cannot be applied to individual cases, but we are tempted to interpret them as such. We are tempted to interpret ego-resiliency and positive functioning *as if* these variables were interacting with each other in a real sense.

The vision is that there is some real entity called "ego-resiliency" that acts in ways to increase another real entity called "well-being." They seem to interact with one another, *as if* these variables, themselves, possessed agency.

But the dynamic process that turns resiliency into positive functioning is not described, nor is it available for analysis. No observation is made. The hows and whys of the process are left unexamined. In other words, the critical evidence that brings together ego-resiliency and positive psychological functioning is never established. It is striking that these relationships are taken as unproblematic. They will end up in a research report, citing Klohnen et al. (1996), and simply stating that ego-resiliency is related to positive functioning in middle age. But, in fact, we have no evidence that it is.

As persons from the same historical period and sharing a similar cultural background, we find it obvious that these ideas should be connected. People with strength of character are able to meet life challenges with dignity and to continue their projects despite the challenges. I can imagine a concrete situation in which a specific ego-resilient person is confronting a life challenge, such as a marital dispute, and how they manage this challenge without destroying their sense of integrity and purpose in life. But what in the data actually says that? Klohnen et al. provide no evidence about what goes on inside the lives and thoughts of resilient people, and how this functions to meet challenges and preserve value in life. The connections are missing.

The essential point here is that we didn't actually observe how or why ego-resiliency and life satisfaction influence each other. We can guess. Perhaps, as Klohnen et al. suggest, people who are ego-brittle cannot cope with changing life circumstances and therefore they are disappointed with their life outcomes. The only information that we possess to draw conclusions is that on average, in our sample, ego-resiliency and life satisfaction tend to co-occur. On average, they tend to co-occur in the same person's reports. We don't know anything else about the dynamics of this relationship as they exist in the lives of real people who are ego-resilient and satisfied with their lives, or those who are ego-brittle and dissatisfied with their lives.

In order to draw inferences about internal mental processes, we need to make a variety of assumptions about how variables interact, subjectively, that we did not actually observe. The actual process, which is going on inside the person's experience and in their relationship with the world, is something of a mystery. We can determine that across a group, these variables tend to be present together or are related in terms of the amounts or quantities of our measures, but we do not actually observe their connection. In fact, the analysis takes place entirely outside of the persons involved. Or, as we can whimsically say, the connections are not taking place "in the head" of the people we are studying. We never observe the subjective or experiential links between processes. Rather, the connections are part of the *experimental imagination*. It is the researcher who fills in the blanks, drawing upon their own life experience, and making inferences about what must be happening in the minds of the persons that they studied.

This is an important critique. Variable-centered methods do not base their theories of psychological phenomena on direct empirical assessments.

But, researchers use their life experience to imagine what must be happening in the minds and interactions of their participants.

I understand that researchers are skeptical about whether or not people are both willing and able to know the actual connections between mental states, motivations, and actions (Nisbett & Wilson, 1977). This skepticism has a long history in psychology, extending back at least to early behaviorism at the beginning of the twentieth century and in psychology's philosophical predecessors. However, it is even more problematic to suppose that researchers have more insight into the subjective experience of the persons they study than do the persons themselves. It is also unscientific.

Although researchers have not observed the thought process in action, as an authentic scientific stance would demand, we stand firm by the scientific methods that our discipline allows and conjecture about what must be happening in the mental world of our subjects. It is essential to emphasize that the problem cannot be resolved by the inclusion of additional mediating or moderating variables or by more sophisticated methods of statistical analysis. The problem is structural and trenchant. An authentic scientific stance requires that we make appropriate observations before drawing conclusions. We must be able to grapple with phenomena in order to describe and explain them. If we are to make psychology a science, then we need to move closer to the meanings that persons articulate, to describe their thoughts and interpretations in more detail, to get to know them and their world better, rather than keeping them at arm's length because we are uncomfortable with their messy, complex, and contradictory lives, or because we are uncomfortable that such explorations are not subject to statistical methods of analysis. Statistics doesn't make psychology a science.

THERE'S NO CONTACT HERE

The critique that I am outlining is applicable to psychology in general, not just personality theory. It is also applicable to the experimental method. From a variable-centered perspective, personality psychology misses the dynamic subjective connections that motivate psychological phenomena. But, when applied to other realms, such as social psychology, the same problem reappears. We miss what we are most interested in describing: the social dynamics that transpire between persons, and how grounded and contextual aspects of meaning making contribute to action and interpretation.

It is in this regard that I turn to the realm of contact theory in social psychology. Contact theory has a long history, beginning with Allport's (1954) seminal work, *The Nature of Prejudice*. The basic premise of contact theory is that when individuals from groups with preexisting prejudices meet one another on equal terms, prejudicial attitudes decrease.

Allport's theory has had a wide impact on social psychology and has been the subject of hundreds of research articles. Pettigrew and Tropp's (2006) quantitative review of contact theory considered "515 individual studies with 713 independent samples and 1,383 non-independent tests. Combined, 250,089 individuals from 38 nations" (p. 753). Pettigrew and Tropp (2006) present convincing evidence that, overall, these two variables are negatively related. Contact between groups is correlated with prejudice reduction.

But what exactly does this mean? Does contact reduce prejudice or not? Pettigrew and Tropp's meta-analysis argues that, on average, it does. But contact does not always lead to prejudice reduction. The relationship is not a perfect one. Under conditions in which status is equal, the effect size that Pettigrew and Tropp estimate is −.28. But, as Pettigrew and Tropp (2008) point out, this effect becomes more substantial when considering data that are more "empirically" rigorous.

In further analysis of this data set, Pettigrew and Tropp (2008) evaluate three factors—knowledge, anxiety, and empathy—which mediate between contact and prejudice reduction. Not all of the 500+ studies measured each factor, so groups were smaller depending on which mediating variable was considered. Their findings indicate that contact works to reduce prejudice by increasing knowledge about the other group, reducing anxiety, and creating a feeling of empathy for others. However, the affective factors of anxiety reduction and empathy are the most powerful mediators.

Pettigrew and Tropp would probably be the first to admit that their meta-analysis is only a rough sketch of the processes that are apparent in intergroup contact. Also, meta-analyses do increase our distance from the evidence; we are further removed from the research, surveying the data of others. But meta-analyses, theoretically, do allow more far-reaching generalizations. Pettigrew and Tropp (2008), rightly, argue that more empirical work is necessary to understand the processes that lead from contact to prejudice reduction. However, they argue, these are clues that should help us to understand at least part of the picture of what must be happening inside of the person and inside of the relational world in which they are embedded. Contact is related to prejudice reduction. This relationship is mediated by anxiety and empathy.

Connecting abstract variables together in time and space as if they are real entities that affect one another is the widely accepted language of mainstream psychology. Contact and prejudice and the variables that mediate between them are taken as givens that can be abstracted from their immediate context and understood on their own—they seem to possess agency—rather than being grounded in the immediate circumstances in which they operate.

By taking these variables as abstracts, we are given little insight into how these processes actually operate in context. We understand little about how persons meet each other in concrete situations, come to know each other, come to see themselves and the other in a new light and to make changes in their view of the other—or not. The phenomenon that we seek to describe and explain remains empty and vague. Complexity is reduced to a platitude.

Pettigrew and Tropp (2008) title one of their publications, "How Does Intergroup Contact Reduce Prejudice? Meta-analytic Tests of Three Mediators." But, from my perspective, they never answer their question. How does contact reduce prejudice? We never really find out. How does this process work? What are the dynamics involved? What does it say about human nature? What does it say about how to help these two persons sitting in front of me to better understand each other and to see each other as human beings with legitimate aspirations? What does it say about how to ameliorate conflict?

Contact doesn't really reduce prejudice. Like the relationship between ego-resiliency and well-being, these variables don't really interact with one another; they are descriptive abstractions plucked from the actual contexts in which they operate. We don't know enough concrete details. We don't know how the process actually works, or why it works (or doesn't). The complexities are glossed over. It would be a significant contribution to our knowledge of human psychology to know and describe the hows and whys of such a critical question. But, in the variable mold, these matters remain undescribed—beyond the purview of the analysis.

The context is wrong. On the level of the psychological variable, we can only have a picture of how two variables co-occur. It is a bird's eye view. At the very least, we have committed Lamiell's (2003) fatal error and have mistaken group averages for what, we suppose, must be happening at the level of the person and social interaction. What is missing is a notion of how these processes translate into concrete descriptions of the situation of contact and how such contact changes persons.

Psychologists need to reintroduce complexity into their observations. Real life is messy. Reducing life to a couple of variables doesn't make the world a more regular place; it just makes our research artificial and out of touch. We need to deal with the complexity of life rather than run away from it. We need to make complexity problematic in order to describe what is really happening.

The external path, which tells us that these variables co-occur, can only go so far. We need to understand the dynamics that are internal to the situation and internal to the person in order to truly understand this phenomenon. For example, even if we know that certain structural aspects, such as reducing anxiety of the other in situations of contact, produce a modest reduction of prejudice, we still have not done our job. How is anxiety negotiated and played out within the concrete circumstances of particular persons meeting one another?

Scholars studying dialogue groups in areas of conflict, particularly Israel, also recognize that "a fundamental problem of research based on the Contact Hypothesis is that most of these studies relate to the outcome rather than to the process of the encounter" (Maoz, 2004, p. 438). Maoz (2004) continues, "when there is no clear description or conceptualization of what takes place during the encounter itself, it is very hard to draw unequivocal conclusions about changes that result from the encounter" (p. 438). Maoz is absolutely correct that, if contact is truly related to prejudice reduction, then, in order to understand the phenomenon, researchers must describe the process of what happens in situations of contact and their results; even more than that, however, researchers need to make the connections clear. Can we show the interpretive lines between contact and prejudice reduction? Can we make explicit how situations of contact produce this effect in persons? Can we describe how contact helps persons arrive at new ways of seeing the other? In other words, can we disclose the phenomenon?

Studies that lift the curtain and describe the process of what actually happens in dialogue with the other and how persons reflect on contact are exceedingly rare. But there are some encouraging signs of a more descriptive, narrative, account of how the situation of contact is structured and the sense that persons make of contact.

Steinberg and Bar-On's (2002) descriptive analysis of dialogue groups moves further in the direction of exploring the meaning of contact. This is a critical step. The research focuses on the kinds of conversations that they have witnessed in the context of encounter groups with Arab and Jewish Israelis, but the ideas apply more widely than just Arabs and Jews. Steinberg and Bar-On ask, what are the various kinds of interactions that one finds during conversations between Arabs and Jews? In other words, they are dealing with a layer of complexity in the varieties and processes of contact that could possibly lead to the accentuation of prejudice or its reduction.

They present a classificatory system that analyzes the conversations of two groups of Jewish and Palestinian Israeli students at Ben-Gurion

University of the Negev who met each other for 3 hours, once a week, for an entire academic year. Their classifications represent the types of conversations that are repeated in their data and "reflect different ways of viewing the self, the other and the relationship. The six categories can theoretically be located on a scale progressing from simplistic to more complex perceptions" (Steinberg & Bar-On, 2002, p. 209). Some dialogues are characterized by "Ethnocentric talk" or "Attack." But the categories do not need to be linear.

Although their goals are more descriptive, when viewed through the lens of contact theory, Steinberg and Bar-On might argue that whether or not contact reduces prejudice depends on the type of conversation that persons find themselves engaged in. Some conversations are conflict producing, while others are, potentially, influential in producing harmonious relationships.

One of their classificatory themes, which they call the "Dialogic moment," is important to discuss. As they define it, a dialogical moment is

> [a] discussion between equals, characterized by sharing feelings with the others, differentiation among individuals, listening, reacting in a non-judgmental way and trying to understand the other's point of view, which leads to a moment of cognitive and affective understanding, of "real meeting" . . . participating in the other's experience without losing the "self." (2002, p. 204)

Steinberg and Bar-On describe this kind of encounter as one in which the participants are able to experience the other's perspective, including the most painful moments of their story, as more immediate and important than their own pain.

One of the most significant aspects of this research is that it starts to break down the notion that a complex human event, such as an encounter, can be reduced to two or more variables and how they relate to one another. I am also appreciative of the creative way in which the authors put together their data and present concrete examples that justify their categorizations.

They are moving in the right direction, but this research could be stronger if it included a full account of the context of the conversations and how these interesting categories connect with how persons understand themselves and the other. In other words, a full accounting of contact and change requires that we understand not only that there are different kinds of conversations, but also who participates in the conversations, why, and what participation means to them.

Using the data set described previously in Steinberg and Bar-On (2002), Maoz, Steinberg, Bar-On, and Fakhereldeen (2002) follow the developing relationship between two of the participants over the course of a semester and their interactions within the sessions. Avner and Nasser, a Jewish and a Palestinian Israeli, are the central actors and contributors to one of the groups. Although their relationship began on a confrontational footing, and within the encounter group it continued to be competitive and at times conflictual, there were also some moments when their positions softened, as they became more aware of the contradictions in their identities and open to self-criticism. And, importantly, the two became friends outside of the group.

Maoz et al. (2002) do not document any dialogical moments in the conversation itself. But, as the semester progressed, "each of them was able to acknowledge and reveal a more complex construction of his own collective identity and include in the dialogue parts of himself that were silenced up to that point" (p. 956). The conflict that Avner and Nasser were able to enact and work through in the context of the encounter group seems to have had beneficial effects in breaking down each person's "monolithic" identity and opening a window to seeing the self and other differently.

Bekerman and colleagues have studied contact and identity in the newly formed "bilingual" primary schools in Israel. Beginning in 1998, a handful of primary schools have opened with the intention of providing equal education and creating lines of contact between Arab and Jewish youth (Bekerman, 2009). These schools take a "strong additive bilingual approach," to bicultural education, striving to place both languages on an equal playing field (Bekerman, 2009, p. 237). For example, each classroom has two teachers—a Palestinian Arab speaker and a Jewish Hebrew speaker—and, ideally, an equal balance of Arab and Jewish students.

Bekerman offers an intensive approach to studying contact and identity that combines both ethnographic observations and narrative interviews in an effort to understand the kinds of conversations that teachers and students co-construct and the consequences of being a student in such an setting on identity and political and social attitudes. In contrast to encounter or dialogue groups, which can either be a single session or repeated meetings over a period of time, the school setting allows for sustained contact over an extended period of time and includes structured classroom discussions and informal, more spontaneous, interactions outside the classroom.

Bekerman and his colleagues are concerned with describing what actually transpires in the schools and how the setting has influenced various aspects of students' lives, attitudes, and identities. In one study, Bekerman (2009) analyzes classroom discussion of historical events, such as the death of Yassar Arafat the day after the news became public. For Bekerman, the larger lesson is really that "the integrated schools offer opportunities for students and teachers to grapple with historical [sic] conflictual narratives" (2009, p. 245). However, individual teachers have different approaches to negotiating conflict within the classroom. Similar to the different styles of those leading encounter groups, some teachers are more accommodating of different positions and try to engage in a real exchange, while others are more cognizant of the power imbalance and represent the Palestinian position forcefully, not only to legitimate and empower this position, but also to provoke conflict. Comparing the approach of two Palestinian teachers, Bekerman (2009) writes that "it is difficult to say whether Nun's accommodating approach or Ul's more oppositional approach better facilitates the development of critical perspectives among the students" (p. 246).

However, it is clear from Bekerman, Habib, and Shhadi's (2011) research that students at the bilingual schools are different from their peers. In comparative interviews with 16 Palestinian and 8 Jewish students in the fifth and sixth grades at the bilingual school and 12 Palestinian and 8 Jewish students at monolingual schools, one of Bekerman et al.'s (2011) most provocative findings is that students at the bilingual schools hold more complex views of self and other. For example, on the one hand, Jewish students at the bilingual school "not only allow for Palestinians to be included in the category of Israeli, but they also add to this their Diaspora roots." And, on the other hand, "Palestinian . . . children at the bilingual school play with hyphenated definitions—Arab/Palestinian-Israeli—though they are very aware that, at present, this definition is not accepted by all" (p. 12).

Hammack's (2011) research on Palestinian and Israeli youth who attended peace camps in the United States nicely complements research that focuses on the situation of contact. Hammack grounds his analysis in personal narratives taken from interviews after the experience. In other words, he deals with reflection—what it all means. Hammack compares pre-camp and post-camp interviews with these youth and explores their construction of identity over time. Has their experience in peace camp influenced their group identity? Does camp experience challenge youth to adopt a new conception of self and others? Of belonging?

Hammack presents a rich analysis of his interviews, the meanings that individuals give to their life experience, their depictions of family, life in Israel-Palestine, social relationships, and peace camp. He also takes into account the role that his presence as an interviewer played in the joint construction of the interview, as well as developmental theory and the power dynamics inherent in the current historical and social context. The analysis is a complex one that begins from what Hammack has learned about each person in his conversations, one by one, but with an understanding of the larger social and cultural forces that influence how interviewees construct their identities.

Based upon his interviews, Hammack concludes that social forces after peace camp, which contradict the message contrived by the camp's organizers, often shape the meaning of the experience itself. Contrary to the wisdom that contact reduces prejudice, although the message of peace camp might be internalized in the short term, in the long term the identities of these youth often become more polarized after the experience of contact. His skeptical conclusion argues that the day-to-day cultural setting, where social forces pit Jews and Arabs against one another and demand an allegiance to one side or the other, are too all encompassing to sustain the experience and ideology of peace camp. This was especially true in the case of Palestinian youth.

Hammack's research helps us to see the persons involved, long after the situation of contact, but loses certain aspects of the situation of contact during peace camp. Other approaches, such as that of Steinberg and Bar-On (2002), are more focused on the dialogue and the situation of contact, and neglect how persons reflect upon the experience and what it means to them. It is worth noting that the tension between privileging the situation of contact, moment by moment, and what contact means afterward, in reflection, replicates the debate between "small" stories and "big" stories in narrative psychology (discussed in detail in Chapter 8). The situation of contact focuses on the process of the conversation, how it unfolds, while reflection focuses on the larger meaning in the person's life. A more complex step would be to consider larger units of analysis that involve both persons and social interactions.

As I will argue, there is much to be gained by bringing together the descriptive analysis of conversations with the in-depth descriptions of life stories over time. How can we conduct research that allows us to see persons in concrete social interactions? Or, alternatively, to see the social world in the person? Studies like Maoz et al. (2002), Hammack (2011), and Bekerman et al. (2011) attempt to move us in this direction. But we are only part of the way there; more work is needed in describing the phenomenon and the links across these domains. Certainly, the work is difficult and, perhaps, this standard is too high to ask of any single piece of research.

Still, this line of research demonstrates the weaknesses of remaining at the level of variables in order to understand the social and intellectual problems posed by contact theory. In order to get beyond vast generalizations that don't apply to any specific case, we need to get our hands dirty and begin to explore social reality as it is constructed by persons in concrete situations. The insights that we gain are edifying and useful and move us beyond the bland and highly abstract claim that contact reduces prejudice. Thickening up what we know about the situation of contact and thickening up what we know about how, but also when and where, persons reflect upon contact, are exceedingly useful for constructing more nuanced, and realistic, pictures of how the phenomenon actually works, that is, how contact and prejudice play out in persons and in social context.

We need to find new approaches that allow us to describe the dynamics internal to specific encounters and particular persons. We need to observe, as close as we possibly can, where the action is happening, how such meetings unfold and progress and are understood, processed, and reflected upon by the actors. This is the appropriate context—inside situations and inside the reflections of the actors involved.

RETHINKING METHOD AND THEORY

Methods configure approaches to subject matter. They are ways of thinking about or seeing something. But they are never neutral. Methods are a reality-building project, which through their acceptance and application come to constitute a world by their own rules, logic, and facts. All of reality may not be up for grabs—there may be "brute facts" (Searle, 1995). But it is also true that the methods we choose are constitutive of the reality that we discover. Psychologists tend to assume the independence of method and theory, presuming that we could use any possible theory to explain what are taken to be pure observations. I assume exactly the opposite. Method and theory are locked together in a reciprocal process of mutual definition. Methods, themselves, are theoretical propositions that make a variety of assumptions and, in turn, configure theory.

At the same moment that methods provide direction for observing one phenomenon, they obscure others. One part of reality lights up, while another is covered over. Variable-centered methods may help us to document the incidence of a single variable in a population or the co-occurrence of variables. But, at the same moment, they conceal the subjective universe of the person and the function of interpretive and reflective capacities in human psychology. As I have argued, variable-centered methods follow an outer, external, path that obscures the fundamental process of human meaning making.

The language of variable-centered methods (the experiment, the survey, validity, reliability, tests of statistical significance, and p-values) is part of the linguistic and social practice of psychologists and produces results as much as the data observed. It is through these socially derived practices and means of configuring the world that psychologists make discoveries.

Forcing psychological processes out of context and out of the head, variable-centered methods impoverish our investigation of how psychological processes function inside persons, and how they play out in social relationships and the complex inter-relationships that ensue between person and world. By consequence, we never get a sense of the way that the interpretations of the persons we are studying change outcomes. We never get to ask, how does interpretation make a difference? Does it make a difference?

One of the strongest arguments for a narrative perspective, developed in detail in Chapter 9, is that narrative promises, somewhat counterintuitively, to make psychology more rigorous and scientific by paying close attention to the phenomena themselves. Narrative psychology argues that researchers need to explore aspects of human subjective experience, intention, and interpretation, in order to have an accurate and, indeed, scientific, accounting of the basic problems in human psychology, of thinking, acting, and feeling.

Variable-centered approaches move our attention away from what is truly critical to know. In order to understand human psychology as it is, we cannot continue to rely on a variable-centered orientation as a model for research and theory. A narrative perspective is essential in this effort.

Narrative attempts to make explicit the connections that motivate lives. It endeavors to move beyond the misguided notion that two objects, variables constructed by researchers, could possibly relate to one another. Unlike humans, lifeless variables do not possess agency and cannot interact. But, drawing on their own life experience, researchers construct a story of how these variables must relate to one another. Narrative examines the reasoning and interpretations of human actors engaged in the project of meaning making, and the ways in which these actors put life and world together in words and deeds. Narrative researchers observe how (and why) persons arrive at, reason through, and articulate meanings in context. Although imperfect and in need of constant critique and reflexivity, the focus is on the person's experiences, not the researcher's, and the connections that he or she makes. The process examined is a dynamic one; researchers try to interpret how this meaning is linked to other meanings, how it is realized in this situation, and how it configures relationships, reconstructs the past, and guides future actions. Meaning is always moving. And once an interpretation is made and pinned down, in speech or on paper, we can be assured that our portrait is no longer faithful to experience now (or then). It has changed. But these are the complexities of life. Although we recognize the limits of our interpretations, we aspire to reveal, if only just a glimpse, how persons make sense of themselves and their lives. This is exactly what is lacking in variable-centered approaches to psychology. As I will argue, narrative analysis attempts to disclose the multilayered psychological, social, and cultural dimensions in the interpretive actions of actual human actors. It is a potent corrective force for the crisis in contemporary psychology.

PART II

CHAPTER 3

Turning to Narrative

As I have argued, the problems with contemporary psychology are deep and structural. The choice is a clear one. Psychology can continue business as usual and continue to misinterpret psychological phenomena, or it can endeavor to rediscover itself in an alternative psychology and begin the critical work of studying persons in context. This is the position that I develop in the following chapters. I believe that psychology needs creative and innovative, as well as sound and pragmatic, strategies for understanding what persons do, say, and think.

But what would such an alternative psychology look like? In my view, the contours of this renewal are best described as a narrative perspective—one that is finely attuned to the descriptive analysis of how persons, in context, interpret themselves, others, and the world.

So, what is it? What is this thing that we call "narrative psychology"?

Problematic as they are, I adore "what is it" questions. They are pesky little questions that lead us to wonder about the bases undergirding our thinking. Of course, one can keep asking, "but what is it—really?" And there is some danger in being too persistent. But posing the "what is it" question doesn't need to produce endless deconstruction. It can also be the beginning moves of putting together the pieces of a puzzle in a new way that allows us to move forward productively, building a revised structure from a more stable foundation. This is my intention in asking the question.

What does the expression "narrative psychology" mean? Indeed, it is exceedingly difficult to give a single answer because "narrative psychology" is used in so many different ways. Of course, such a response is unsatisfying, and I don't intend to leave the matter unresolved. Some of my comments are critical of the current state of narrative psychology, but this is with an eye toward a sharper and more vital field of inquiry. My aim is to set the narrative perspective on the right footing so that it can claim a place in the conversation at the center of psychological science. Narrative has a central contribution to make in our understanding of human beings and it is imperative that we empower it to assume this position. But before narrative can make a real contribution, we must understand what narrative is and what it can do.

WE'VE ALWAYS DONE "IT"

One way of answering the "what is it" question is to respond that we have always done "it." And there is something to this argument. Psychologists have always studied narrative—or, at least, for a long time and, at least, something *like* narrative.

Historically, a small group of psychologists, some quite prominent in the field, has always been concerned with aspects of storytelling in human lives. Indeed, many of psychology's enduring theoretical discoveries (e.g., Allport, Erikson, Freud, James, Janet, Maslow, Piaget, Rogers, etc.) were based upon the close examination of rich oral and written expressions.

The obvious narrative predecessor is the psychoanalytic tradition of examining words and meanings. Psychoanalysis, especially seen through Ricoeur's (1970) reading of Freud, influenced the development of narrative in multiple disciplines, including psychology. The use of life documents in the study of psychoanalysis dates back at least as far as the discovery of psychoanalysis and the publication of Freud and Breuer's first psychoanalytic case studies (Breuer & Freud, 1893–1895/2000).

Typically, Freud's case studies are based upon clinical observations, but they also include the innovative use of autobiographical and historical documents. Beyond their influence on psychoanalytic theory, Freud's case studies are claimed as part of the intellectual heritage of researchers interested in a later-day variety of case-based research called "psychobiography" (Schultz, 2005). Freud's interpretation of a childhood memory of Leonardo di Vinci is often cited as one of the earliest examples of psychobiographical analysis (Runyan, 2005).

Case studies form a critical source of demonstrating and communicating psychoanalytic theory. Erik Erikson's influential interpretations of the development of (1958) Martin Luther and (1969) Gandhi are outstanding examples of the descriptive and theoretical power of case-study research.

Although the influence of case studies is felt mainly within psychoanalytic circles, psychodynamic portrayals of human development have had a profound and lasting impact not only inside psychology, but also outside, in philosophy, history, and literary studies.

A less obvious predecessor—and I believe equally, if not more, important than psychoanalysis—is the tradition of idiographic study in personality psychology, which is sometimes referred to as the Allport-Murray-White tradition, or personological psychology. Beginning in the 1930s, Gordon Allport, Henry Murray, and Robert White, and their students at Harvard University's Department of Social Relations, developed innovative methods for studying personality, which pay close attention to a person's words and stories.

Allport (1962), the most accomplished theoretician of the group, advocated for a methodologically balanced approach to the study of personality. On the one hand, he argued for the study of dimensions or concepts that could describe characteristics across individuals and could serve as the basis for comparative analysis between persons (which he called a "nomothetic" or "dimensional" approach). On the other hand, he argued for the close study of individual lives in order to describe persons on their own terms from the inside out (which he called an "idiographic" or "morphogenic" approach). In this tradition, nomothetic and idiographic approaches are viewed as complementary and necessary ways of studying human beings.

In light of the quantitative (nomothetic) standard, which prevailed then as it does now, the introduction of an idiographic psychology had a critical edge to it. Allport argued that psychological knowledge is incomplete without complementary investigations of individuals. Knowledge discovered in nomothetic research cannot be translated back to the person. Knowing that people with low IQ are, on average, something (for example, more violent) does not help us to understand Molly's or William's development or whether or not, given their IQ, they will (or will not) become violent. Each person develops differently. To do justice to this uniqueness, Allport urged psychologists to study the events and experiences that define the person's life history.

Allport's (1942/1951) major theoretical statement on the principles of idiographic research, *Personal Documents in Psychological Science*, was published by the Social Science Research Council (SSRC). The work is Allport's contribution to the debate on qualitative methods in the social sciences organized by the SSRC and kicked off by Thomas and Znaniecki's *The Polish Peasant in Europe and America*, a five-volume manuscript published from 1918 to 1920 (Stanley, 2010). The scientific merits of the Polish peasant documents was debated by Allport, but the SSRC also published manuscripts written by other luminaries in the social sciences, such as Blumer (1939) and Gottschalk, Kluckhorn, and Angell (1945).

Allport (1942/1951) limited the scope of his commentary to those documents written in the first person. In other words, "personal documents," which he defined as: "*any self-revealing record that intentionally or unintentionally yields information regarding the structure, dynamics, and functioning of the author's mental life*" (p. xii). Allport (1942/1951) and his associates, including Jerome Bruner, considered the extant literature of the time, using personal documents and considering when and under what circumstances the in-depth study of what people say about themselves should be used in psychological research. Some of Allport's concerns are common with historical research. When should we put credence in the source? In what circumstances should such data be used? Other concerns are more disciplinary. How reliable and valid are the data? How representative are they? How do we handle the problem of interpreter bias? Can it be scientific?

Allport's approach was hard-nosed and methodical. Allport contended that even idiographic analysis could be systematic, scientific, and predictive. Influential as Allport's legacy is to contemporary psychological theory, from the perspective of the current historical moment, the issues and many of the recommendations for idiographic study feel out of date. However, presciently, Allport understood the necessary use of personal documents, not only as the beginning point for nomothetic projects or as an endpoint for testing nomothetic research, but also as a means for getting at the phenomenon itself. His chapter "The Case for Personal Documents" begins with the following words:

> The only reasonable thing to do if one wishes to study a phenomenon is to put a specimen before one's eyes and look at it repeatedly until its essential features sink indelibly into one's mind. . . . The subject matter of psychology is particularly elusive. . . . Subject matter so unfathomably complex needs more than the usual amount of concrete inspection before analysis and abstraction begins. . . . In the personal document can be found the needed touchstone of reality. Unless concrete psychology progresses along with abstract psychology, the discipline is likely to run wild. (p. 143)

The particulars are necessary not only for describing the depth of complexity that we witness in human lives, but also for keeping us in touch with the phenomenon itself. The concrete is our "touchstone of reality" for remaining grounded in the phenomenon.

Allport's colleague at Harvard's Department of Social Relations, Henry Murray, made several innovative contributions to narrative psychology's pre-history. Like Allport, Murray was in favor of the use of multiple methods for the study of personality. He favored an intensive approach, combining in-depth interviews, paper-and-pencil measures, and projective tests. Research participants would come to the lab for several days. Typically, a team of researchers organized the tests, interviewed participants, and consulted with each other for data analysis (McAdams, 2008).

One of Murray's enduring contributions is his development of the Thematic Apperception Test (TAT). In the 1930s, Murray and Christiana Morgan developed the TAT, a personality instrument in which persons are asked to tell imaginative stories out loud to ambiguous and sometimes bizarre pictures meant to stimulate unconscious processes (Murray, 1943). Indeed, we haven't completely sidestepped psychoanalytic theory. The TAT is a storytelling task that is supposed to reveal something about the conscious and unconscious conflicts and desires of the storyteller. Murray and Morgan provided a road map for the analysis of TAT stories, asking various questions: Who is the hero of the story? What needs does the hero express? How does the person portray the environment (which they called the "press")? What is the interaction between the hero's needs and the environmental press? (McAdams, 2008).

Murray and Morgan's method of interpretation is open-ended and descriptive. It was intended to provide a picture of the experience of the person and categories for describing some 20 personal needs. And it does provide a rich picture of the person's inner world. There is also a story elicited. The story feels contrived, but it is a form of storytelling. Although the TAT is still used in some clinical settings, in research settings the TAT, if used at all, is quantified into three motives (achievement, power, and intimacy). McClelland, a personality psychologist with a strong interest in measurement theory and the TAT, reshaped Murray's test in a different direction (Winter, 1998). In many ways, McClelland's repurposing of the TAT is instructive for understanding the way in which some personality psychologists have taken narrative from a qualitative project to a quantitative one.

McClelland was interested in the potential uses of the TAT to describe unconscious conflicts and systems of deep meaning. However, he found Murray's analyses to be diffuse and unconvincing, reading too much into the data itself and guided by the subjective impressions of experts rather than observable facts in test responses. McClelland made several changes to the administration of the TAT, including group testing with written responses and manipulating subjects in order to elicit and observe thematic changes in stories; his most important development was a detailed codebook for interpreting responses (Winter, 1998).

The project of studying personality through rich personal documents probably has its highest expression in the work of Robert W. White—in particular, White's (1952/1966) *Lives in Progress*, in which White follows Murray's method of intensive study of the person to interview a group of 20 Harvard students, first as undergraduates and again 10 years later.

The memorable characters of Joseph Kidd, Hartley Hale, and Joyce Kingsley serve as rich cases for exploring the development of personality and growth over time. White's case histories are well worth reading. They are insightful, showing the value of closely analyzing life documents for understanding personality. White moves between direct, revealing quotes taken from his interviews to detailed analyses of each case and general lessons drawn from the cases.

His case studies are developmental tales, told chronologically from early childhood to the present in adulthood. Who is Hartley Hale? How did he become the person that he is? What is the "backbone story"? How did he interact with peers in childhood? Why did he stutter? What were his expectations of marriage, and why is his marriage the way it is currently? How did his personality grow over time and why?

White (1952/1966) provides an intimate and complex understanding of personality. His interpretations integrate biological, psychodynamic, and sociocultural theories. He writes:

> We want to understand one man, Hartley Hale, as well as it is possible with the materials at our disposal. We want to know the story of his life and to search behind that story for whatever we can find by way of explanation. Before we can move in a responsible manner in the realm of general ideas it is necessary to become exhaustively acquainted with at least one fact, and if personality is our theme this fact can be nothing smaller than a person's whole life in all its uniqueness and all its complexity. (p. 28)

The quote highlights the underlying conceptions of White's research, but also of Allport's and Murray's, and the differences between White's understanding of "story" and current understandings in narrative psychology.

White is interested in personality—how and why people think, act, and feel the way that they do. When White says "story," he seems to be talking about the facts of Hartley's life. Someone's "story" is the repository of fact, the elements of a history (i.e., what really happened to them). In White's work, life documents or life histories are vehicles for getting at personality. These are worthy goals. But is this really narrative?

Many narrative studies are identical to White's, using narrative as a method only. Missing is a notion of how the action of telling shapes mental life or is useful for the interpretation of self, identity, and life experience, or how cultural stories enter our repertoire of stories to tell. In a sense, these early notions of story lack an idea of the power of narrative to construct. How do persons make sense of who they are? How do persons, together and separately, interpret life experience? Tell their identities? How are cultural meanings used to make sense of life? In short, there is no overarching narrative theory to match the narrative method. From our contemporary perspective, White's case studies seem unfocused. They are fascinating (though meandering) in their insights about the individuals considered, and they lack the critical sense of the constructedness of our lives and what we tell about them.

PSYCHOLOGY'S TURN TO NARRATIVE

Although there has always been an interest in the close study of persons, the impact of these approaches on mainstream psychology has been meager. From the perspective of the mainstream, this line of research is marginal. It is harshly judged and often mistrusted. In fact, most mainstream psychologists seem to treat case studies with contempt. They are viewed as unscientific and therefore outside of academic psychology. Case studies are slurred as mere literature, journalism, or, perhaps, philosophy—but definitely not scientific psychology.

Mainstream psychology fashions itself as a science in the style of physics, looking for certainty and truth, the laws that govern human nature for all time. Toulmin (1992) argues that this search for certainty in the social sciences, for real truths, was a response to the enormous social changes brought about by industrialization and the chaos and mass death of the first and second world wars. The upheaval compelled scientists to search for indisputable solutions to the problems plaguing Western civilization.

Although many disciplines have abandoned the search for universal truths, psychology still clings to the hope of developing theories that reveal the eternal laws that guide thought and behavior. The close study of words and meanings involved in narrative research does not yield certainty. Interpretive analysis does not possess the hard, cold, objective feeling of truth that numbers do.

In the 1980s, some psychologists began to self-consciously focus on narration. The "narrative turn" did not begin in the field of psychology. "Narrative" is not usually considered a basic psychological process in the same category as intelligence, memory, perception, personality, language, behavior, or thinking. Narrative is thought to be more social or cultural and, therefore, not part of the basic architecture of human nature that psychologists seek to describe. Psychology is a latecomer in recognizing the significance of narrative.

In the 1970s and 1980s, across the humanities and the social sciences, a wide-ranging discussion unfolded on the meaning of narrative for the construction and representation of the past (Hyvärinen, 2006, 2010). The 1980 publication of a special issue of the journal *Critical Inquiry*, which was later republished with the title *On Narrative* (Mitchell, 1981), was important in disseminating these ideas across disciplinary lines (Bruner, 1991; Hyvärinen, 2006).

The wave of interest in narrative in the discipline of psychology is, in large measure, a response to innovative theoretical and empirical work on narrative that begins in the fields of literary studies and linguistics and spreads to philosophy, history, the social sciences at large, and finally to psychology. However, as Hyvärinen (2010) cautions, the turn toward narrative in literary studies, history, the social sciences, and culture should not be interpreted as a continuous plotline. Rather, in turning toward narrative, each of these groups has reinterpreted the idea of narrative in a new fashion. Psychology is no exception. Psychology reinvents the narrative wheel.

This interdisciplinary conversation on narrative was a tremendous resource for psychologists, who, reading outside their discipline, saw the obvious applications for narrative in psychology.

Still, I don't want to give the impression that a singular plot line can capture the development of narrative psychology. Certainly, in the 1980s, the idea of narrative was "in the air," but there were other ideas and intellectual movements also floating about at that time, often with common personnel and intersecting interests. The late twentieth century witnessed not only the "cognitive revolution," but also the "linguistic turn" and the "interpretive turn." Not only was the "narrative turn" almost contemporaneous with these other "turns," but they often shared a general discontent with reductive methods and with theories of knowledge invested in the project of building universal, true, laws about the world.

Several foundational works on narrative psychology were published in the 1980s and early 1990s. Cohler's (1982) seminal chapter, "Personal Narrative and Life Course," was one of the first manuscripts published in what would later become known as narrative psychology. Drawing upon an impressive range of literature from philosophy, literary studies, history, psychoanalysis, and life course developmental psychology, Cohler argued that we need to consider lives as texts that are told and revised in response to periods of crisis and rupture, brought out by developmental transitions and personal experiences. Persons strive to make sense of their past, but can only do so from the present moment, constantly retelling and revising their stories into a *presently understood past*. Drawing heavily on Ricoeur, Cohler argued that narratives have a dual interpretive task: to account for the past in a way that makes subjective sense of experience for the person, but that narratives must also be followable by listeners. Cohler emphasized that the coherence of our personal accounts, as understood by the self and the other, is one of the hallmarks of mental health, and that disintegration of the personal narrative was akin to disintegration of the self and could lead to mental illness (see Schiff [2014] for further reflections on the impact of Cohler [1982]).

Shortly after, Freeman (1984) published "History, Narrative and Life-Span Developmental Knowledge." There are some shared themes and concerns with Cohler's (1982) essay; Freeman was a graduate student at the time, and Cohler as well as Ricoeur counted among his professors. Freeman (1984) proposes a "hermeneutic solution" to life-span studies where development is viewed not only in the direction of a past oriented toward a future, but also in reverse, in the sense of meaning making. The role of the interpreter is to reach an intersubjective understanding of the person—fraught though it is in Freeman's view—through the practice of empathy.

Both Cohler (1982) and Freeman (1984) draw upon a philosophy of science that is critical of mainstream psychology, arguing for methods that emphasize subjectivity, interpretation, and understanding. How do persons understand time and the course of development? Narrative is theorized as a way of integrating disparate aspects of the self through time and in response to changing life circumstances in order to find a sense of self-consistency or coherence.

Another seminal early contribution is Mishler's (1986) *Research Interviewing: Context and Narrative*, which strongly critiques the idea that interviews, both structured and unstructured, collect transparent information. Rather, Mishler argues that interviews are a site of performance and storytelling—narrative—where meaning is built from the interaction between interviewer and interviewee in the frame of the conversation at hand. Mishler's (1986) work is informed by linguistic theory and the methods of discourse analysis and has been critical for connecting these traditions with narrative psychology.

Although the subject of an intense critique and re-evaluation (De Fina & Georgakopoulou, 2012; Georgakopoulou, 2007; Norrick, 2007), Labov's (1972; Labov & Waletzky, 1967/1997) structural analysis of personal experience narratives continues to have a wide impact on narrative psychology. Labov argued that personal experience narratives can be structurally defined, minimally, as two linked complicating actions that recount a past event in the order in which they occurred. Fully developed personal experience narratives contain the additional structural elements of an orientation, abstract, resolution, evaluation, and coda, as well as multiple complicating actions (for various perspectives on Labov's influence on narrative in psychology and the social sciences, see Bamberg, 1997).

Also during the 1980s and early 1990s, several clinicians, including Spence (1982), Schafer (1980, 1992), and White and Epston (1990), reframed psychological therapy as the reconstitution of a failed narrative, which is reconstructed by clinician and client through conversation about the past. Polkinghorne's (1988) *Narrative Knowing and the Human Sciences* is noteworthy in its attempt to ground narrative practice in a theoretical, hermeneutic, philosophical tradition and, like Cohler (1982) and Freeman (1984) as well as Gergen (1985), a philosophy of science based upon the humanistic principles of understanding, rather than the natural science model of explanation, prediction, and control.

Using Eriksonian developmental theory and the in-depth study of lives from the personological tradition of Allport, Murray, and White, McAdams (1985) introduced his highly influential life-story model of identity in *Power, Intimacy and the Life Story*. McAdams connects the problem of modern identity to the personal narrative, arguing that the life story is a vehicle for grappling with the question, "who am I?" As he writes, the personal narrative

> is an individual's story which has the power to tie together past, present, and future in his or her life. It is a story which is able to provide unity and purpose. It is a story which specifies a personalized "niche" in the adult world and a sense of continuity and sameness across situations and over time. (p. 18)

For McAdams, a life story is characterized thematically, in terms of the complexity of the account, the highly differentiated (what he calls "nuclear") episodes recounted, the dominant characters or imagos, the ideological setting or backdrop of the story, and the variety of scripts, such as generativity, included in the life story.

However, the term "narrative psychology" was first introduced by Sarbin (1986) in the introduction to his edited volume, *Narrative Psychology: The Storied Nature of Human Conduct*. Drawing upon Pepper's notion of root metaphors as worldviews that provide the resources for the interpretation and "study" of "all other areas of fact" (Pepper, 1942, p. 91, as cited in Sarbin, 1986), Sarbin reviews and contrasts the various root metaphors (principally formism, mechanism, and organicism) that psychologists have historically used to understand human action. For Sarbin, narrative is akin to the "historical act," sharing "approximately the same semantic structure" (1986, p. 7). As he wrote, "I propose the narratory principle: that human beings think, perceive, imagine, and make moral choices according to narrative structures" (p. 8). In light of the criticism that narrative psychology employs a naïve or naturalistic conception of narrative, rather than one drawing upon narratological research, it is interesting to trace the development of narrative psychology to such an explicit attempt at reconceptualizing the basic metaphor of psychology itself.

Narrative dramatically entered the vocabulary of developmental psychology with the publication of *Narratives from the Crib*, in which Nelson (1989) and other contributors analyzed the linguistic productions, both monologues and dialogues, of a young child, Emily, recorded during her second and third years of life just before bedtime and naps. Emily's recounting of everyday happenings were analyzed not only as a case study in the growth of grammatical competence, but also for their capacities to interpret self, other, and world, and to regulate emotional life.

However, the writings of Jerome Bruner, especially in (1986) *Actual Minds, Possible Worlds* and (1990) *Acts of Meaning*, were seminal in reaching a large audience of psychologists. Bruner was one of the most influential psychologists of the twentieth century and was one of the leading figures in the cognitive movement in the 1950s and 1960s. Among his enormous accomplishments, he introduced psychologists to the thought of Vygotsky and applied the principles of sociocultural analysis to the study of child development (cf. Bruner, 1983). Bruner's status played a critical role in legitimizing the nascent narrative movement in psychology.

Bruner (1986) distinguished narrative as a mode of thinking and reasoning about life distinct from the scientific or paradigmatic mode and (1990) ascribed this tendency to inborn and universal human capacities. Premised upon social and cultural resources, both literary and folkloric, narrative represents humans' special ability to construct a sense of self, world, and life itself within a specific social and cultural horizon. Bruner insisted that the study of narrative is psychology's point of entry into the study of meaning making in its everyday forms. As he put it (1990), "what I want to argue instead is that culture and the quest for meaning within culture are the proper causes of human action" (p. 20). From Bruner's perspective, narrative is the way that cultural meanings are enacted in order to make sense of social life and one's place inside it.

Acts of Meaning provides the rationale for engaging in narrative research, but Bruner's critical assessment of cognitive psychology is perhaps the book's most significant achievement. Bruner charges that the cognitive revolution was a failure because cognitive psychology had become preoccupied with information processing and artificial intelligence, abandoning the spirit that birthed the movement, which, according to Bruner, was the study of meaning in context.

In an inspired stroke of the pen, Bruner deflates the cognitive movement down to size. The cognitive movement is not what it set out to be. In fact, according to Bruner, it misses what is most important to study, that is, the study of meaning in context. Human beings are not computing machines but meaning makers. For Bruner, the narrative turn in psychology is the true heir of the cognitive revolution, and the narrative turn toward meaning constitutes a second cognitive revolution. For Bruner, narrative is the key to recovering the true spirit of the cognitive revolution.

The early 1990s also witnessed the launching of journals and serials that would become the main outlets for the publication of research in narrative psychology. In 1990, *Narrative Inquiry* (originally named *The Journal of Narrative Life History*), edited by Michael Bamberg and Alyssa McCabe, began publishing research articles in the interdisciplinary space between sociolinguistics, developmental psychology, and social psychology. Although inclusive of a wide range of approaches, *Narrative Inquiry* tends to feature interdisciplinary articles with a discourse analytic or linguistic focus. In 1993, Ruthellen Josselson and Amia Lieblich began publishing the series *The Narrative Study of Lives*. Interestingly, the idea for an outlet to publish research on narrative psychology was developed in conversation with Jerome Bruner during the time that he was delivering the lectures at Hebrew University of Jerusalem that would later become *Acts of Meaning* (Josselson & Lieblich, 2009). The series, later co-edited with Dan McAdams, published 11 volumes from 1993 to 2007. The chapters in the volumes of *The Narrative Study of Lives* were all unique contributions, some theoretical but mostly case studies that employed a whole-life method of analysis and were written, in large measure, by psychologists. In contrast to *Narrative Inquiry, The Narrative Study of Lives* was more discipline specific and less concerned with the problems of method in studying narratives.

Since the 1980s and 1990s, narrative psychology has grown considerably. As Lieblich, Tuval-Mashiach, and Zilber (1998) note, beginning in the 1980s and intensifying in the 1990s, there was a sharp increase in the number of publications found in psychology journals with keywords related to "narrative."

But has psychology undergone a narrative "revolution?" In my opinion, revolution is hardly the right metaphor. At least at the current moment, we are still waiting for the revolution. Psychology is far from being revolutionized or revolutionary, but appears to be doing the same old thing. Even my preference for a narrative "turn" is a strong assertion, perhaps too strong, and needs to be qualified. A turn would indicate that a significant change has occurred and that a new direction is evidenced. Psychology has not yet turned narrative. Reductionist approaches still dominate psychology, while more complex approaches to lives are forced out from the center. Some psychologists have turned to narrative study. It is only in this sense that one can speak of a narrative turn; numerous psychologists have integrated some conception of narrativity into their scholarship. As a whole, however, the field remains unchanged.

CURRENT USES OF THE NARRATIVE CONCEPT

Although I view the explosion of research and writing on narrative since the 1990s optimistically, it also carries with it the danger of incoherence. If everyone is doing "it," what is the "it" that they are doing? Indeed, the question is exceedingly difficult to answer. There are so many different, and contradictory, ways of approaching narrative in psychology. Once again, the "what is it" question surfaces.

Part of this incoherence may reside in the term "narrative" itself. Pinning down the meaning of narrative is extremely problematic—there are no steadfast rules to identify it when we see it (Squire, Andrews, and Tamboukou, 2013). Even in the realm of post-classical approaches to narrative in literary studies, the latest trend seems to be a preference for more open and flexible, "fuzzy," definitions of narrative (Herman, 2009; Ryan, 2007). This seems right to me. As I will argue, structural definitions of narrative are very slippery concepts.

In any case, narrative psychology has its own definitional problems. The term "narrative psychology," historically but also currently, maintains a variety of senses. Perhaps even worse, there is more than one way to describe the fragmentation of the narrative concept in psychology.

In their excellent theoretical review of narrative perspectives in psychology and sociology, Smith and Sparkes (2008a) provide one model for describing the divisions. Although they state that their analysis is not comprehensive, they manage to capture the range and character of a broad swath of research going on in this interdisciplinary space.

They describe five contrasting perspectives on narrative: psychosocial, inter-subjective, storied resource, dialogic, and performative. Their key contrast is the weight placed on individuals and social relationships. They see a continuum from perspectives with "thick individuals" and "thin social relationships" to those with "thin individuals" and "thick social relationships." Each of these perspectives has its own definitions of what narrative is, the purpose of narrative, and how narrative functions to produce and sustain aspects of personal and social identity.

Smith and Sparkes's (2008a) analysis of the various theories is astute and diplomatic. Indeed, the main objective of the review is to open the field to a dialogue between the various perspectives on narrative in order to debate the merits of each of these approaches. Although they are careful to note that these divisions are likely to continue, the ultimate objective could be interpreted as discipline building, through description and consciousness raising. They write, "Qualitative researchers need to understand what the debate is about, make informed choices in their adoption of a certain perspective, and have a position; they do not have to resolve the issue itself" (p. 29). The review is very helpful in making the debate clear.

However, I take a somewhat more critical stance on the divisions in narrative psychology. I see less order and more conflict in the chaos. Another possible way to describe the fragmentation of narrative psychology is to view the split along the lines of the major perspectives in psychology, such as cognitive, personality, and social-cultural psychology. In the following, I discuss what I take to be the major approaches to narrative in psychology, with the object of clarifying the contrasting definitions of narrative that underlie these points of view.

Cognitive Approaches

One way of interpreting Bruner's (1986, 1990) call to study narratives is to conceptualize narrative as a cognitive structure or cognitive process. Narrative is something in the mind, something that minds do to structure and interpret experience, the self, others, and the world. Framing the approach as "cognitive" connects narrative psychology with the cognitive sciences, with its pretentions to discover the universal properties underlying human thinking. Cognitive approaches view narrative as an internalized form, which can provide a finely tuned portrait of thought processes. Narrative is a window into the mind (Chafe, 1998). It is how the mind operates. A cognitive approach asks these two questions: How do persons structure their stories such that we can gain some insight into the actual processes of thought? And how do storytelling and story structures shape cognitions?

In an influential line of research, Habermas and colleagues (Habermas & Bluck, 2000; Habermas & Hatiböglu, 2014) study the underlying processes of autobiographical reasoning (global temporal coherence, global thematic coherence, global causal-motivational coherence, contextualization) in which persons make connections between various aspects of the life story in order to craft a more coherent and integrated account of the self. Autobiographical arguments are the connective tissue that holds together the various facets of a telling about the self and the past, organizing one's life experience in more abstract and synthetic terms. In longitudinal research following the same persons from age 8 to 69, Köber, Schmiedek, and Habermas (2015) have shown the emergence of autobiographical reasoning in early adolescence, growth through early adulthood, and relative stability through late midlife.

For others, narrating provides insight into how children think about persons and their mental states (Nicolopoulou & Richner, 2007), how readers comprehend narratives by analyzing the plans and goals of story characters (Trabasso & Wiley, 2005), how narrative form helps persons to comprehend the extension of self through time and other people's minds (Fivush & Nelson, 2006), and how narratives are told as a window into styles of making sense of traumatic memories (Greenhoot, Sun, Bunnell, & Lindboe, 2013).

Many cognitive approaches are concerned with aspects of development and the social world. Narrative skills develop over the life course. They are internalized through social interaction and become modes of thinking about the world. Following Vygostky, the tools for narrative thinking are scaffolded through children's participation in face-to-face conversations, which lead to distinct modes of talking about the past and conceptualizing selfhood (Fivush & Nelson, 2006; Miller, Fung, & Mintz, 1996; Wiley, Rose, Burger, & Miller, 1998;). For example, Reese and Fivush (1993) argue that parents have distinct conversational styles of interaction with girls and boys that become internalized gendered styles of talk and processing experience. Furthermore, such patterns can be found across diverse groups as late as adolescence (Fivush, Bohanek, Zaman, & Grapin, 2012).

Personal(ity) Approaches

In personality psychology, McAdams (1996, 2001) has argued that the life story is a level of personality. This conception of narrative is heavily influenced by Erikson's (1950) theory of psychosocial development and by the personological psychology of Henry Murray. Beginning from Erikson, personality psychologists have examined the adolescent and adult stages of Erikson's theory, particularly identity and generativity, from a narrative perspective.

From this perspective, the life story is a representation of one's identity. It is shaped by childhood experiences but is established in late adolescence when questions of identity are pressing. The life story is internal, something that persons "have" and use in more or less consistent ways over time. Persons strive for coherence, unity, and purpose in their life stories and their identities (McAdams, 1996, 2001).

McAdams (2001) proposes a three-level model of personality that takes into account Cantor's having and doing sides of personality, as well as larger configurations of selfhood. He argues that personality can be fruitfully understood as three separate but interrelated levels of analysis: traits and dispositions (level 1), personal goals and projects (level 2), and life stories (level 3). Level 1 corresponds to the descriptive tools of trait psychology, culminating, according to McAdams, with an agreement that personality is universally composed of five overarching clusters of traits, or the "Big Five." Level 1 is Cantor's "having" side of personality. Level 2 takes into account the critique of social and cognitive psychologists that dispositions cannot fully explain action, but that we must include time and context. Level 2 is Cantor's "doing" side of personality. Finally, level 3 is the life story, where persons are given the opportunity to put together their past into a coherent narrative that gives their lives unity and purpose. McAdams argues that there is a place in personality research for traits, cognition, context, and stories. It opens a way for conceptualizing the close study of life stories as a legitimate approach in personality research and provides a means for understanding how experience is organized into larger themes and plot lines.

McAdams and his colleagues have investigated problems such as narrative coherence and generativity, using a hypothesis-testing framework. In the Allport-Murray-White tradition, McAdams uses a variety of kinds of data in order to study lives. Some of this research is qualitative and concentrates on whole lives; other methods are survey based and correlational.

In one influential study, McAdams and his colleagues (McAdams, Reynolds, Lewis, Pattern, & Bowman, 2001) identify two distinct "narrative strategies," redemptive and contamination sequences, that persons use in order to configure episodes of their life stories. On the one hand, redemption narratives interpret difficult experiences as bringing some advantage. Structurally, the plot line moves from a low point to a high point. On the other hand, contamination narratives interpret positive or advantageous life events in a negative or destructive manner. Structurally, the plot line moves from a high point to a low point. They ask, is there a relationship between one or both of these narrative strategies and aspects of well-being, life satisfaction, and self-esteem?

McAdams et al. (2001) selected 74 American adults, between 35 and 65 years old, on the basis of their scores on three measures of generativity, "the strong concern for and commitment to promoting the well-being of youth and the next generation" (p. 474). The participants were asked to imagine their lives as books and to parse their lives into chapters. Each person was then asked to describe eight specific happenings, stories, in their lives, such as the high point, a turning point, and important scenes from different developmental periods. Each of the moments was coded, 0 or 1, for the presence or absence of redemption or contamination. For each person, a total score for redemption and contamination was derived by summing across all eight stories. Scores on redemption and contamination were correlated with self-report measures of psychological well-being, such as life satisfaction, self-esteem, sense of coherence, and depression.

In other studies, telling "good" stories, narrating memories of growth, is related to aspects of life satisfaction and happiness (Bauer, McAdams, & Sakaeda, 2005). Personality traits have been connected to themes in life stories (McAdams, Anyidoho, et al., 2004). The theme of agency increases in narratives told after psychotherapy and is related to mental health outcomes. Furthermore, such increases in agency were shown to pre-date improvements in psychological well-being (Adler, 2012).

Smith and Sparkes (2008a) call this group of researchers "psychosocial." I agree, but I see a distinction between personality approaches and interpretive approaches (which I describe in the following), whereas Smith and Sparkes put both in the psychosocial perspective.

Cognitive-Personality Approaches

Interestingly, there are continuities between personality and cognitive approaches to narrative, which may or may not merit a separate grouping. Some researchers and theorists blend cognitive and personality approaches. Singer (2004) argues that a new generation of "narrative identity" researchers has emerged who draw upon script theory (e.g., Tomkins), the cognitive traditions of autobiographical memory research (e.g., Neisser and Conway), psychosocial theory (e.g., Erikson) and personologically oriented narrative study (e.g., McAdams). What distinguishes this group of researchers is that, like the cognitive psychologists, they are more concerned with the processes or strategies that underlie stories. But, like the personality psychologists, these problems are framed as issues of identity and self-development over time. For example, researchers have studied the developmental trajectory of narrative "meaning making" in adolescence;

McLean and Breen (2009) found an increase in self-event connections over adolescence, and Pasupathi and Wainryb (2010) found growth in the evaluative content of autobiographical narratives from age 8 to 10.

Perhaps this calls into question my categories, which distinguish between personality and cognitive approaches to narrative. Or, my preferred explanation, it further complicates matters by introducing yet another fractal distinction in narrative psychology.

"Interpretive" Approaches

An interpretive (or hermeneutic) approach contrasts, and converges, with cognitive and personality approaches on several dimensions. Admittedly, the label of "interpretive" is not perfect. In contrast to the other categories, I am not certain that researchers in this area would identity themselves as "interpretive." Nevertheless, researchers using an interpretive approach see narrative as a process in which persons construct a vision of themselves, the world, and others through concerted acts of interpretation (Brockmeier & Harré, 2001). The focus is on how persons interpret their life experience and make these interpretations explicit. Narrating is viewed as a vehicle for sense making. Although some interpretive researchers are concerned with sticking close to the life and words of the person, others are interested in uncovering the hidden meanings of the text (Josselson, 2004).

Another important distinction with personality and cognitive approaches is along the lines of the philosophy of science that underlies the interpretive approach. For interpretive researchers, narrative is generally viewed as a critical tool for challenging mainstream psychology's statistical methods for studying life experience. Interpretive approaches argue that only through the close examination of words in context can psychologists better understand psychological experience. The emphasis is on rich and detailed narrative texts and what their close analysis can teach us about life experience and interpretation.

Although sensitive to the social and cultural world, and sometimes theorizing about the connection between the person and social processes, this research tends to be concerned with the dynamics of identity as seen through the life of a single or multiple persons. These approaches favor whole portraits of lives, attempting to reflexively understand how persons describe themselves in words and why. Preference is given to the inclusion of a large corpus of textual data and its analysis. Typically, interviews are not broken into themes or narrative structures, and are not coded, but are analyzed in a more holistic fashion to understand the meanings behind the words.

A good example of the interpretive approach is found in Freeman's (2010) description of his interviews with two artists, Samuel and Leah, who have both confronted the sense that their artistic vitality and careers have come to a dead end. Interviewed in their sixties, Samuel and Leah recount their early success and optimism and their eventual loss of faith in their artistic development and self. The reader learns about Samuel's idealized ambitions for success, his self-diminishing comparisons with artistic luminaries such as Picasso and Rembrandt, and his inability to focus his creative energies on new projects of value. The reader also learns about Leah's beginnings as part of an avant-garde group of artists, her disillusionment with the commercial realities of art, and the deconstruction of her work in the search for her own artistic style. In both interviews, contamination looms large as a potential story for framing the past, which we can understand in terms of the particular concerns, events, and reflections of the person. Freeman evocatively calls this state "narrative foreclosure," which is "the conviction that the story of one's life or life work, has effectively ended" (2010, p. 125).

Although Samuel is unable to move beyond the profound disappointment that his ambitions will never be realized, Leah has found a way to imagine new narrative possibilities. The contrast between where Samuel and Leah are now in their lives is one of the most captivating features of Freeman's interpretation. But, even more interesting, Freeman deals with both cases with the same theoretical apparatus. Reflection has different effects and consequences. It can provide the means for our own imprisonment or our liberation.

Freeman argues that storylines, acquired from our immersion in social, cultural, and linguistic communities, direct our understandings of self and others. For example, artists aspire to recognition. Aging is a time of diminished creativity and decline. If you haven't made it by mid-life, you'll never make it. Artistic talent is the basis of success. Or, value is determined by a dollar amount on the marketplace. Samuel and Leah have inherited social narratives of this kind, which now exert a "narrative force" on how they reflect upon their past and futures. For Freeman, the difference between Samuel and Leah is in their willingness to engage these myths about who one is and should be, to expose their influence, and to begin the hard work of imagining new possible narratives of the past and future. Freeman calls this process, of de-idealizing these ingrained storylines and imagining alternate realities, the discovery of "narrative freedom."

Interpretive researchers study problems such as the role of significant others in the creation of our personal identity (Josselson, 1994, 2007), understanding of one's sense of agency (Lieblich, Zilber, & Tuval-Mashiach,

2008), how social positions and differences crystallize understanding of self and other (Hammack, 2011), and the role of history and social memory in self-understanding (Cohler, 2008; Schiff & Noy, 2006).

Although many interpretive researchers share Habermas's and McAdams's concern with coherence, this is not necessarily the case. And, recently, the preoccupation with narrative coherence has come under increasing fire (e.g., Hyvärinen, Hyden, Saarenheimo, & Tamboukou, 2010). Also, researchers take various positions, on the contention that the life story is an internalized form that persons have, often emphasizing the situatedness and malleability of life stories over time.

Social-Cultural Approaches

The social-cultural approach overlaps with many aspects of what Smith and Sparkes (2008a) term the "performative" and "storied resources" perspectives. Also, the lines between interpretive and social-cultural approaches are not clear. In general, these approaches share a common philosophy of science that is critical of mainstream psychology, seeking to develop more nuanced theories and methods of understanding human psychology. Perhaps because of this shared critical perspective, there is sustained conversation, and engagement, between interpretive and social-cultural approaches.

Although the distinction between interpretive and social-cultural approaches is fluid, I see the main difference in the emphasis on the situatedness of telling. Social-cultural psychologists tend to be interested in the conversational dynamics of narrative and the historical-cultural context of the narration. How do narratives take shape in the real, everyday context of storytelling? And how do relational, social, and cultural processes shape the narrative produced?

In this approach, narrative is a resource for positioning oneself in regard to the evolving conversation at hand (Davies & Harré, 1990; Wortham, 2000) and to identity discourses (Bamberg, 2004). For example, Bhatia and Ram (2009) describe the re-negotiation of cultural identity and belonging of Indian-American immigrants, in particular the accessibility of being "White" and "American," after the attacks on 9/11 and the shift in cultural definitions and group alignments in the post–9/11 world.

Smith and Sparkes (2008b) present a nuanced analysis of Jaime, a 40-year-old man with spinal cord injury resulting from a rugby match, and the constraints (and affordances) of socially shared resources and the physical body for making sense of self, life, and the future. Although just after his injury Jaime narrated his injury as an obstacle that he would overcome, he is unable to sustain the sense of hopefulness that his severely damaged body will somehow be repaired and gives up, withdrawing into social isolation and darkness. As Smith and Sparkes point out, the hopeful, restitution narrative is the preferred one of the medical community and the social world, while the despairing, chaos narrative, which Jaime now tells, is uncomfortable to listen to and borders on the untellable. Jaime's pain coming from a phantom limb and his inability to perform the taken for granted physical tasks of maneuvering about spaces, or even to hold his children, are serious and present checks on his ability to rewrite his life story into a more optimistic direction. But so does the social world, which has difficulties listening to such stories and interacting with the disabled, and a dearth of models for imagining alternative narratives.

For social-cultural researchers, narratives are cultural discourses that are performed in concrete situations (Mishler, 1999). Narratives are activities that are embedded in conversations and are told in concert with others for particular reasons (Georgakopoulou, 2007). Ochs and Capps (2001) write in their critical analysis of everyday narratives:

> The content and direction that narrative framings take are contingent upon the narrative input of other interlocutors, who provide, elicit, criticize, refute, and draw inferences from facets of the unfolding account. In these exchanges, narrative becomes an interactional achievement and interlocutors become co-authors. (pp. 2–3)

Narrative is viewed as conversation or dialogue, as malleable, open-ended, situational, and relational. It is not a fixed entity that endures through time (Gergen, 2009). In social-cultural approaches, narrative is not inside the person; persons don't have narratives. Persons may perform their understandings of self in concrete situations, and there may be continuity between situations. But the basic action of narrating is a form of co-action in which the narrative comes into being between persons, in a specific time and place (Gergen, 2009).

Beyond Categories

Of course, there are also linguistic approaches to narrative, such as small story research (Bamberg & Georgakopoulou, 2008) as well as those interested in syntactic regularities in language across a large number of transcripts (László, 2008; Pennebaker & Seagal, 1999; Ramírez-Esparza

& Pennebaker, 2006), neurological theories (Dennett, 1991; Gazzaniga, 1998), and clinical applications (Madigan, 2011). Still, narrative has found its way into not only the related disciplines of gerontology (Kenyon, Bohlmeijer, & Randall, 2011; Kenyon, Clark, & De Vries, 2001), sociology (Denzin & Lincoln, 2008; Gubrium & Holstein, 2009), and social work (Riessman, 2008), but also medicine (Charon, 2008) and philosophy (Hutto, 2008; Nelson, 2014). And, once again, there is substantial overlap with narrative psychology, which further exacerbates attempts at easy categorization.

FRACTAL DISTINCTIONS

The diversity of approaches to narrative in psychology is extensive—and exhausting. It is dizzying. I am afraid that my review has only scratched the surface of the complexity and diversity of narrative in psychology.

The multiplication of theories has been accompanied by a multiplication of methods of analysis. Indeed, there is no single method of narrative research. Some methods focus on whole lives, others on parts of the life story. Some approaches focus on linguistic structure, turn taking in conversations, or theme, while others are experimental or survey based.

We need to ask the question: Is there a center of gravity to the concept of narrative psychology? Domains of research can and should tolerate dissent and contradictions. Not everyone should be doing the same thing. But doesn't narrative psychology have to be about something? I think that it does. If that is the case, what is the something that narrative is about?

In the *Chaos of Disciplines*, Abbott (2001) argues that disciplines are not rationally formed, but reach a sense of incoherence over time through a process of distinction and division that he labels "fractal distinctions." Divisions found within a larger intellectual domain are often recapitulated in smaller groupings.

In other words, smaller groups maintain the same conflicts and tensions that plagued the larger one. For example, Abbott argues that the larger distinction between qualitative and quantitative approaches in sociology is also found in both subgroups of qualitative and quantitative sociology. In other words, there is a qualitative-quantitative sociology and a quantitative-qualitative sociology. Over time, the conceptual terrain tends to become muddied and metaphors become mixed.

In my reading of the evolution of narrative psychology, "fractal distinctions" are the rule. In the realm of theory, narrative is constantly revisiting the ideological conflicts between personality, social, biological, and cognitive psychology. Arguably, each one of these perspectives in psychology has its own version of narrative; there is a narrative-personality-psychology, a narrative-social-psychology, and so on. Or, even better, there are multiple narrative-personality-psychologies and multiple narrative-social-psychologies, and even narrative personality-cognitive psychologies and narrative interpretive-social psychologies.

Once again, in the realm of method, divisions between variable-centered, linguistic, whole life, and thematic-content approaches are evident. There is a fractal quantitative-narrative method and a fractal qualitative-narrative method.

However, I should be careful about overstating the fractures. There are some overarching commonalities that should be emphasized. I would suggest that despite the many differences, post-1980s narrative psychology shares a common, constructionist, ontology that narrative practices bring into being core aspects of self, other, and world.

But this does not resolve the issue of definition. If we base our answer on what has already been written, the "what is it?" question is nearly impossible to answer. Furthermore, I believe that by leaving the waters muddied, we find ourselves diverted from the central motives that launched the narrative psychology movement.

It is not my intention to put this debate aside. The goals of this book are to offer an open and vibrant vision for the narrative perspective and to place the narrative perspective in the landscape of the discipline. I want to offer some suggestions that aspire to provide coherence and energy to a domain of inquiry in need of clarity. Narrative is not just everything. There are many good reasons for narrative in psychology, which have the potential to move the discipline forward in new and exciting directions in order to make real progress in our understanding of human beings. In my view, narrative psychology is, at its core, the study of meaning-making practices—how persons, together with others, articulate and inhabit interpretations of life.

NARRATING LIFE

Narrative psychology should be thought of as an integrative perspective where, on the one hand, theory about storytelling is grounded by appropriate and detailed evidence and, on the other hand, textual data are conceptualized as part of a telling in a social and cultural context.

Reductive methods break persons into variables and miss an understanding of how psychological processes are part of personal experience and social context.

In a sense, narrative research makes up for the substantial weaknesses that one finds in variable-centered approaches. The emphasis is on seeing how experience and interpretation unfold in the context of a person's life and in social and temporal context. Narrative research does not seek to break down experience into its component parts, but rather to see life as a dynamic process that unfolds in space and time, in the contexts that make experience meaningful, in order to describe and understand how it all works.

But narrative is more than this. It is more than a research tool for approaching psychological data. It is a way of seeing persons, understanding actions, thinking through the ways that words are enacted and their effects. It is a way of understanding human psychology and human nature.

Narrating is about making sense of self and others. Or quite simply put, it is about interpreting life experience and making these interpretations known. In this sense, narrating is directed toward understanding life. My reformulation of narrative connects together narrative and life, arguing that narrating provides the means for imagining and making present life experience.

Certainly, I am not the first to connect together narrative and life. Bruner's (1987) well-known essay "Life as Narrative" argues that a notion of life is constructed through narrative practices and that narratives provide recipes for persons to navigate experience. Still, it is interesting to take note of how the word "narrative" is used in psychological study. We speak about life narratives, life stories, life writings, and life histories. Indeed, the philological origins of the words "biography" and "autobiography" literally connect the notion of writing with life. Rosenwald and Ochberg (1992) titled their edited book *Storied Lives*. Josselson and Lieblich (1993) eloquently titled their book series *The Narrative Study of Lives*. Kenyon and Randall (1997) have written about the process of "restorying life."

The notion of "life" is already in the foreground of multiple conceptions of narrativity. Typically, the idea of life is not further developed. But these formulations reveal a critical property of narrative.

I would like to offer this thought. Life is exactly what narrative approaches to human psychology attempt to disclose: what it is like to be a living and breathing human being—what it is like to be me, to have my experience, to live where I do, in this country, in this language community, in this conversation, in this moment of time, in this family, at this age.

Narrative grapples with what it means to have a life, to make life, and what our experience of life means to us.

As a concept, life evokes philosophical approaches to psychology, such as Dilthey's (1989) call to examine lived experience and employ biographical approaches to understand the "psychophysical life-unit." In the related tradition of phenomenology, Husserl and Schutz developed the evocative notion of a "life-world" as the basic concept for describing the structure of human experience and the forces that influence it (Husserl, 1954/1970; Schutz & Luckmann, 1973). Sociologists have employed the idea of the "life course" to describe the impact of historical and social events on personal trajectories. And in anthropology, we find "life ways" and "life plans." What draws these approaches together is the desire to understand human beings beyond the narrow frame of the individual at a single moment in time in order to see the connectedness of human experience.

Life is a process. We think about lives as unfolding through time and across situations. Life evolves and changes, forms and reforms. It is dynamic.

Life is natural; it is programmed into the genes and our bodies. Life speaks to the sense of being alive—the sensation that blood courses through my veins, that my heart beats, that I have a body and that I am physically present in the world. Furthermore, I know it. I know that I am alive. I am cognizant of the experience.

Life includes my lifetime, from my birth to death, my past, present, and future. It describes the part of my lifetime that I find myself in right now. And it speaks to my sense of how I connect together these points in time.

But life is also more than just me; it is also social. Life invokes a rich network of social relationships that participate in my life. I participate in their lives, too. We are bound together and share life together.

Life is more than the person and more than the social world. There is a sense in which we share certain aspects of our lives with others, but that other aspects are more privately held. Even if the idea of the "private" or "interior" is, itself, socially constructed, we hold some facts about our lives close to ourselves. There are aspects of life that are unsaid, perhaps even unspeakable.

Life encompasses historical and cultural facts, the political situation in which I live, the state of intergroup and economic relationships, the language that I speak, and the power to voice a point of view.

Telling is an attempt to speak life, to articulate a version of what it means, and to navigate through our ambiguous and sometimes tumultuous life-world. But the relationship is not only one way. Narrative is directed to life and, of course, life is configured by narrative. Or, as Bruner (1987) puts it, "in the end, we *become* the autobiographical narratives by which we 'tell about' our lives" (p. 15). In narrating, we show and describe life, making aspects of experience known in words. In life, we make use of the realm of meanings, which shape our understanding of present experience and provide the resources for acting out and reflecting upon actions and events. And we also author new stories that spiral back into life for new productions. Life and narrative entangle each other in the most intimate sense. The connection between narrative and life is direct but complex, mediated through cultural and social circumstances and the person's ability to creatively imagine alternative possibilities.

From my perspective, narrative psychology is the study of how life is experienced and interpreted through close attention to what people reveal in concrete tellings and the study of how life is shaped and configured through meanings and stories. The basic questions are focused on the realm of meaning, about how life is experienced and interpreted.

There are numerous advantages to framing narrative as the telling of life. Here are just a few. First, directing narrative study toward the study of life avoids the problem of reductionism. Psychological processes are no longer the equivalent of the assay, extracted from individuals, stored in tubes and manipulated by researchers, but instead are dynamics that implicate multiple levels of analysis in complex ways. Second, the entrenched social scientific vocabulary that separates persons, social interactions, and culture, perpetuating a fallacious opposition between these realms, disappears. We are free to appreciate the intricate ways that these levels of analysis work together. And, of course, we don't merely tell about what has happened to us in our world; much of what we know and tell comes from life that we have experienced living in the world along with others. Finally, I believe that conceptualizing narrative as the articulation of life brings disparate groups of narrative researchers together. Putting aside our differences, this is something that we can agree on. It is an idea that has the power to give narrative psychology definition and vitality.

In this chapter, I have tried to address the history and conceptual fragmentation in narrative psychology and to explore some of the tensions that complicate definitions of narrative psychology. I believe that conceptual work in this area is necessary.

Although the "what is it" question will likely remain, perpetual soul searching is, ultimately, counterproductive to getting to the real work of applying narrative to effectively address the pressing problems of human psychology. We should be clear about what we are doing and why. It is my hope that innovative theorizing will provide some provisional answers to these problems. Providing at least provisional closure, which inspires students and researchers and provides a sense that we understand what narrative is, should help us get on with this work. It may sound idealistic, but we live in a historical epoch desperately in need of new ways of understanding human life. Narrative psychology has a critical role to play in these conversations.

CHAPTER 4

How Narrating Functions

Most approaches to narrative accept that there are some structural properties that distinguish narrative from other forms of talk. It seems logical. After all, the narrative concept is often associated with structural theory and linguistic analysis. Some of the most influential investigations of narrative began in folklore (e.g., Propp, 1928/1968), literary studies (e.g., Barthes, 1966/1975), and linguistics (e.g., Labov & Waletzsky, 1967/1997), where narrative is often conceptualized as having basic underlying structural or formal characteristics.

Recent scholarship in literary studies tries to move beyond prescriptive, cut-and-dry definitions of narrative, instead opting for larger, more inclusive conceptions that hold together a wider array of forms. One strategy has been to specify minimal defining features of narrative that leave the term open to multiple possible usages. Phelan and Rabinowitz (2012) offer the following definition: "*Narrative is somebody telling somebody else, on some occasion, and for some purposes, that something happened to someone or something*" (p. 3). Phelan and Rabinowitz evoke the purposive act of telling, from a particular context, for a particular reason, and to a particular other/others, a past happening. However, emphasizing the openness of narrative, they insist that their definition is "default" rather than "definitive." For Prince (2008), narrative must include "the logically consistent representation of at least two asynchronous events" (p. 20), to which he later adds that the events must also follow from one another without being logically presupposed (Prince, 2012). Abbott (2008) is even more minimalist and more concrete. "Simply put, narrative is *the representation of an event or a series of events*," which, he continues "*is the key gift and it produces the building blocks out of which all the more complex forms are built*" (p. 13). Following Genette, Todorov, Propp, and others, Abbott describes narrative as the overarching category that includes the story, those events or actions recounted, and narrative discourse, "those events as represented" (p. 16). Although in psychology and the social sciences the terms "narrative" and "story" are used in imprecise ways, often interchangeably, many literary narratologists argue that a distinction between the two is key (Hyvärinen, 2013).

Some post-classical narratologists have gone even further, arguing that either/or categorizations of narrative can be problematic, especially around the rough edges of the narrative universe. Herman (2009) argues that the lines between narrative and other forms of speech events, such as explanation and description, are permeable. Although the prototypical cases are clear, there is a large middle ground of mixed forms, "narrative explanations" and "descriptive narrations." Differences are subtle, of degree rather than kind (Herman, 2009). Similarly, Ryan (2007) argues for a fuzzy-set definition of narrative that comprises multiple dimensions, including spatial, temporal, mental, formal, and pragmatic. The fuzzy set excludes some forms of discourse as non-narrative, such as repetitive events or instructions. But the definition becomes very open, a "tool kit for do-it-yourself definitions" (p. 30) in which narratologists can choose to emphasize or de-emphasize certain aspects of narratives.

In narrative psychology, although a structural basis is widely accepted, researchers point to vastly different structures. For example, the approach most frequently taken in personality psychology emphasizes that life narratives are structured by arranging personal experience memories into a coherent configuration. Structure is found in the creation of a plot line from these disparate events. In more linguistically oriented approaches, smaller structural units of speech are typically emphasized. Narrative structure could be the arrangement of complicating actions to tell about a past incident, or how speech turns by different participants work to create meaning. For cognitivists, the structure is an internalized form that allows persons to reason and to understand the self and the social world. There is a narrative structure to memory or planning. Interpretive researchers and social-cultural researchers also rely on notions of structure. There is a patterning or organizing of themes, structure in the linguistic arrangement of speech elements, or one that emerges in storytelling.

The contrasting structures are at odds with one another and, apparently, are responding to the fractal divisions in psychology at large (see Chapter 3). Although we can't seem to agree on what constitutes narrative structure, structure is assumed to be identical with narrative. We just assume that there must be something definitive and structural there, and we can't see past the idea.

It is my contention that psychologists, and other narrativists, have placed too much emphasis on the structural properties of narrative and not enough on what narrative accomplishes. This is one of the main critiques of Georgakopoulou (2007), who, rightly, argues that researchers should broaden their understanding of narrative to study speech as it is actually used in context. She contends that forms of narrative that don't resemble finely polished narratives, what Bamberg and Georgakopoulou (2008) call "small stories," are as, or even more, interesting because small stories provide us with a view into the common everyday practice of narrative.

I believe that Georgakopoulou and Bamberg are on the right track, but I would like to take the idea one step further. In a sense, focusing on story type perpetuates the notion that we can uncover the fundamental structural properties of a narrative, small or big. In my opinion, structure cannot fully capture the narrative impulse. Rather, it is what we do with words. What does narrative accomplish? How do people do narrative? What do narratives mean? Telling serves what end or purpose?

Let me emphasize that the formal properties of how meanings are told can be valuable clues to why it is told, that is, the intentions and the evaluation of the narrator. They are important, useful descriptively, and complementary. And we would be imprudent to disregard structure. As I will argue, structure and function exist in a dynamic relationship.

Telling experience in narrative form might possess distinctive properties, such as the ability to experience the world of another person in depth and color (Fludernik, 1996; Herman, 2009). Or, it may provide the means for configuring the units of experience together into a meaningful whole (Cohler, 1982; McAdams, 1996, 2001). It may even be true that experience itself prefers narrative forms of configuring events in order to make sense of the world (Carr, 1991; Freeman, 2010; Hyvärinen, 2006).

All of this may be true. However, I want to argue that the structural components of narratives are not what make narrative special and ubiquitous, and should not be privileged as the defining characteristic of narrative. In order to focus on meanings, I advocate what could be thought of as a functional approach to narrative. At its core, I believe that narrative is interesting because of the meanings that we are able to express and articulate with and through narrative. For me, the important question is this: How does narrative work or function to communicate and reveal aspects of human experience and manage meanings? In other words, narrative is important because of what can be done or accomplished with narrative; this is the essence of what I have in mind.

A functionalist account of narrative asks, how does narrative work to accomplish meaning making? In doing so, I conceptualize narrative as a dynamic process (Schiff, 2006, 2012). Rather than a form or structure, narrative can be thought of as a verb, "to narrate," or the derived form "narrating," rather than the noun form "narrative" or the adjective "narrativity." The focus shifts to the process—how and why persons express themselves in a certain fashion. Also, as I will argue, to narrate calls forth the conceptual similarities with the related forms "to tell," "to show," and "to make present." The assumption here is that narrative is not an epistemological category, or at least not exclusively so, but an ontological one that "refers to a constitutive element of the human way of being in the world" (Meretoja, 2014a, p. 6).

In narrating, persons disclose and develop interpretations of life experience. Importantly, we move from understanding narrative as a static object and begin to view it, more accurately, as the process or activity of making meaning. Narrative is a doing, a happening, an eruption. As I like to think about it, *narrating is an interpretive action, articulated in space and time.* Brockmeier and Meretoja (2014) write, "the stuff of narrative understanding appears as an ongoing flow of interpretive and self-interpretive acts: a stream of attempts to figure out what one's and others' experiences, intentions, emotions, beliefs, desires, and anxieties could possibly mean" (p. 11). Drawing upon Heidegger, Arendt, and Ricoeur, Brockmeier and Meretoja (2014) argue that narrative understanding is a form of poetic activity, using "the Greek term *poíēsis* (which stems from the Greek verb *poiéō*, 'to make') to describe this process of configuring and negotiating of meaning-making" (p. 11). This sense of poetic composition, as Ricoeur (1984) argues, is at the core of narrative, in which persons are making sense of experience and world in order to "make" life and "make" selves. Narrative poiesis, as Freeman (2010) writes, is "that sort of constructive, imaginative activity that is involved in our various efforts to make sense of the world" (p. 43)

Function directly addresses the meaning of narrating. In other words, what can persons do or accomplish by narrating experience? Indeed, why should we tell or do anything at all? How does narrating work through and express meaning in a specific time and place? What is the language game that we call narrating (Rudrum, 2005)?

Such a move does end up including a wide range of expressions as appropriate for narrative study that others might exclude or overlook, verbal but also nonverbal, that make present life experiences and interpretations of life. Narrating can take the form of verbal expressions that are structurally non-narrative, such as poetry, song, eulogy, proclamation, aphorism, chronicle, explanation, and reflection. For example, Abu-Lughod's (1985) ethnography of the Awlad Ali Bedouins of Egypt describes the centrality of highly formulaic poems, *ghinnawas,* or "little songs," as the mode for interpreting and communicating a range of feelings, often sorrowful, without the risk of losing honor. Likewise, nonverbal performances, including gesture, dance, and bodywork, and perhaps even music, can tell a story. For example, Langellier's (2001) sensitive analysis of women tattooing scars left by a mastectomy, where the tattoo itself plays a role, equally, in the performance of the story of trauma and healing and is an event to be storied. If we center on narrating as an interpretive action, closing off our study from such expressions illogically constrains our pursuit. Emphasizing functions broadens the scope of the narrative perspective in psychology, opening it up further beyond the walls of structuralism, and specifying our research on the fundamental problems of human meaning making. Structural approaches can be very useful in describing how language or other actions are employed to realize a story, but cannot provide us with definitive answers about the purpose of narrative in human lives—nor should we expect them to. Structural analysis provides clues for creatively describing what people are doing with words. But meaning is another matter.

Still, even if scholars could articulate a way of marking narrative forms of speech from other forms of speech, I would be skeptical of the significance of such a discovery. Especially for psychologists and other social scientists who are interested in narrative because of the way that narratives are involved in how persons make sense of life, the issue of form is secondary. The arrangement of speech elements into a structure is not the foremost property of narrative.

Indeed, it may sound paradoxical that I am advocating for narrative study but at the same time arguing against a structuralist definition of narrative. However, this is exactly the point. As Sarbin (1986) argued in his original formulation of narrative psychology, narrative should be understood as a metaphor for human psychology. Narrative stands in for the notion that human beings are meaning makers who configure their life experience using the forms that their social and cultural world have passed down in order to describe and show their lives. The idea of narrative psychology helps us to understand this phenomenon. As a figure, the concept of narrative is fitting, but we should remember that we are dealing with metaphor. It would be a mistake to take the expression too literally and reify narrative forms or structures as the only, or the most efficient, modes of meaning making.

In his conceptual history of narrative, Hyvärinen (2010) observes that there are at least four separate narrative turns, each with its own history and distinct understanding of the concept. In the social sciences, the conceptual development of narrative proceeded on its own path. Rather than appropriating the terms delineated in literary theory or linguistics or coming up with a concrete definition of narrative itself, psychology, like the other social sciences, appears to be content with an imprecise metaphor. Narrative stands in for something else. It is a convenient placeholder, an empty vessel, configured for the purposes of each user, who can define the term in any way that he or she likes.

An interesting implication of Hyvärinen's thesis is, if narrative is a metaphor, then, why narrative and not something else? Couldn't another metaphor work equally well? I am not going to argue against the concept of narrative. The narrative metaphor is not, necessarily, incorrect or misleading. In fact, I believe that the narrative metaphor is essential for understanding psychological processes and social reality, but it needs some precision.

The theoretical framework that I describe attempts to ground the metaphor so that narrative can be applied productively to describe life experience in more complex and accurate terms. On the one hand, the narrative metaphor should be sufficiently open to include a broad range of research and dissent. On the other hand, it should be specific enough so that we know what narrative is, why we are doing narrative research, and it should direct us to innovative ways of understanding human lives in social context.

As I see it, the concept of narrative should focus on how narrating works to make, and make present, meanings—in particular, meanings about life experience. I take this to be the principal mission of narrative psychology and basic to what makes it such an attractive concept.

INTERPRETIVE ACTIONS

But how can we do this? How can a narrative perspective in psychology be constituted so that it allows researchers to describe meaning making in language that is both rich and concrete?

I argue that we need to take seriously the notion of narrating as a dynamic and contextual interpretive action. In this spirit, Brockmeier (2013) has recently advocated for a "narrative hermeneutics" (cf. Brockmeier & Meretoja, 2014). He writes:

The heart of every process of interpretive understanding that reaches a certain level of complexity is a narrative process. Yet the narrative nature of interpretation is only one side of the coin. On the other side is the interpretive nature of narrative, that is, at the heart of every process of narrative understanding is an interpretive process. Examining this twofold movement is the gist of what I call narrative hermeneutics. (p. 126)

On the one hand, narrative hermeneutics argues that narrative forms are necessary in order to account for complex life experience. On the other hand, narrative hermeneutics argues that narrative is always a mode of interpreting and understanding. Taken together, the idea of narrative hermeneutics orients us to the process of interpreting and understanding that is so central to the narrative project.

I want to amplify Brockmeier's "twofold movement" of narrative hermeneutics. Beginning with the second point first, narrating is a fundamental interpretive action that touches upon most aspects of our lives. Narrating is our tool for attempting to understand the world and our place inside it, for configuring versions of self and life. In my estimation, the narrative concept is interesting for psychologists precisely because narrative is the primary means by which persons are able to create understandings of their own life and life in general. Narrative hermeneutics captures this fundamental narrative impulse.

Although the first assertion—that narrative is necessary to account for complex life experience—is certainly true, I want to play with the borders between narrative and interpretation, which, on the basis of my analysis of narrating as an interpretive action, become permeable and fluid. Narrative may be distinct from interpretation, but the threshold is easily traversed. This is because (1) narrating is an ongoing activity, forever incomplete, that always has the potential to put interpretations into new and changing relationships; and (2) narrating is always embedded in a specific social and cultural setting, which evokes and shapes the emergent content and form of what is told and how it is told.

In our day-to-day life, we make interpretations on the fly in order to understand the world around us. For example, we may understand a painting, such as Edvard Munch's *The Scream*, on a visceral level. We are affected by the colors, the movement of the brush strokes, the physical expression of the subject's face. But once we move to explaining what the painting means to ourselves, or what it meant to the painter or the history of Western art, we are moving into a narrative that sets the painting in some context, which requires us to make assertions about the emerging "story." Interpretation becomes more than mere interpretation; it becomes an engagement with narrative in order to make sense of something—and we start to tell a story.

Upon viewing the painting, I might softly and simply whisper, as many others have, "painful." Certainly, this is an interpretation of the painting—albeit a fairly banal one. This is obviously a statement that interprets my reaction to the painting, the expression of the main subject of Munch's painting, Munch's psychology, a characterization of the historical epoch in which the work was created, and so on.

But is it narrative? The statement itself contains no event and no temporal continuity, there is no past or projected future. And I have provided no hint that this utterance is connected to other kinds of context that would connect this statement to other events or elements.

What I would like to suggest is that my interpretive statement, "painful," is at the cusp of narrative. It doesn't tell us much—at least not yet. But it is an interpretive action, potentially part of a larger effort after meaning and not easily distinguishable from narrative. Rudimentary and vague as it is, my one-word utterance shares a lot with narrative. It uses discourse in order to refer to something about my experience or, perhaps, about the world. The utterance doesn't give us that much to work with—hardly anything, in fact—and it is difficult, if not impossible, to understand what the utterance might mean. If we rely upon definitions of minimal narratives, "painful" comes up short an event (Abbott, 2008) or, perhaps, two events and the connections between them (Prince, 2012). Additional information and linkages would help us to better understand what's so "painful." But, as in other matters, knowing more is often helpful.

"Painful" could just remain a vague and senseless expression, or it could be actualized as a more well-developed narrative. In the realm of cultural memory, Assmann (1995, 1997) distinguishes between cultural artifacts that lay dormant in the cultural storehouse, such as an archive, and their actualization when they become used. Someone needs to discover and champion cultural knowledge in order to bring it into collective awareness. To be active, cultural memory must be realized through its use. In a similar fashion, to move from the banal to a fully fleshed-out narrative, interpretations require attention and engagement.

Ryan (2005) makes a similar distinction between "being a narrative" and "possessing narrativity":

> The property of "being" a narrative can be predicated of any semiotic object, whatever the medium, produced with the intent to create a response involving

the construction of a story. More precisely, it is the receiver's recognition of this intent that leads to the judgment that a given semiotic object is a narrative, even though we can never be sure if sender and receiver have the same story in mind. "Possessing narrativity," on the other hand, means being able to inspire a narrative response, whether or not the text, if there is one, was intended to be processed that way, and whether or not the stimuli are designed by an author. (p. 347)

For Ryan, on the one hand, all narratives are constructed—in someone's mind or subjective experience. We consider something narrative because, *as readers*, we take into account the intentions of the author: he or she wanted to tell a story. It is a matter of debate, point of view, and context, whether or not something is narrative. In other words, it is a second-order interpretation to say, "this is a narrative." And, on the other hand, there are many "stimuli," with or without intent, which can become narrative. They possess narrativity, that is, the potential to be understood as a story but not yet formulated into narrative. Life, at some level, always possesses narrativity or a pre-narrative potential (Ricoeur, 1984).

Often, the story includes an event, bundles of interrelated events, or habitual events (Herman, 2009). But it is not always or necessarily true that story has an event-like character (real or imagined). Stories can be less event-like and more about the basic conditions of life, such as feelings, a state of affairs in the world (actual or possible), a life direction, denoting the character of a person. The stories that narratives actualize can sometimes be vague—even very vague—incomplete, mundane, and static. This may not be the highest aspiration of narrative, but it is a large portion of the narratives that we recount in everyday life. Literary and filmic narratives, typically, are much more elaborately constituted with multiple layers of description and action. As Brockmeier (2013) reminds us, things get more interesting as experience becomes more complex, and a well-elaborated narrative emerges that begins to make connections between events in the past, present, or future.

I recognize that I am pushing the envelope on what can be called narrative or story, but exactly at what point does it move from "possessing narrativity" to, squarely, "being" a narrative? Pushing the envelope forces us to recognize that narrative and story are emergent qualities and perpetually open to newly assigned interpretations.

We cannot understand narrative as merely the verbal utterance or the word on a page. It isn't a text type, but an impulse to articulate meanings. The story cannot be found only in words. Words need to be ascribed with the context that they deserve. Articulating the word "painful" is only part of the context, which realizes or makes present an interpretation. Other parts of the context are the person who said it and the situation, the when and where, it was said (i.e., the temporal and spatial context).

The engagement is not only in the words. Narrative is not just in the verbalized phrases, but also is part of subjective experience and part of the social world. My verbalized "painful" might be the beginning of a non-verbalized internal dialogue about how I studied Munch's painting as an undergraduate in a course on the history of Expressionism. This might be all there is to the story, or there may be additional elaboration about how the painting affected my 20-year-old self's view on life and my place in historical time.

If I were viewing the painting with another person, he or she might ask me what I meant by "painful," and this might start a conversation about the view of the future and progress in Europe during the late nineteenth and early twentieth centuries. Or perhaps, it might trigger speculation about my mental state and why I might feel pained at this moment in my life. Or, of course, my utterance could be ignored, dropped, and given no further elaboration. The many potential stories in this narrated opening could be left unexplored. In any case, my initial static and ambiguous utterance comes alive and starts to take on definition when I begin to engage with other meanings in a particular context—internal or social. The contextual facts of my subjectivity and the social context in which I speak are in no way trivial. They are integral to the concept.

Miller and her colleagues (Miller, Chen, & Olivarez, 2014) have argued that what we know as the personal narrative in adolescence, and beyond, has its origins in early childhood conversations about personal experience. These conversations about the past are more circumscribed than narratings in later developmental epochs; they involve the recounting of particular episodes in the child's/the family's daily life. As early as two years old, children are making substantial contributions to the recountings of past experience. But, of course, these narratives are never told alone. Early recountings include the support of parents and other experienced tellers to scaffold the child's developing narrative competencies into a story. Miller uses the term "co-narratives" in order to emphasize the joint production of these early tellings.

In this context, what is especially striking about these narratives is that parents and children work together to produce a story when there otherwise might be no story. They work together to define the boundaries of exactly what should be included in the taleworld (Young, 1986, 2004). The end result is narrative, but what the story is about emerges in the dialogic relationship between parent and child. There is no story without both participants in this interactional context. In a different interaction, nothing might emerge. In essence, parent and child work together to make a story. Tentative interpretive moves are actualized into a story through their interactional work.

Fivush and Nelson (2006) present an illustrative conversation between a two-year-old boy and his mother, which becomes a story of the boy's trip to his Dad's office at the Chrysler building in New York City. The narrative is taken from Engel's (1986) research and is quoted with the original author's permission.

C: Mommy, the Chrysler building.
M: The Chrysler building?
C: The Chrysler building?
M: Yeah, who works in the Chrysler building?
C: Daddy.
M: Do you ever go there?
C: Yes, I see the Chrysler building\picture of the Chrysler building\
M: I don't know if we have a picture of the Chrysler building. Do we?
C: We went to::: my Daddy went to work.
M: Remember when we went to visit Daddy? Went in the elevator, way way up in the building so we could look down from the big window?
C: big window.
M: mmhm.
C: When::: we did go on the big building.
M: mmhm, the big building. Was that fun? Would you like to do it again? Sometime.
C: I want to go on the big building. (Fivush & Nelson, 2006, p. 245)

Like my "painful" reaction to Munch's painting, the tentative move of the child's "Mommy, the Chrysler Building" is ambiguous in its meaning. But this statement enters into dialogue with the boy's mother, who makes something out of it.

Fivush and Nelson (2006) use this conversation as evidence of the way that mothers scaffold the elements of an event into a concrete narrative with characters and a plot line. The scaffolding cuts very deeply. The mother treats this utterance as a meaningful statement from a conversational partner who is trying to take the floor and directs the child toward an event and an evaluation. The words themselves do not indicate a clear point or intention to tell anything. There might not have been a story, but the dialogical context actualizes a jointly told narrative.

I don't think that we should (or can) limit these observations to childhood or a few rare cases. Rather, this is true of the storytelling process in general. Narrating is thoroughly contextual, dialogically infused, and never written just in the words themselves. A number of factors, particularly contextual ones, actualize basic narrative moves into larger and more complicated ones.

It is difficult to determine if a given interpretive action is part of an ongoing theme or plot line because there is always the opportunity for such interpretations to be understood in some way, by somebody, as fitting into a story. And, in some sense, understanding an interpretation as narrative ultimately depends on including a particular somebody in the calculation, that is, a person who frames, and understands, the words or actions as part of a story. Perspective is critical.

For our two-year-old, "Mommy, the Chrysler building" might have already been part of a story—part of which was not verbalized but imagined and framed as such internally without further elaboration—maybe even the identical story as the one that was drawn out in the conversation. Or, as the exchange seems to indicate, perhaps the interpretation "Mommy, the Chrysler building" only became a story when his mother entered into the conversation. We could imagine other points of view on this utterance that engage it and build a more comprehensive narrative or leave this articulation as just an odd fragment that is out of context. The mother takes an active role, using her life experience and competencies in storytelling in order to interpret what the child should tell about and leads the child to an appropriate set of events.

Seeing an expression as a narrative requires seeing it as a part of the ongoing context of talk. Interpretive actions can potentially engage plot lines or themes, but it may not be immediately evident how they do so.

Making narratives involves more than recounting specific events or ordering histories (past, present, or future). Storytelling is a way of orienting us to what the world is like, what life is like, and who we are. The story isn't only in the substance of what is actually said, but also in what is implied. Often, the implications are schematic, deeply implied, rather than an explicit recounting of events. And interpretation, both by others in the immediate context of the telling and researchers removed from this context, is necessary in order to make what is said into a story.

TEXT AND CONTEXT

Ricoeur's (1984) analysis of mimesis in *Time and Narrative* can help us shed some light on the dynamic relationship between the composition of a narrative text and the contexts in which it exists. In large measure, Ricoeur follows Aristotle's analysis of dramatic forms of tragedy, comedy, and epic as mimetic activity, which he views as the art of poetically rendering and representing events and actions. Like Aristotle, Ricoeur puts the central emphasis and highest value of mimesis in the imitation and organization of actions. The imitation of "what" happened, the *muthos* in Aristotle, and plot or emplotment in Ricoeur. But, as Ricoeur argues, the accent is on the activity of composing or making: "poetics is thereby identified, without further ado, as the art of 'composing plots'" (Ricoeur, 1984, p. 33). "Narrative" is "exactly what Aristotle calls muthos, the organization of events" (p. 36).

Although the recapitulation of actions emploted as a narrative object is central to the Ricoeurian conception of narrative, Ricoeur's very productive move is to place the Aristotelian conception of mimesis in a dynamic interpretive context. He introduces two other conceptions of mimesis (mimesis1 and mimesis3) at the borders of the mimetic configuration of action (mimesis2, which is an expansion of Aristotle's *muthos*).

In his generous interpretation of Aristotle, Ricoeur claims that he finds evidence for mimesis1 and mimesis3 in Aristotle's works, which, Ricoeur writes, "testify to the impossibility, for a poetics that puts its principal accent on the internal structures of the text, of locking itself up within the closure of the text" (1984, p. 48). In a sense, narrative as the emplotment of action is located between two contexts. Configuring (mimesis2) is both prefigured (mimesis1) and reconfigured (mimesis3).

Mimesis1 argues that any representation of action is always based upon our understanding of the world of action itself in its everyday form. Persons must have a native understanding of action, which is socially and culturally grounded, in order to be able to recapitulate action in narrative. Mimesis1, quite simply, is those pre-understandings that persons have acquired in their participation in the world.

Ricoeur uses examples from psychoanalysis and the law in order to argue for what he calls the "(as yet) untold story," which rightly belongs to mimesis1. In life there is a pre-narrative potential that has the ability to be formed into a narrative from the "bits and pieces" of everyday life (p. 74). Something happens to someone before the story can be told "whose beginning has to be chosen by the narrator" (p. 75).

Mimesis2 does not "radically alter" (p. 65) the Aristotelian model. But, as Ricoeur writes, "the plot transforms events into a story. The configurational act consists of 'grasping together' the detailed actions or what I have called the story's incidents. It draws from the manifold of events the unity of one temporal whole." (p. 66) And, later, "[t]hanks to this reflective act, the entire plot can be translated into one 'thought,' which is nothing other than its 'point' or theme'" (p. 67).

Finally, this configurational activity is always in the context of how the text affects readers/listeners. "Mimesis3 marks the intersection of the world of the text and the world of the reader or hearer" (p. 71). It is the competence and capacity to follow the story.

Narratives are actualized, in mimesis3, in the reception or reading of a text. Although readers are guided by their prior knowledge of action and narrative, which "govern the story's capacity to be followed . . . it is the act of reading that accompanies the narrative's configuration and actualizes its capacity to be followed. To follow a story is to actualize it by reading it" (p. 76).

Although the composition of action, of grasping actions together as more than incidental, is the pivotal force behind Ricoeur's hermeneutic reading, it must be contextualized between prefiguring and reconfiguring. There is a dynamic interplay between the three forms of mimesis. There is much more to narrating stories than just the textual object.

The configural dimension is not only in the words, but also in the opportunity to construe and narrativize the words in various ways. In other words, it is our interpretive reading/following of what is said that allows us to actualize it into a narrative. The reason that interpretation and narrative are so entangled is because, congruent with the ongoingness of life, interpretations are always incomplete. And, given the right circumstances, interpretive acts have the potential to be put in relationship with other meanings. Following Ricoeur, we can view structure as an evolving part of the contextual process in which narrating is embedded. But, because life is ongoing and highly socialized, structure is in continuous evolution. The text is always woven into a context that frames and reframes the text itself.

NARRATING AS MAKING PRESENT

In what follows, I further elaborate the thesis that narrating has various meaning-creating functions that can be described in concrete terms. But I am not going to make the claim that I have all the terms right. I am not going to provide a taxonomy of narrating functions to end up as a pithy chart. My description is not meant to be exhaustive.

However, we can point to a wide range of narrating functions. Particularly, I have in mind functions such as forming a personal or collective identity, developing a sense of self-continuity and coherence in time, and communicating a past. Webster (1993) argues that reminiscing about the past has the function of reducing boredom, preparing for death, recalling bitter memories, connecting with others, teaching/informing, identity/problem-solving. Tellings can also make arguments, express a point of view, persuade or seduce, pleasure and entertain, build social bonds, establish social facts, or argue for what really happened.

These notions should be considered beginning points, which could serve as ways of thinking about narrating to be refined and rethought in research. I hope to provide some tools to describe, in detail, exactly how narrating works as a sense-making practice. The power of thinking about narrating functions is to allow for creative ways of describing and researching meaning making.

Despite the caveat that my account will necessarily be incomplete, I begin my account with the assertion that a basic function appears to underlie many, if not all, varieties of tellings. As I see it, the foundational property of narrating is to "make present." This is narrating's primary function.

The idea of "making present" is inspired by phenomenological and hermeneutic philosophy, particularly Heidegger (1926/1962) and Ricoeur (1984), but also the work of Freeman (1993, 2010). Although I retain some of the meanings emanating from this tradition, I extend the idea of making present to new domains.

The notion that narrating functions to make present has many nuanced consequences for what narrative means and how it works to express and make sense of life. I now turn to a description of three related ways of conceptualizing making present and a discussion of some of the implications of these ideas. I argue that making present has at least three interrelated aspects that can be put together to view narration as a whole.

Making present is

1. *Declarative*: Making present gives presence to subjective experience;
2. *Temporal*: Making present gives meaning to the past, present, and future; and
3. *Spatial (social)*: Making present co-creates shared and divergent understandings of the world.

MAKING PRESENT AS SHOWING

First and foremost, making present can be thought of as a variety of showing. Telling makes known. It is declarative. It establishes: I am this; I know this; I have seen or experienced these events; these are my thoughts or reflections; this is what I imagined or dreamed; even, this is what I have been told by my friend.

In narrating, we establish the subjective facts of our life experience. We communicate the feel and texture of our lives. For me, this is how it is or was. When we tell, we make experience and interpretations of life present in a social scene of action, using the terms of some particular linguistic, historical, and cultural community.

Presence has the sense of taking shape, of giving corporality: "*to give presence to*." Narrating puts knowledge into play in the real world. Experiences, feelings, inchoate thoughts take form. They gain substance. They become something other than internal wanderings, becoming active as they are entered into the here and now of the social world.

There is a certain sense in which telling externalizes and objectifies our subjective experience and projects it into the world of social life. The words live on past their internal value, beyond the closed-off space of the untold. In such a way, narrations can be considered by the self and by others as a reference point or marker. In their "objectivation" (Schutz & Luckmann, 1973), one's subjectivity is transformed, through an interpretive action, and now can be taken as an object and analyzed. Experience is en-textualized in speech or action and can be commented upon, returned to in conversation, and taken to other contexts.

Of course, there are various media in which interpretive actions are en-textualized with different consequences for the distribution and enduring presence of the action. Talking to my friend on the telephone is more circumscribed and subject to the memory of my friend than a taped interview broadcast on television to one million viewers.

Certainly, an important aspect of narrating is telling experience in order to make known what we have lived through. Memoirs and autobiographies are often primarily interested in making life experiences known. This is especially true in cases of hardship, extreme violence, and injustice.

The accumulation of journals and stories from the trenches in World War I are voluminous. Even more exceptional are the stories of concentration and death camp survivors after World War II, who provided written and oral testimony of their experiences. In the language of Holocaust studies, witnesses make present their memories through their testimony.

Listening to and reading survivor stories, whether literary or oral histories or interviews that I have conducted, I have been struck, as have others, by survivors' need to tell the story as a way to make their experiences known to others. In such a way, others can become witnesses to their experience. This is a common sentiment. In an analysis of open-ended interviews with 20 Holocaust survivors that I conducted in 1994–1996, I noted that 7 of the 20 survivors explicitly discussed the telling of their story as a weapon against the repetition of future atrocities, which I called a *pro-memory* stance (Schiff, 1998).

One of my interviewees, Ben, whom I discuss in much more detail in Chapter 7, was born in Sosnowiec, Poland, in 1923. Ben lived with his family for a short time in the ghetto before he was sent to Krakow Plaszow. Ben and other prisoners built the camp, which has since become famous, mostly, from the film *Schindler's List* (1993). Ben spent around two years in Plaszow. Later, he was transported to Czestochowa to an ammunition factory. After the war, in Kielce, Ben survived a pogrom. Ben met his wife in his hometown and moved to the United States. Ben owned a successful shoe store and is now retired. Ben's brother lives in the United States and he has cousins in Israel, but most of his family was murdered during the war. He has one daughter and two grandchildren.

My interview with Ben is emotionally charged. It begins with a searing indictment of Western powers for collaborating with the Nazis in the extermination of the Jews. Ben reserves the same emotional approbation for American Jews.

> They didn't care, so they made a Final Solution, they gave the go ahead, they gave Hitler the green light what to do the Final Solution. Otherwise a lot of the Jews would be saved. A lot of the Jews I blame here too. I'll tell you the truth, I'll be honest with you. I never told this to anyone, you are the first one, which you are going to hear about it, but even now it's public, people know about it that the US and England and Russia they're to blame for it too. Otherwise Hitler would have never done it. Never. They just looked away.

Ben continues to think about the past often—his incarceration, the murder of most his family, the anti-Semitism that he experienced after the war, leaving his native Poland—and it still troubles him. He suffers from insomnia and high blood pressure. Ben is also very emotional about telling his life story. He does not often speak publicly about his experiences. As he tells me, he only spoke to me at the rabbi's encouragement: "He told me you are a nice young man. OK I'll do this. I couldn't refuse, but otherwise I wouldn't."

Near the end of the interview, in response to my question about one or two things that people should know about the Holocaust, Ben responds:

> To tell them this story, what was going on, what's happening, what was happening. To be able to know so that history doesn't repeat itself again. That this should never ever happen again. They should know they should learn. Should teach in school. Which they do now teach in school. Once you teach it and once

the world knows it, and sure there are a lot of them you are going to find they are not going to believe it. But they have to keep talking and telling the story over and over and over again not to forget. Not to be just history. Should not allow it to be history. What happened should never be allowed to be history, never, ever. Should be told for thousands and thousands of years, because like I said before, it's impossible to describe what I have seen, what my two eyes have seen.

A little later in the interview, he continues along the same lines:

What else can you do? That's all you can do. That's all the power you have, is to keep on telling the story to your children and grandchildren and generations to come. Never to forget. Because once it's not told, it's all gone. So they died in vain.

The sentiment driving pro-memory is not limited to survivors of the Holocaust, but captures something about how persons, especially with experiences of suffering, desire to establish that I, or we, have experienced this. Narrating becomes a marker but also, potentially, a corrective force. As Ricoeur (1984) wrote: "We tell stories because in the last analysis human lives need and merit being narrated. This remark takes on its full force when we refer to the necessity to save the history of the defeated and the lost. The whole history of suffering cries out for vengeance and calls for narrative" (p. 75).

Making present is a claim to truth, of holding on to the reality of the past with the goal of not allowing events, in Ben's words, "to be just history." This is one of the nuances of the idea. In making present, speakers are establishing claims about the reality of their experiences or knowledge. Part of the object of making present is to clear a space, to make an argument for, the narrator's understanding of reality. In Chapter 5, I discuss this implication of making present in more detail.

Of course, cynical performances are always possible. The relationship between telling and experience is complex. Narrating makes present, but this presence is always in the context of an absence. There is always a gap between what we know and experience and what we tell (Josselson, 2004). The gap consists of the inability of words to truly capture and represent events and perhaps sentiments, and our inability to speak or write as fast as we think and feel. Narrating is also restrained by the relevance of our thoughts to the current conversation, their tellability in this context (Ochs & Capps, 2001). Power dynamics constrain or limit the ability to speak (Johnstone, 1996). Unconscious desires, conflicts, or traumas may edit internal processes. People lie or willingly conceal. Persons are caught up in the world and are not fully in touch with what they are thinking. When we give voice to an idea, the telling is not a direct representation of experience itself.

Despite the disjuncture between experience and telling, narrating is closely tied to lived experience and our reflections on life. Narrating is, arguably, the closest that we can get to experience and our understanding of those experiences. And, perhaps, that's all there is. There is no denying the fact that narrations are constructions, but they are constructions that articulate aspects of our lived experience, and they become active forces in our internal dialogue and in the field of social life.

Narrating works in presence. And it must. What can be said about absence, except that it is not there? Most of the time, there is not a lot more to add. Even when we are searching for what is hidden and elusive, what Josselson (2004), following Ricoeur, calls a hermeneutics of demysti-fication, we are still dealing with the visible signs of underlying processes. We continue to work with clues that others have made present for us. Still, we need to recognize and attend to the limits of narrating and what it can reveal about human experience. Except under certain conditions—a gifted writer, a revelation, a psychoanalytic insight—narrating might not be able to access the deepest strata of human experience and the unconscious.

THE FUSION OF NARRATINGS IN TIME AND SPACE

Narrating is always making present at some specific time and place; in a very real sense, experience is made present here and now. In the context of a particular conversation, real or imagined, that is taking place at a certain temporal horizon. Considering the idea of making present in relation to time and space adds additional nuances to this function.

It will be helpful to describe making present in time and space sepa-rately. But, in a sense, they always go together to form a complete con-text. Bakhtin (1981) coined the term "chronotope" to describe the fusion between time and space evidenced in literary narratives. But the idea is equally applicable to other varieties of telling.

Young's (2004) analysis of oral narratives makes this point explicit. Beginning from Goffman's analysis of frames, Young argues that there are two frames that surround stories about the past. The widest frame Young calls "the realm of conversation." Indeed, storytelling is part of everyday language in use. It is found within dialogues, which have echoes to other previous conversations and projections to future conversations. The con-versation that we are in right now is part of a long chain of conversations and is meaningful only because it stands in reference to them. Smaller than the realm of the conversation is the storyrealm, which Young defines as "tellings, writings and performances—that is, of recountings of or alludings to events understood to transpire in another realm" (p. 77). The storyrealm is the here and now in which tellers use language in order to conjure another world. The taleworld is this other realm. It is the world of characters and actions that we take to have transpired in another space and time.

Although my definition of narrative is more expansive than Young's, her analysis evokes the embeddedness (Georgakopoulou, 2007) of where telling happens. Taleworlds are made present in a specific time/space horizon. They are made present here/now or there/then—in a definite chronotope. We can begin to imagine and concretely describe the when and where of narrating, when and where narrators make a lifeworld present.

In terms of temporality, making present means literally bringing experience and evaluation into the present, in present time. In terms of spatiality, making present means building shared tellings and understandings of self, other, and world.

MAKING PRESENT IN TIME

The relationship between narrative and time is a central concern in narrative study. Some researchers argue that narrative is the vehicle for bringing together the present, past, and future into a coherent whole (Cohler, 1982; McAdams, 1996).

Freeman (2010) argues that one of the proper functions of narrative is reflecting on and making sense of the past. For Freeman, understanding is always from the perspective of the present, looking backward, which he calls hindsight. Reflection provides the space for creating new and meaningful understandings of the past. Hindsight is a kind of "recuperative disclosure." He writes that poetry and hindsight can be "agents of insight and rescue, recollection and recovery, serving to counteract the forces of oblivion" (p. 44). He continues, a little later:

> Or, to put the matter more philosophically, it is a *making-present* of the world in its absence; it is thus seen to provide a kind of "supplement" to ordinary experience, serving to draw out features of the world that would otherwise go unnoticed. (p. 54, italics added)

Telling the past, putting it into words, is a way of recovering aspects of our past from forgetfulness.

A basic definition of memory would place the past in the present, folding the units of time together. Memory makes present the past. Or, as Terdiman (1993) writes, "the complex of practices and means by which the past invests the present is memory: *memory is the present past*" (p. 8).

What we recall from the past, and when we recall it, reconfigures the meaning of the past. The past is reflected upon in new ways, through subsequent life experiences and the present. The past is rewritten by how things have turned out since that time, how our life is now, who we are now.

Time is never just clock time, but it is also human time. The now of the clock corresponds to a point in my lifetime and the lifetimes of others who are co-present with me. Making that past present in this now, we tell a developmental story in which we look over once again those past experiences and give them new laminations of sense and significance. But we always do this from the present. Time moves forward and backward; clock time keeps moving forward, but retrospective time, human time, moves backward (Mishler, 2006).

Ricoeur (1980) compares the act of recollection to the act of reading a book that we have read before. Drawing upon Kermode, Ricoeur argues that we cannot know the meaning of a story or novel until we know the ending. But, in life, we already know the ending, or at least, our current understanding of how events have turned out until the present now. In such a way, interpreting our life from the present becomes an act of "reading the past backward" (Schiff & Cohler, 2001). The past is always colored by our knowledge of the present and becomes something new in the act of recollection. As our lives develop, so too do we develop new reworkings of the meaning of the past. The past is never just the past but, as Cohler (1982) argues, it is always a "presently understood past" (p. 207).

MAKING PRESENT IN (SOCIAL) SPACE

The past that we make present and the timing of when we make it present rewrite the meaning of our lives, our identities. However, we are just looking at one part of the chronotope. As I have argued, narrating makes present in time and space. We need to consider both in order to form a complete context. In every "now," there is a "here."

In order to understand the "here," it is critical to highlight that space is highly socialized. Other people are the most salient aspect of where we make present our life experience. We are "here" with others, both real and imagined.

This is one of the profound implications of Bakhtin's dialogical theory. All speech is part of an ongoing dialogue and is addressed to others (Bakhtin, 1981; Noy, 2002) from whom we expect a response. Our words seek out an answer and are only really comprehensible in light of a response from others (Gergen, 2009). As I have already argued, stories are co-told or co-narrated with substantial input from others present and narrating along with us (Georgakopoulou, 2007; Ochs & Capps, 2001; Miller, Fung, & Mintz, 1996; Wiley, Rose, Burger, & Miller, 1998). Narrating is a social activity that is grounded in the actual context in which it occurs, and it has very clear and concrete social meanings.

Making present in space implies locating ourselves in a given conversation. The imagery is one of being physically present in an ongoing "scene of talk" (Herman, 2009), a social performance (Bauman, 1986) in which we enter into and exit from conversational turns (Sacks, Schlegoff, & Jefferson, 1974). We gain our "footing" in the conversation at hand (Goffman, 1981). We "position" ourselves in relation to what is being said, to the others present, and to larger identity discourses (Bamberg, 2004; Davies & Harré, 1990; Georgakopoulou, 2007; Wortham, 2000).

Of course, conversations are not only mine. They are not invented from whole cloth in the present. The words and stories that we possess are social, inherited from our predecessors by virtue of our participation in a world rich with sense and meaning. From the very beginning, we find ourselves immersed in this world. We are born in the midst of ongoing conversations that precede our own personal existence. Through participation in this world and in concert with others, we discover the language and stories of life. These conversations are concrete and face to face. Through repeated interaction with others, we come to know the stories of our community, what a story is, and how to tell such stories. The stories are enacted, made alive, for us in a certain time and space.

Through the enactment of stories, we learn about the basic facts of our existence: what a self is, the roles and desires of others, how the world works, the meaning and goals of life. These stories are resources for understanding who we are and the meaning of our existence. As MacIntyre (1981) famously put the matter, "deprive children of stories and you leave them unscripted, anxious stutterers in their actions and their words" (p. 216).

Although co-narrations are, theoretically, a stage in the child's ability to independently tell stories about his or her past, co-narrations are much more prominent than is recognized. There are some sound theoretical and empirical reasons to argue that all narrations, even in adulthood, are co-narrations.

Georgakopoulou (2007) argues that narrative psychology privileges narratives in which there is a single speaker, who tells a significant life experience to an interested and attentive listener. According to Georgakopoulou, the problem with this model is that everyday narrative practices are strikingly different, involving multiple competing speakers who negotiate basic issues of story ownership and evaluation. Meaning emerges from the interaction in which multiple persons make present life experience, together, regardless of whose experience it was/is/will be. Speakers take up roles or positions in storytelling to produce a negotiated account. Narrating is a co-narrating, a kind of "co-action" (Gergen, 2009), even in the research interview (Mishler, 1986). It involves balance, mutuality, and negotiation between participants.

Although our narratings are never free from the constraints of the conversational dynamics, from power or storytelling rights and with whom we are speaking, making present in social space has the effect, and often the intent, of influencing the conversation at hand and others—including those who are present and those who will only hear reports of the conversation. We cast others and ourselves into positions and alignments, propose roles and versions of the past, self, and life, and test them out in the context of others and their responses (Bamberg, 2004). To make present in social space is a tentative attempt to direct or redirect these meanings in order to have a social impact.

The end result is to make present together joint understandings of self, others, the world, the past that are mutually shared between the participants. But this is not the only result. Narrating also gives form to divisions and disagreements in these understandings, making visible aspects of power, status, and authority (Georgakopoulou, 2007; Holland, Lachicotte, Skinner, & Cain, 1998). Co-telling doesn't lead necessarily to consensus—far from it. It can also be a vehicle for bringing forward and expressing competing versions of reality that remain unresolved.

STRUCTURE—REVISITED

I want to return to the opposition that I constructed between structure and function. I have argued that narrative psychology should be concerned with the process and use of narrative. Although structure should not be thought of as an end in itself, how narratives are formed and told can be critical insights for describing and understanding questions about the meanings of narrating. In other words, structures have functions. In the following,

I want to make a couple of brief comments about the relationship between structure and function. Certainly, there is more to be said.

First, structure appears to have a link with the length and complexity of narratives. I have argued that showing or making present experience is essential to narrating and of substantial value in understanding life experience. Making present includes intricate and detailed narratings, such as life stories or autobiographies, and shorter interventions into everyday conversations. At the level of more basic narrations, many elements of narrative convention are not as prominent or, perhaps, necessary. Mediation, artfulness, and structure are still evident, but such articulations of experience have more in common with the structure of speech turns in conversations than with the novel.

But, once we consider more complex tellings, with multiple actions and characters across time and space, the artfulness of forming a narrative takes on increased salience. To deal with complexity, of the kind that life relentlessly presents us, narrative conventions provide the tools for managing and expressing the thickness and density of our experience. As Brockmeier (2012) has argued, narrative is the form of discourse best suited to capturing the complex activities of human action. "No other sign system could handle and communicate the complexity of these syntheses in such a comprehensive, economic, and effective manner" (p. 443). Narrative structure is helpful in dealing with the messiness of human experience in order to infer the meaning of actions, motivations, cause and effect, and connections. Such conventions become more evident and necessary as complexity increases.

Second, expressions that are structured using particular conventions, such as those resembling a Labovian personal experience narrative, might possess properties, such as repeatability, which in turn have consequences for understanding ourselves. Although stories are responsive to the situation of telling and the audience, substantial portions of narrative structure and content are repeated across tellings (Chafe, 1998; Norrick, 1998; Schiff, Skillingstead, Archibald, Arasim, & Peterson, 2006). In other words, people might not tell exactly the same story twice, but central elements of stories are carried to new contexts and over time. Similarly, borrowed, vicarious, narratives, from face-to-face conversations and from the media, are routinely integrated into the telling of our personal experiences. Putting words into a structure may help us to remember and use the story in diverse contexts. The longevity of particular stories, and particular aspects of our lives, might be enhanced by our ability to articulate those experiences in a conventionalized and transportable structure.

A third way that structures serve functions is in the ability to create and experience other worlds. Herman (2002, 2009) argues that one of the basic elements of narrative is the capacity to create imagined, fictional and nonfictional, worlds, or storyworlds. There is something seductive about good storytelling; good stories transport readers/listeners to another place and time. This ability to shift from the here and now and into another storyworld relies not only upon the listener's, or reader's, desire and interpretive skills, but also on linguistic, structural, aspects of the narrative itself. Narratives, literary and oral, often provide indicators for readers to shift to their focal point of consciousness to the storyworld (Herman, 2002).

IS EVERYTHING NARRATIVE?

A functionalist approach to narrative does include a wide range of verbal and nonverbal practices that would be disregarded in current research. In some ways, the range of possible narrative scholarship does become larger, but it also closes off other avenues. In any case, a functionalist perspective does not imply a radical opening of the narrative concept.

First, one should view the functionalist position against the backdrop of what is currently practiced. In psychology and the social sciences, the current use of the narrative concept is woefully imprecise. As I argued in Chapter 3, conceptions of narrative psychology are so diverse that the term seems to have no meaning outside of the researcher's desire to frame their study as "narrative." At the current moment, in psychology and the social sciences, everything is narrative.

In contrast to current practice, functionalism gives shape and grounding to narrative. It does so in a way that is inclusive, welcoming creative ways of approaching meaning making. Using this definition, researchers can recognize narrating, by attending to what an interpretive act accomplishes, and know the reasons that they are studying narrating, to understand the hows and whys of meaning making.

Still, distinguishing between what is narrative and what is not narrative on the basis of function will continue to be tricky because it relies on interpretive criteria. Do these words function to articulate and make sense of life experience? A given application can be disputed, but I don't see this as particularly problematic. A good definition stimulates innovation. Functionalism serves as a guide for research and thinking by orienting us toward what is really essential about narrative, that is what narrating can do, and inspiring creative research on meaning making.

Still, not everything becomes narrative. But it does mean that the more we stop and pay attention to interpretive acts, the more we can start to interpret them as narratives. Still, typing loudly on my computer is not, usually, a narrating. However, given the right context, it can be. Stepping on the breaks of my car is not, usually, a narrating. But, once again, it depends on the context. A verbal greeting, "hello," buying a bread at the bakery, ordering a steak at a restaurant, or many of the habitual expressions that we make present in our day-to-day lives are not, usually, narratings. But if we enlarge our scope of how these actions participate in the ongoing and embedded project of making sense of life, they can be, if we engage with them and begin to understand them as such.

In my estimation, the answer to whether or not something is narrative moves from a focus on the text in isolation to the way the text is understood. Whether or not something is narrative depends on whether or not we understand it narratively. The burden is as much on how the interpretive action is constructed and produced as on how it is interpreted and consumed, as Ricoeur makes explicit in mimesis3.

In her analysis of storytelling in social media, such as Facebook and Twitter, Georgakopoulou (2017) argues that these new tools engage others in acts of distributed, joint storytelling. Georgakopoulou observes that about 95% of text messages and two-thirds of status posts on Facebook walls are either stories or beginnings that introduce storytelling activity.

In order to capture the situated and evolving nature of storytelling in online media, Georgakopoulou (2017) introduces the term of narrative stancetaking, which she defines as

[a] moment of position taking when a teller more or less reflexively mobilizes more or less conventionalized communicative means to signal that the activity to follow, the activity under way or the activity that is indexed, alluded to, deferred, silenced is a story. (p. 38)

Narrative stancetaking describes the way that expressions become stories through social processes in which the activity is mutually defined as storied or potentially storied. The emphasis is not on what is said, but what is implied in the context, the position, or the attitude of speakers and listeners toward what is said and how it is said.

I have argued that the primary function of narrating is making present. Narrating is an interpretive act in which life experiences and understandings of life are articulated and made meaningful through their declaration in our present circumstances and in collaboration with co-actors. Making present is not the only function of narrating. To give just a few other possibilities, narrative functions to establish close bonds, to organize past events, to give color and pathos to our lives, to attribute cause and agency to our experiences, to establish social identity, and even to lie and conceal. But I would argue that all of these functions are related to, perhaps even require, making present at their core.

What are the implications of this theoretical analysis for narrative research? Where does it suggest that narrative research should go? I firmly believe that narrative scholars should focus on the process of meaning making—on what narrative does and how it accomplishes this—in the concrete circumstances in which meaning making happens. How do persons, in time and space, make sense of life experience?

In my opinion, this is what narrative research is all about. This is the unique contribution that narrative research can make to the advancement of psychology and the social sciences at large. Narrative allows us to take an inside path to understanding how persons connect together aspects of their life and world. Quantitative methods using statistical analysis can't study how persons construct a world, think about themselves, and connect themselves to their social world. From the perspective of a narrative psychology, this is what narrative does best. And I believe that it can do so in a way that valorizes the complex experience of persons while holding true to the kind of systematic observation required by science.

Although my description has been theoretical, narrative should not be. Further work on narrative functions should be grounded in observations of interviews and other conversations. Once again, the goal is not a taxonomy, but rather to use the idea to think through the problem of how meaning is accomplished in time and space, turning toward the concrete circumstances in which life experience is made present and closely tying our observations to human lives in context.

CHAPTER 5
Making It So

In one of his aphorisms in *Hermeneutics: The Handwritten Manuscripts*, Frederich Schleiermacher (1986) writes, "Every child comes to understand the meanings of words only through hermeneutics" (p. 52; originally published in 1805 and 1809–1810). The aphorism strongly suggests the connection between what interpreters do in the analysis of texts and what everyday people do, even children, in coming to understand what things mean in the world. It is interesting to contemplate how persons, children, are positioned. Children seem to figure things out on the fly, always in the midst of life. Out of the flux and flow of life in all its ambiguities, we come to understand the world.

Schleiermacher is pointing out an essential aspect of the everyday, in and out, work of interpretation. Understanding is a process that unfolds through our sustained interaction with the world and others. Interpretive practices are necessary; they are everywhere, normal and natural. Indeed, even children need to be interpreters, even at the beginning of life, in order to figure out what the world is all about.

This need to understand the world, for our very survival and well-being, is not unique to childhood. It is part of the everyday orientation that persons take toward the world. We are constantly trying to figure out where we are in the world, the situations that we are in, and what our lives are all about. What kind of world do I live in? What is expected of me? What is this object? Who is this person? What are they saying to me?

The effort is constant from childhood to old age. However, sense making is most evident at moments of rupture or crisis, when we don't understand where we are or what is happening, and there is a pressing need to put together a convincing account of life experience. What do I know about the world? Where am I? What kind of world is this?

Primo Levi's (1947/1993) description of his first days of incarceration, as described in *Survival in Auschwitz* (originally titled *If This Is a Man*), can be read as such a rupture experience, where the meaning of life needs to be quickly rearranged into a new configuration. The situation is bizarre, absurd, disturbing. Skeletons in striped pajamas scurry about performing their duties. The men are incomprehensibly and brutally separated from the women and children. Everyone is dying of thirst, but the only water is not potable. The strange mix of languages. Hundreds of shoes are mixed together for redistribution. The body and hair are cruelly, and ridiculously, shaved on each prisoner. The tattoo. In the upheaval, Levi seems to be searching for the right words, the right metaphor, for the experience that is unfolding before him. It is so out of the ordinary and alarming. Is it like a dream, a game, a madhouse, hell? At moments, Levi uses the trope of the theater, like acts in a play. But is it a comedy or a tragedy, or some newly invented form?

Levi struggles to understand, what kind of world has he arrived in? What is the logic of this world? Who are the actors? What are their roles? What is his role in this world?

"Driven by thirst," Levi reaches for an icicle stick, only to have it taken away by a passing guard. When he asks why, "'Warum,'" the guard responds, "'Hier ist kein warum' [there is no why here]" (p. 29). This is a variety of knowledge, albeit of the negative variety, which Levi takes as a summary statement in his developing understanding of life inside the camp. Here is a world where there is no why. Taking the tone of a scientist observing the social norms of the camp, Levi comments, "The explanation is repugnant but simple: in this place everything is forbidden, not for hidden reasons, but because the camp has been created for this purpose. If one wants to live one must learn this quickly and well" (p. 29).

There are rules that constitute the laws of the alternate universe of camp life. The laws are mostly senseless, illogical from the perspective of the world outside the barbed wire fence, and brutal in their absurdity. Levi details the many strictures and forms of behavior necessary in order to avoid selection and to stay alive. They included a detailed knowledge of the social organization, "guests of the lager are divided into three categories," the forms of address, "never ask questions, always pretend to understand," how to eat bread, holding the bowl "under our chins ... so as not to lose the crumbs," and due to the rampant stealing and the need to guard one's few possessions, "sleeping with our head on a bundle made up of our jacket and containing all our belongings" (p. 33). Even at the beginning of his internment, Levi writes, "We already know in good part the rules of the camp, which are incredibly complicated. The prohibitions are innumerable" (p. 33). This knowledge became so internalized that inmates were able to regulate their bladders during sleep to avoid urinating in a full chamber pot that would lead to being forced to exit the barracks in the freezing cold to the latrines. It was incredibly costly to misconstrue a rule and lose one's soup bowl or spoon or to keep ill-fitting shoes. But figuring out the "Gordian knot of laws, taboos and problems" (p. 35) was a critical act in one's ability to live a day in the camp.

I am not suggesting that grown adults in the contemporary world are like children or concentration camp inmates. But these examples highlight the everyday epistemological stance of persons in the world. Persons need to figure out the world and their place within it. We figure things out and constitute knowledge about the self and others, but also about the world in general—narrating is key in this process. But how does narrative do this?

In this chapter, I build upon the idea of making present in order to address one of the central problems in narrative studies: how narrating produces accounts that guide us about what life is, was, and will be. Narrative is commonly described as possessing the capacity to build worlds (Bruner, 1987; Herman, 2009), or truths (Spence, 1980), or to construct realities (Gergen, 1994; Shotter, 1993). In this chapter, I ask how, exactly, does narrating create a sense of truth or a sense of reality? Or, to put the matter closer to everyday experience, how do interpretive actions help us take apart, fix, and re-fix what life is and means?

These are central questions about the nature of our lives. Some might say that they are existential or philosophical questions, which either can't be answered or are better left to the humanists in philosophy and literature. Obviously, I don't believe that's true. Psychologists can and should study the big questions about human experience. How persons work, together and alone, to build up interpretations about themselves and the world and to negotiate those interpretations with others is at the core of psychology. And psychology can provide us with insights, which have practical applications. The narrative perspective in psychology can provide a powerful conceptual framework for approaching these big questions in a manner that is concrete, pragmatic, and grounded in empirical data.

I want to be careful to distinguish the problem of the true or objective nature of reality, if there ever were such a thing, which is more properly the domain of philosophy, from the problem of the "sense of" the real as it is subjectively experienced, which is more properly the domain of psychology (Sarbin, 1998). The notion that subjective constructions about the nature of reality are at the core of our day-to-day experience is part of the psychological canon; this, of course, was Piaget's (1952) major thesis. Much narrative research, and much psychology, begins from this premise of individual constructivism in which persons are the active agents in developing their own picture of reality. As an alternative to this emphasis on the primacy of individuals, social constructionists have argued that reality is a project that is built up through the negotiation between persons in social interaction (Gergen, 1994, 2009). Beginning from Vygotsky (1978), social constructionism argues that relationships are primary to introduce and redefine social reality.

As I have argued, I take a functionalist approach to narrative in order to describe how persons manage meanings in time and space. *Making it so* is one of the functions that narrating does—or tries to do. In narrating, persons make present versions of life that assert what is right, true, or real—or what is patently false. Narratings attempt to fix a point of view or unseat a position that is taken for granted within a particular context. Often, narratings are social assertions jointly produced in a concrete conversational setting, and they enter into a contest for authority. But even self-talk, internalized dialogue, what we tell ourselves in dead of the night, is but one move in a conversation (Bakhtin, 1981). It is *a priori* no more authoritative than any other telling. Self-talk must also wait for a response, the next move, internal or social, to determine the sense of the previous utterance. In such a way, there is never a moment in time in which meaning is permanently fixed. Although narrating attempts to fix meaning, it is never really set in stone, but is always open. Rather, the project of making it so is one of fixing and undoing and, once again, fixing and undoing—fixed only until the next moment, the next intervention.

Although the social sciences typically put persons in opposition to social group and culture, focusing on one or the other, a narrative perspective allows us to understand the multilayered, and reciprocal, connections between persons, social relationships, and culture that are implicated in building, and rebuilding, a sense of the real. Narrating provides the means for connecting together ideas and persons, creating versions of life that we, and others, come to see as, at least provisionally, right or true. My main thesis is that narrating functions to create meaningful "resonances" (Schiff & Noy, 2006) or "reverberations" (Miller, Fung, & Koven, 2007) in which the person and the social world "harmonize" (Halbwachs, 1980).

In Chapter 4, I argued that narrating, as making present, enacts inter-pretations. Presenting interpretations is at the heart of all narrative activ-ity, from the everyday to the literary. In this chapter, I build upon making present, to say that narrating is basic to the process of reality building. Making present attempts to make it so. Telling something, especially social instances of telling, is part of a psychological, social, and cultural process that can work to establish that "this" is "so." In such a way, narrating can be thought of as the process for disclosing and fixing particular interpreta-tions. Words have the ability to create and conjure worlds. Simply speaking has a force to impress meaning. The word brings the idea into being, cana-lizing the shape of the idea in a quasi-substantial formation. Narrating says something like "here is something," or "here is a world."

I don't want to give the impression that there is something whimsical or trivial about this process of building up and tearing down meanings. These are interpretations that matter. They matter deeply, supporting fam-ily relationships, identities, and regimes of power. They participate in the project of imagining, establishing, and living in versions of the world, what is really real and what really concerns us. Narrating configures worlds to be lived in. To borrow a phrase from Shweder (2003), like culture, narrative is engaged in what can be thought of as a "reality-binding project"—what life (my life and life in general) is all about. Certainly, we are dealing with an elementary process. But it is a central one and important to reflect upon. For persons, saying is at the basis of truth making.

Although I view a person's articulation in words as the center of this creative effort, telling is never without a social and cultural context, and it is far from a simple matter to determine the distance between saying and, provisionally, establishing that my telling corresponds to what really is. Tellings exist inside other tellings, with a history that they refer to, in deference to or contradiction with, and they address contemporaries and future potential interlocutors. There is also the issue of the medium of the telling, written, electronic or verbal—which gives an interpretive action more or less permanence—and the authoritativeness that is given to the interpretive act through the reputation of the teller. There is also the ques-tion of the physical reality surrounding us, and the documents and arti-facts that constrain, play off, and bump against our narratings.

These are complications that I will take into account. However, for the time being, we can simply describe the process as telling makes it so. Telling is a tentative move in the social world, an opening, which draws upon the experience of the teller in order to declare certain facts about the world.

MAKING LIFE

Describing how narrating forms lived-in realities requires some precision. I don't think that we should be content with vague abstractions. Rather, we need to describe the concrete everyday actions that constitute this dynamic process. How and why do interpretations become so important that we see them as true for us, who we are, and what the world is all about, and live our lives by them? My focus is squarely on the process (how) and functional significance (why) through which persons, in time and space, designate meaning, and the consequences of such designations for making, and remaking, interpretations of life.

I describe three interrelated aspects of arriving at narrative interpretations of consequence.

Encountering

People are born into and inhabit worlds of stories, but not in some abstract way. As I will argue, stories are encountered in our day-to-day life, in specific, concrete enactments, in particular temporal and sociocultural settings.

Imagining

Prior encounters are resources for later enactments, providing the means for forming new interpretations of life. This is the role of imagination, which as Andrews (2014) has eloquently argued, is active in all aspects of our lives:

> It is imagination in its everyday guise, imagination as it is manifested as we think about our lives as they have been lived, and as they might be led, as we try to make sense of people who seem very different from ourselves, and even those with whom we think we share so much. Our imagination, in this sense, is not something which we dust off and put on for special occasions, a psychological tiara of sorts. Rather, it guides us from our waking hour to when we go to bed at night. It is with us always, sitting side by side with our reason and perception. (p. 10–11).

Every interpretation always involves some innovation and reinvention. This is why the word "imagining," as Sarbin (1998) describes, is appropriate in this context.

Resonating

Interpretations come and go. The sense of grounding interpretations, that they are real or reality-like, I call "resonance." Resonance attempts to describe why meanings are held in place—at least provisionally. As I will argue, imaginings can be fixed, even momentarily, because they function to interpret the self and the world.

Although we may be tempted to see a sequence or steps, I make no assumptions in this regard.

ENCOUNTERS WITH MEANING

Meaning always comes from somewhere. There is always a background to what we know and tell. Like Schleiermacher's children, we figure out, on the fly, what is happening in the world around us. But, as Gadamer (1960/ 1993) tells us, meaning making always implies a preexisting structure. There is a paradoxical sense in which we can only build meaning with meaning. Persons are always in the middle of it, in the thick of making sense of the world from what they have established.

The background or horizon of meaning making is essential, but one that is already well elaborated in several lines of literature. For example, the tradition on collective memory in sociology, beginning with Halbwachs (1980), argues that all social groups provide frameworks for remembering the past. In the phenomenological tradition, Schutz and Luckmann (1973) argue that social groups have stocks of knowledge, storehouses of know-how and tradition, which are passed along from generation to generation. In contemporary theories in the social sciences as well, Frank (2010) writes about the narrative habitus, or a site of readily accessible storylines. And Freeman (2010) argues for the narrative unconscious or that set of potential, but yet to be actualized, stories that come from our participation in culture.

I would like to add the event-like character of such encounters. We encounter stories—meanings—in our everyday participation in the world. Just as narratings make present meanings, meanings are made present for us, *always in a concrete experience*, always in some specific time and place. Once again, we find ourselves in Bakhtin's chronotope.

The form for such encounters is typically in face-to-face relationships, concrete conversations, but could equally take place through an encounter with other media, such as books, television, or electronic media. We might speak about shared meanings as part of the cultural background or horizon, but our encounter with meaning is anything but general. We encounter meaning in the specific, in the particular, and we can provide a date, a time and place, for the encounter—even in the case of cultural knowledge.

Certainly, we encounter narratives in the chronotope. But narratives also are told and come to take on certain meanings within the chronotope. In other words, all three aspects of making it so (encountering, imagining, and resonating) must be seen as taking place inside a situation in a specific time-space horizon, a specific here and now.

INNOVATING, IMAGINING, TELLING

The encounter is essential for new productions. Some might even argue that, in large measure, the background determines the production and that applications are, on the whole, automatic. In other words, persons simply restate and apply what they have discovered through their encounter with the world and others. This argument would state that narrating is mostly imitation. However, this does not realistically portray the interpretive process, which, in my view, is always, and necessarily, creative. We are always producing innovative interpretations because life itself demands innovation.

First, persons are constantly required to deal with the fluidity of life. Life is always new. Although there may be echoes between situations, meanings indexed from other times and conversations, strictly speaking, we never experience exactly the same situation twice. No matter how many times we do the same old thing, life maintains this ambiguous quality where meaning requires work and negotiation (Goffman, 1959). Indeed, when do we truly ever have a clear and certain grasp of life?

Second, narrating always entails innovation. Narrating is never just simple representation. Even when recounting the most vivid memory that appears to be etched into our minds, remembering is always more than a direct line to the past. Remembering does not duplicate an exact replica of the past. It is not representational—at least, not exclusively so. Remembering is a reconstruction, a translation. We need to put the remembered experience into words and to make choices that recast experience into another sign system; the rich perceptual world, full of color and emotion, becomes words and gestures, thereby editing the experience and its meaning.

In our everyday usage, we oppose memory against imagination as if these two forces were distinct from one another. Memory is for telling about the real; imagination is for telling about fictions, fabrications, fanta-sies, and untruths.

In cognitive psychology, it is widely accepted that memories are con-structions, which are susceptible to the influence of cultural beliefs and social interactions. But cognitive psychologists also speak about "memory failures" or "sins" (Schacter, 2001). This only makes sense when a corre-spondence theory of memory is employed and the accurate reproduction of past events is identical to memory (Wertsch, 2002). In other words, mem-ory is thought to be opposed to imagination because fabrication diminishes accurate retrieval or representation. However, in my view, memory and imagination exist in a much different relationship. Memory is profoundly indebted to imagination. Memory cannot be realized—the past cannot be made present—without the work of imagination itself.

In a chapter entitled "Believed-in Imaginings: A Narrative Approach," Sarbin (1998) equates the action of imaginings with narratives. He writes:

> The contents [of imaginings] are sequences of actions in which self and oth-ers are involved—narratives with beginnings, middles, and endings. They are fashioned from concurrent perceptions of proximal and distal stimulus events, rememberings, bedtime stories, folk tales, cultural myths, articulated theories and art forms. In short, imaginings are storied constructions. (p. 19)

Prefaced upon our encounter with the world, we are constantly imagining scenarios, spinning stories, in our heads and in our speech. Furthermore, as Sarbin points out, imaginings draw upon a wide range of storied knowl-edge, including what we have learned in our direct life experience, such as personal relationships, events, and situations, and what we have learned in indirect, mediated, life experiences such as friends' stories, television, books, social media, and films.

Imagining means storying both the actual and the possible. The bound-aries between the two are constantly moving and fuzzy. For Sarbin, such imaginings are hypothetical; they have the character of "as if" construc-tions. They are possible ways of interpreting and fashioning life. Similarly, Bruner (1986) suggests that narratives involve the skillful use of the sub-junctive tense. In other words, narratives are always in conversation with what could have been or might happen, and they need to manage the uncertain and the possible. Perhaps, literary and filmic narratives keep us on the edge of our seats because they play upon our sense of what is pos-sible (Sternberg, 1992).

Narrating as imagining is a constant companion as we move through our day, go to work, talk with others, read a book. We are spinning stories as we go about our business. How many stories do we imagine a day? Hundreds? Perhaps thousands? Some of these stories are full-blown narratives with beginnings, middles, and endings, whereas the vast majority are merely a word or a two. If anything, narrating as imagining radically extends the narrative potential of life.

Imaginings have multiple registers for expression. Imaginings are made present in thought, speech, writing, performance, and so on, at a particular time/space in the midst of an ongoing dialogue. They intervene in a conversation. I like the French word for presentations, such as in a seminar—one doesn't say "give" a paper, but rather *intervenir*, or translated into English "to intervene." Imaginings act in similar ways. Imaginings are actions, which intervene in an ongoing dialogue at a particular moment in time and in a particular social setting. The intervention has the potential to establish certain facts or truths, which will endure beyond this particular intervention, to affect us, and to lead the conversation in new directions.

Imagining, like all psychological processes, is something that persons do, and there are vast differences in imaginative abilities. Some people are better at dreaming up different possibilities; others are more contrived and limited in their expressive range. But imagination is more than a personality characteristic. It is a basic component of human experience and is always in context.

Our encounter with the world provides the terms for what we can imagine; there is a sense in which we imagine on the basis of what is already possible to imagine. But the concrete context that we find ourselves in at the moment of imagining is also critical. Persons imagine, but they always do so in context, at a particular time and in a particular place.

In terms of time, the present opens up and closes off possibilities. For example, at this time in my life, it is hard for me to think that I will ever be a professional baseball player or filmmaker. Yet, these are possibilities that at one point in my life, I (somewhat) seriously considered. Temporally, imagining is constantly evolving. It is in development, never a fixed target.

Imagining also works within social space. We imagine together, in the company of others, who shape and reshape our interpretations. One of the most striking findings from Georgakopoulou's (2007) ethnography on Greek female teenagers is the sheer number of stories about possible futures that these young women spoke about together. Amazingly, the largest group of story types that she observed were about imagined future scenarios. Georgakopoulou's informants worked closely together in order to describe, in great detail, what could and might and would happen. In conversation, they dreamed up what the future would look like, how it would unfold, and what it would mean. Imagination is very much a social phenomenon. What speakers can tell is limited by the social context and by what counts as a tellable story for this particular listener or listeners (Norrick, 2007).

RESONATING

Most imaginings are furtive, stuttering attempts to interpret life. They are the smallest of "small stories"—tentative, probing interpretations, rising up here and there, typically dying an immediate death before surrendering themselves to forgetfulness. Other imaginings, however, become part of larger threads or plot lines close to our heart and central to our identities.

This is a very interesting problem. We imagine much more than we feel to be really true about ourselves or about life. We are constantly imagining and narrating, constantly living in the realm of the possible. Also, somehow, we know that the vast majority of our narrative wanderings have no implications about our lives, how the world really is, who we really are.

Sarbin (1998) argues that some imaginings become believings through a process that he terms "hypothetical instantiation," where through deep play the "as if" is slowly removed and the possible becomes internalized as the actual. The hypothetical becomes real. He suggests that *"believings are highly valued imaginings"* (p. 23) which are connected to our self-narratives.

I agree with Sarbin; imaginings become believings because an imagined narrative fits into another configuration. They resonate. Here, resonance stands in for that sense of accord or fit. Subjectively, resonance is what we might think about as a "truth-feeling." *Something feels right about that. It accords or it is true for the person.* When a meaning or story resonates, it comes to fill a function, often in multiple domains. Meanings might serve as complements to identity or other deeply held beliefs about the world, or serve as interactionally managed truths about the world.

Resonance is also chronotopic. Imaginings resonate in a particular time and social space. In terms of our past or identity, resonance means that, at this time in my life, this is true for me. It fits with how I understand myself and my place in the world. Interpersonally, resonance is an agreed-upon fact that is worked out in a conversational context. In this conversation, this is true.

Although the idea of resonance is appealing, I want to suggest a more complex relationship between the sense of self and imaginings. Multiple relationships are possible. The sense of fit is not the only possibility. We may experience discord or dissonance between imaginings and the self when a story does not work for us, or causes us damage, pain, or confusion. And, of course, there are other possibilities

COUPLE STORIES: ENCOUNTERING-IMAGINING-RESONATING

In this section, I apply the theory of making it so, and the process of encountering-imagining-resonating, to research interviews. My concern here is with the reality-making function of narrating. How and why do interpretations become so important that we see them as true for us (who we are and what the world is all about) and live our lives by them?

The data analysis is an opportunity to reflect on these ideas but is not intended as proof of the concepts. Rather, it is a way of showing how the concepts work. I discuss issues of interpretation, trustworthiness, and sound arguments in narrative research in Chapters 6, 7, 8, and 9.

In the following, I examine *making it so*, twice, using interview data from two related projects. The first set of interviews included seven couples with no restrictions on ethnicity or the length of their relationship. Interviews for this data set were collective, both partners and two interviewers were present during the entire interview. The second set of interviews included three mixed Jewish and Arab couples at the early stages of their relationship. Interviews for this data set were individual, with separate interviewers for each of the partners. In both projects, interviews were structured as a conversation to elicit the couple's story and reflections on the course of their relationship. And, in both, the interviews were conducted in French and translated.

The *couple's story* is my central point of reference in describing the processes of encountering-imagining-resonating. A couple's story describes who the couple is and what brings them together. It includes those central narratives that define the couple, the pivotal choices they have made, and the enduring traditions that provide their lives with meaning. It is a joint construction of who "we" are that is negotiated and performed in concert with one's partner. Neither partner owns the couple story. But, couples seem to arrive at a decision about notions of authorship rights and authority in concert with one another.

The couple story is, essentially, an imaginative product, which relies upon the joint efforts of both partners. How do they imagine together the story of who they are? The story of their past, present, and future? Although both partners play a role in authoring what the couple story is all about, each partner also needs to find a place for themselves in the story of the couple and to live in the story that they helped to co-author. Couple stories are about the collective identity of the relationship, but personal identity is also deeply implicated. In this way, we are talking about the fit or resonance-dissonance of the couple story for each partner. How does the story function to serve the needs and desires of each person's identity? What does the story allow or deny? What room does the couple story leave for identity construction?

The analytic path that I follow begins from the group interviews and a more microanalytic, moment by moment, interpretation (Clement and Marine) before moving onto a macroanalytic interpretation (Steve and Salima) in the individual interviews.

CLEMENT AND MARINE

In order to develop these points, I begin with a microanalytic view on the couple story. In the conversation are two interviewers, myself and one of my students, Fanie Collardeau, and a recently married couple, Clement and Marine. At the time of the interview, Marine was 8 months pregnant with their first child. Both Clement and Marine are in their early twenties. The conversation lasted over 2 hours and provided a detailed description of how the couple met, the disputes that characterized their relationship, and their thoughts about their respective families of origin.

The interview is more like a dialogue with Marine and Clement, with Marine, for the most part, taking the lead of the interview. They also engage each other and ask questions of one another. The interviewers add very little by way of direct questions. As the transcript indicates, the discussion is animated, and both Marine and Clement are active contributors to the dialogue.

In this context, I want to consider how the couple story emerges from the interactional setting of the interview context in which Marine and Clement negotiate the facts of the story to be told and the meanings that they assign to their relationship and each other. I want to focus on two central portions of the transcript in which the meaning of the couple story is at stake and becomes an item for contestation and reconsideration. In both instances, there is a socially agreed-upon, mostly consensual, interpretation that emerges in the dialogue that makes use of stories and meanings encountered in other circumstances before this conversation, imagines innovative explanations and scenarios, and, ultimately, establishes common ground, what I have called "social resonance." The two exchanges, found near the beginning of the interview transcript, contain moments of ambiguity where competing meanings are contested.

Marine and Clement's interview begins with the typical negotiation for who will lead the direction of the conversation. After an initial presentation of the purpose of the interview, Clement jokes, "Is this a therapy?" and "What percentage of interviews end up in divorce?" I don't want to make too much of these statements, other than, as will become clear, Clement makes a number of ironic, jocular remarks during the course of the interview. The general tone of the interview is humorous, a lot of laughing can be heard, but there is also an undercurrent that could be interpreted as cynical or sarcastic. Clement's humor is sharp and sometimes biting.

After we present the project and sign the informed consent, Marine asks if we have a hypothesis for the interview, and we once again make it clear that we are just there to listen to their thoughts and reflections. They decide that a good place to begin would be the story of how they met. Clement says, "How did we meet already. That's a good start. So, I'll start, otherwise she will tell everything and I won't have anything to add." Marine seems to acquiesce to Clement and cedes the floor. Clement continues, "Well, we met at the house of one of my friends, at a dinner. One of my very good friends and Marine didn't have any friends at that time." From the very beginning, Marine objects, "Pff. Nonsense. No." She moves herself back into the position as the main authoritative storyteller, correcting Clement's assertion that she "didn't have any friends"; rather, she didn't have any friends in the area, and through one of Marine's mother's friends had reached out to other local high school students.

The moment of their meeting not only brought Clement and Marine together for the first time, but also established a "fusional" teenage group in which both were implicated. Clement and Marine discuss the structure of the group and the main members and describe the period as a stage in their adolescent development. At the end of their high school years, they finally got together for 2 months, before going on to university in different cities. In fact, Marine left France to study abroad.

The story continues in a straightforward fashion, with Marine taking the lead and directing which events are tellable and to be included in the interview.

> MARINE: I left to study abroad. It was a little, either I stay in France
> or go abroad and during that time I said to myself that I would
> stay for Clement. After I said between the two choices, I'd rather
> go abroad (to a more prestigious university). So, I left and then
> we found each other. So I did my studies but we still stayed in
> contact and all that but each one had their own life.

CLEMENT: We saw each other every December 25th at Christmas Mass.

MARINE: At Christmas, yes that's right, we would see each other at the Mass. He had his girlfriends and I had a boyfriend. We each had a little our lives apart from each other. And, me, I came back here. I worked for a year over there and came back. And we saw each other again. He was with someone else and we saw each other again.

CLEMENT: (laughs)

MARINE: What?

CLEMENT: No, nothing, go ahead, start.

MARINE: No, no, he was with someone. No, we saw each other again, we saw each other during Easter vacation when I was. Yes, you were with someone else. That was very important, fidelity.

CLEMENT: We are speaking about who there?

MARINE: Felicity.

CLEMENT: Ah, OK, you skipped directly to the next step after.

MARINE: But, of course. And, suddenly, everything, in other words finally, finally, he broke up with this other girl in September and then in September we were together. That's it. So that's (year). Oh no that was (year).

The sequence of recounted events ends here and Clement applauds Marine, apparently for her mastery of the dates, but it is not entirely clear what the applause means. Although the account seems coherent, my interview partner, Fanie, has been carefully listening and noticed the lacuna in their account marked by Clement's "Ah, OK, you skipped directly to the next step after."

After the account concludes and there is a pause in the conversation, Fanie, carefully and gently, asks, "I am just wondering because you said 'you had skipped a step' so I was only wondering what that step was?" They respond:

CLEMENT: No, but because in fact there was a moment.

MARINE: No but because we would get too much into the details.

CLEMENT: Yes, we get into the story of Dawson's Creek (the American teen television series).

MARINE: It isn't very interesting.

CLEMENT: But, yes, of course, it's interesting.

MARINE: In fact, yes, because it really—

CLEMENT: It very much—

MARINE: It very much had consequences on our couple.

Fanie's intervention into the conversation redirects the flow of the narrative into new subjects that were hidden by the clean schematic account in which Marine was the main narrator. At first, Marine resists the notion that the details are relevant or interesting to their couple story but with a little insistence from Clement, "but, yes, of course, it's interesting," Marine quickly reconsiders her original reticence to enter into the details and the account becomes infinitely more complex.

In a sense, Fanie's question works to support Clement's position that a step has been missed and opens the floor for alternative versions of their story. In this exchange, Fanie becomes a central player in the recounted story. Through her gentle intervention, she participates integrally in the process of imagining the contours and meaning of the couple's past history. She creates an opening for a second story that is more complete but also more acrimonious and disputed.

Rather than being a simple narrative of meeting and dating before taking a break for studies and coming back together again, Clement and Marine's couple story is filled with drama, heartbreak, other lovers, perceived deception, misunderstandings, and conflict. These are the details that were glossed over in the previous account, which was largely authored by Marine, and that, as they both agree afterward, loom large over the character of the relationship.

The episodes missing in Marine's account are given colorful description in what is largely Clement's account of the years in between. Although the tone of Clement's account is at times bitter and confrontational, almost like a lawyer deposing a witness, and there are points of continued disagreement, in large measure Marine affirms the telling with a steady refrain of "yes" and "that's true."

CLEMENT: In fact, the story is that when I went out with this girl, who I was with before, I started to date her during a university wide weekend. . . . And, I, maybe ten days later saw Marine. . . . And for once, I want to say, I succeeded in going out again with her. Yes, because she led me on for years. She forgets to say that but during two years if we went out together only for two months it's because she put up a number of obstacles—

MARINE: That's true.

CLEMENT: It's incredible. Typically, I stop after the first let down. I am super shy but with her. She doesn't have any pity. She really put a lot—

MARINE: It's true.

CLEMENT: She really played the princess. All that. For that. You could have accepted and we would have saved some time.

MARINE: Yes, that's true. It's true, it was long and hard. Right.

CLEMENT: And, I was persistent—

MARINE: Yes, it paid off.

CLEMENT: And, in fact when I, when I saw her, I was with this other girl for two weeks, not even. That's where our stories differ, it is that in the fact that we went out for four or five days.

MARINE: Yes, we saw each other a bit.

CLEMENT: No, you're joking, it was intense. It was. "Ah." And, I didn't see the other girl since, but I didn't officially break up with the other one. And in fact, Marine told me that she was going back abroad to finish up some things and pack her bags.

MARINE: Because you need to know that I lived in this other country. I had a job there, I had an apartment there and in these five days I told him that frankly, I would really like to come back anyway and that I will come back for you. And I said that I will come back. But, I needed to end my job, my affairs, so finally, but there we don't agree at all.

CLEMENT: Right.

MARINE: And we still don't. We still don't have the truth of the story.

CLEMENT: We agree to disagree (in English).

MARINE: Right. But I said that I will come back, I will finish things up and all and that when I come we will be together.

CLEMENT: Right that's it, but only that she didn't come back when she said she would.

MARINE: So, it's there that we don't agree. I gave—

CLEMENT: And in fact, you should know that Marine, at that time, wasn't a person that you could have confidence in, seriously none, zero. I loved her but I had absolutely no confidence in her.

MARINE: That's it.

The conversation represents the couple's negotiation to establish the events, sequence, and meanings of their early relationship and the role that each played during this tumultuous period—what really happened. Of course, they are also telling these facts within the context of a research interview, with two outsiders listening in the room. But there is a sense that the couple story is being worked on, imagined, in the interview itself.

They are discussing firsthand experiences, which they each encountered from their own perspective. However, this is not the only material that they are working with. It is not the first time that they have discussed the events in question. The tenor of their remarks indicates that they are revisiting previous discussions and points that they have made in the past. This is also made explicit in their words: "But we don't agree at all" and "We agree to disagree (in English)." Meanings, anterior to the present conversation and embodying previous negotiations, are brought forward into the context of the present, of the here and now of the interview situation, and made present for revision, recasting, and reimagining in the presence of the interviewers. They are made available for dispute, but also as the grounds for potential agreement and synchrony in point of view. But the conversation doesn't end in a shared version of the past—the closing words are more dissonant than resonant.

At this point in my analysis, we can say that, at least, the conversation has unearthed something that is already known and understood by Clement and Marine. Fanie's intervention into the interview created an opportunity for a retelling, and reimagining, of the couple's story found in the second, more detailed, version. I have shown that, given the right circumstances, different versions are possible, but I have not provided convincing evidence of the potential to arrive at innovative conceptions of reality, explicit in my notion of making it so. I turn to that task now.

Clement and Marine wrap up the complicated history of how they finally started a stable couple relationship. There are some closing stories, which conclude the topic, about the aftereffects of Clement's ex-girlfriends and whether or not Marine and Clement were friends first before they became a couple, and so on. Marine then directs the talk to the interviewers.

MARINE: OK then. Go ahead and ask us some questions.
BRIAN: It's a complicated story but interesting.
CLEMENT: (Singing) *The story of life.*

Marine, then, herself, reframes the interview to the larger purpose of the interview, saying, "But, OK, and since that time how do we construct our couple?" I follow up and ask, "What is the role of each person in the couple?" Marine answers:

You need to know that we were a couple. We are very different today than what we were before. At the very beginning, well, during many years, we had a relation very—in fact, really, we didn't get along very well. We fought a lot. Finally, really, we were, we were. It was super passionate really. We fought a lot. It was like all of a sudden, I slam the door, I leave, I come back, I leave again, we fight.

It was really. It was a little tiring in fact. But, we never really left each other. We left each other 2 days, and would come back and in fact everything has settled down. But, since when?

Clement tries to steer the conversation to an incident of leaving Marine on the side of the road on one of their travels. Marine rejects this attempt and returns to the same point.

MARINE: Really we had a relationship. At the beginning not really simple at all. We fought a lot.
CLEMENT: It was—
MARINE: At the same time, when it was good, it was perfect.

Rather than directly answering my question about roles, Marine offers an overriding portrayal of the course of their relationship, contrasting the earlier period of their relationship, when "we fought a lot," with their current life together, when "everything has settled down."

At this point in the conversation Clement offers the following assertion, Marine is a "*chat sauvage.*"

CLEMENT: No, but you need to know that Marine is a real feral cat. Now, we wouldn't think so but she was a terror before. It was—
MARINE: But, explain yourself because—
CLEMENT: A feral cat, do you see what it is? It is an expression which says that you were, that you couldn't stand to be confined at all.
MARINE: Yeah, I had some problems keeping promises. But, I always had. I don't like to say to myself that I am in a situation that I can't get out of. Finally, it's true that I would run away.
CLEMENT: There were many times and you recognized it afterward. The fights were just to make you feel alive.
MARINE: No, it wasn't just to make me feel alive. It was just not to feel stuck in something.
CLEMENT: Yeah, that's right.
MARINE: In a relationship, yeah that's true. I needed an escape route but that has really changed.

In the exchange, Clement makes a rather bold claim in which he attempts to fix an aspect of Marine's identity. She is this, she is a "*chat sauvage.*" The label of "*chat sauvage,*" which we would translate in English as "wild or feral cat," is a provocative assertion that casts Marine as a certain kind of character. A feral cat is part of general knowledge, witnessed on the street or read about in books. It is certainly something that Clement knows about, that he has encountered somewhere, and so do the others in the room. However, the reasoning behind Clement's intervention in the conversation and how or why Marine is a feral cat are not clear.

Marine is certainly surprised by this strange accusation. It is also not clear if she is offended—the assertion could be read as sexist—or if she is just asking for more details, but she calls the assertion into question. Clement elaborates, "you couldn't stand to be confined at all." Marine agrees, "it's true that I would run away." Clement moves to expand on his initial assertion, adding, "The fights were just to make you feel alive." Marine rejects this expansion, and the two seem to agree on the original assertion that Marine was the kind of person who did not like "to feel stuck" and "needed an escape route." We also get a sense of their/her personal history. There is a sense of temporality, "Now, we wouldn't think so but she was a terror before."

The exchange is inherently interesting and raises many questions about not only how this couple negotiates conflict and contrasting interpretations, but also how they see their past and each other. It also displays the way the composition of the text is the result of joint authorship (as I argued in Chapter 4). Each move, Clement's labeling of Marine, her request for more information, his explanation, her agreement, and so on, are interpretive acts that have an effect on the structure of the text produced and how they (and we) understand Marine. The text evolves and could still evolve, with each move implicitly carrying the tag "until further notice."

There is an active way in which what is established in the conversation as true about Marine and about their relationship is configured and reconfigured, imagined and reimagined, fluidly through coordinated acts of interpretation and reinterpretation. Although Clement appears to have more interpretive authority in the exchange, Marine attenuates his claim and focuses it to, what appears to be, an acceptable conclusion for her. It is their active reimagining of one another's interpretations that produces a version of Marine's character and a chapter in the couple's story, past and present.

The exchange is meaningful in establishing an overarching theme about Marine and giving it a pithy label. But the theme is evidenced in other language, such as, previously, using different words, when Clement says, "And in fact, you should know that Marine, at that time, you couldn't have confidence in, seriously none, zero."

Still, the *"chat sauvage"* has what we might call social resonance; it becomes a consensual conversational fact that parties agree upon as a correct interpretation. There is an explanatory point to the telling. It fixes her character in a particular identity that has descriptive power.

It is then used as an interpretive tool. At two later points in the transcript, Clement returns to the *"chat sauvage"* as an interpretation of Marine's personality. First, he uses it as a rejoinder to explain Marine's expressed discomfort with the closeness of Clement's parents' marriage. "Don't forget that she is a feral cat." Second, he recalls it to explain Marine's ambivalence and anxiety about planning a formal wedding ceremony and party. "She is really a feral cat."

The interview data show how versions of reality come into being through the concerted effort of imagining together and how versions of reality are worked out in talk, becoming synchronized and accepted, resonating, as an appropriate or accurate version of the real that is, in turn, available for use and translation into other circumstances and contexts.

In discussing Marine and Clement's couple story, then, I have presented two instances where interpretations are contested and reworked in order to arrive at alternative and, more or less, consensual versions of the couple's past and the character of the protagonists. The group interviews highlight the real-time social processes at work in making it so. In both instances, others are centrally implicated in the process of encountering, imagining, and resonating. What we take to be the real or true story—true about Marine and Clement's past and true about Marine's character—is the negotiated product of imagining a world along with others.

Still, it is not clear from the transcript how Marine and Clement see the *"chat sauvage."* How enduring is this agreed-upon fact? In other words, the notion of the *"chat sauvage"* has social resonance, but does it have personal resonance? Does Marine now see herself, in some metaphoric sense, as a "chat sauvage"? Does she see the idea as descriptive or insightful in any sense? The bridge that connects together more immediate and situational productions and more long-term and internalized understandings is not straightforward. Personal resonance is my attempt to clarify some aspects of this puzzle. I have argued that there is an emotional or intellectual sense of fitting together that can describe how encountered imaginings come to be accepted as true.

Although I cannot directly answer these questions in the couple story of Marine and Clement, I can provide some insight into the process of personal resonance through an exploration of individual interviews with partners from another couple.

Steve and Salima resist commonly held notions that mixed Jewish-Muslim couples must have deep conflicts in their relationship with one another or with the external world. The first descriptors that come to mind in describing Steve and Salima's couple story are simple, easy, and natural. These words are appropriate in regard to each stage of their story: their first meetings, the relationship with their families, Salima's conversion to Judaism, politics, and so on.

Certainly, there are a number of ways to understand their interviews. But I think that it is fascinating to look at Salima's movement into Judaism and her adoption of Steve's family story as the guiding narrative for their couple story and a central one for her own identity as an example of making it so. As I will describe, Salima's Judaism is a lesson in how encountered meanings can be seen as relevant and possible and come to define one's selfhood. Her Judaism is a story encountered in a specific time and space. Although she certainly had contact with Jews and Judaism before dating Steve, the self-definition, to be Jewish and have a Jewish family, is one that she made in her encounter with Steve's family narrative and their decision to build their lives together.

Salima never would have converted to Judaism on her own. She never would have thought of it as a possibility for herself. But imagining together the story of their couple is a pivotal moment for her identity. Together, Steve and Salima dream together about what their life could be. They establish the important issues and themes of their common life. They explore possible futures and then rally around these choices. Because these choices are functional and necessary in multiple domains (Salima's identity, their relationship to each other and to their extended families), they become lived-in meanings. In other words, their imagined construction fits well; it resonates in numerous domains.

In order to understand Salima's Judaism, it is essential to consider the couple story and to begin with Steve. It is Steve's Jewish identity that forms the core of the couple's story and is a central meaning in the construction of Salima's identity.

Steve began his interview by describing his strong commitment to a Jewish identity. Steve's identity is set in the history of his family and their conscious effort to protect and pass along their Judaism. This story, borrowed intact, is the central narrative of Steve and Salima's couple story. Jewish heritage is preserved by the powerful image of handing religious practice and tradition from person to person and across time and country. Their narrative is reminiscent of Zerubavel's (2004) contention that relationships are "lines of contact" or "links" between persons and cultural ideas. Persons inherit histories because they have been, literally and figuratively, "touched by" others. As Steve recounted:

> Like I was saying, we were never practicing Jews. My father was born in North Africa. They were never very religious, my father did his Bar Mitzvah and afterwards came to France. They settled here and everything. My parents met in France. When I was born. Actually, it was very important for my father, he had warned my mother actually, that I had to be Jewish. It was kind of the precondition if you will. So, when he told her that, my mother said "it's cool, no problem." . . . After, I was born. With regards to religion we were always in a Jewish environment. Afterwards, when he considered what to do about choosing my religion, it was imposed on me by my parents. But I didn't, I don't suffer from it, I don't suffer from that today. They said to me. It was also the wish of my grandfather before he died, even if he wasn't religious, but it was still important to him for his grandson to be Jewish. Because actually, I am the last carrying my family name. . . . It's [also] important that our family is Jewish and everything. It's important for my father and for my grandfather. (Pause) So I took classes at the synagogue.

Steve's Jewish identity is passed along, from person to person. Like Steve, his father and grandfather both married non-Jewish women. Also like them, Steve has perpetuated the family's Jewish character. He has inherited the responsibility for keeping the tradition, the name, and the family's "line" alive. Equally, he has inherited a story that connects his family and himself to Jewish tradition. His promise to his father echoes his father's promise to his grandfather to continue Jewish tradition.

Steve's Jewish heritage foregrounds Steve and Salima's couple story. These burdens are incorporated into the plot line of the couple's present and future. The family is and will continue to be Jewish. The family name will live into the future. However, the problem with patrilineal descent is that it complicates the Orthodox Jewish narrative, in which the mother's religious identity is decisive. Only Steve's father is Jewish, so he was not technically Jewish under Orthodox law.

At the age of 12, his father decided that Steve needed to convert to Judaism in order to claim a Jewish identity that would be recognized by the religious orthodoxy. He went through the arduous process of religious conversion, taking courses every Sunday for 7 years and, eventually, a ritual cleansing at the *mikvah*, the Jewish ceremonial bath.

Despite his repeated affirmations that he did not and does not suffer, the experience appears to have made a profound impact on his sense of self. Rather than simply being born Jewish, his identity required years of commitment and study during his formative years. It is arguable that his perseverance through conversion has made his identity stronger. Also, this commitment, at such an early age, is a decision that Salima clearly respects.

As they recount, the beginning of their relationship was natural. The couple met at Steve's aunt's house in North Africa, near where Salima grew up. Salima's mother and Steve's aunt are close friends. Throughout the years, Steve has traveled to North Africa to visit his aunt and cousin. He met Salima before they started dating. Salima's family would often come to his aunt's house during the Jewish holidays, but they never considered each other candidates for a romantic relationship. Salima is a few years older than Steve and was involved in a serious relationship, with a Jewish boyfriend, for 6 years. For Salima, all of this forms the background to her conversion. Her encounter with Steve's family narrative is not her first encounter with Jews and Judaism or mixed relationships.

In their first meetings, their religious difference did not play a role; although Salima was cognizant of Steve's religious background, Steve did not know hers and assumed that Salima was Jewish. This was Salima's version of their "first" meeting:

> We had already crossed paths before a couple of times. My husband is younger than me. He's three years younger than me. And actually when I met him before, I was with my ex-boyfriend. So I probably didn't pay much attention to him. [Laughs] Actually when I met him we were both coming out of a breakup, both him and me. And actually it happened, I don't know, it wasn't love at first sight, but it was something which happened very, very, very naturally. It happened very naturally. I mean, well, we were attracted to each other from the beginning, without it necessarily being a physical love at first sight, or even psychological. But, we wanted to be together and the more we were together, the more we wanted to be together. We shared a lot of things, we talked a lot. What I appreciated in him straight away is that he's someone who talks a lot. It's not necessarily the case, because there are a lot of, of men who don't talk a lot. So, it was nice. I really liked that. . . . It happened very, very naturally actually. . . .

Both Steve and Salima's accounts pointed out that it wasn't love at first sight. The relationship did not immediately turn passionate and sexual. The beginning of their relationship was characterized by a lot of talking. They really enjoyed each other's company and were interested in conversing. They fell in love but were content to let the relationship evolve without forcing it forward.

At the very beginning, their conversations turned to serious subjects, particularly religion, values, marriage, and how their lives together might be structured. In other words, imagining—and if and if and if. They found common ground long before their relationship became serious. The couple's decision to commit to a Jewish identity occurred very early in the relationship.

Imagining, and committing to, a Jewish identity was a decisive chapter in their couple story. When asked if, at the time he met her, he thought Salima's religion would prevent their relationship from developing, Steve responded:

> STEVE: We actually talked about all of this very early on. We quickly
> settled things. So that there wouldn't be any problems later on. . . .
> If you don't talk about this quickly, about these questions . . . then
> it'll be a fight. Whereas if you say these things at the beginning,
> when things are cool, you talk. "Couldn't we do this?" Without
> each person getting annoyed. . . . So it's also important to bring
> the issue up, to talk very, very freely, and very simply, to say,
> "Well, for me this is important, these values are also important,"
> well, it's also, it's exchanging . . . maybe not being quite so intran-
> sigent, quite so hard like, "You know, I want to do this, I want us
> to do it like this, and it'll be this way, it won't be any other way."
> Well, that's not the right way to do it. . . .
>
> INTERVIEWER: And do you remember a conversation, a specific dis-
> cussion, when you talked about all of this?
>
> STEVE: Well, no. Well, we said, "You know, if we want to keep going
> with this relationship and we want to get married, we have to ask
> ourselves these questions." . . . I said to Salima that it was very
> important for me, that I had made a lot of effort for this, taken
> lots of classes and everything. And for my father it was impor-
> tant. Like I was telling you before, I am the last person carrying
> my family's name. That in the end, the values and the things
> that are important, the fundamental values, they're actually the
> same. . . . There weren't any fights. It was very cool, the discus-
> sion, and actually we went in this direction easily, simply, with-
> out me having to insist more than that. Salima was in love with
> me, I was in love with her. She knew what I had done . . . for the
> conversion.

This spirit of openness and free discussion is an evaluation that is found in both Steve and Salima's descriptions of these early conversations. If, ultimately, Salima converted to Judaism and adopted substantial aspects of Steve's family's narrative and identity, she did so by choice and admiration. Steve portrayed the decision as a free one, and Salima would probably agree with this interpretation.

The identity was not forced upon her. There was no struggle or fight. The discussions were frank and honest. But, after all, it is Steve's identity and heritage that Salima chose.

It is important to note that the adoption of Steve's religious and family identity accomplished something for Salima. It resonated with her. This move toward Steve resolved issues in her past, complementing and completing her identity. Like a key fitting into a lock, her newfound Judaism provided her with a clear identity.

Both received substantial benefits from Salima's conversion. Steve found a way of carrying forward his family's heritage in which Salima could play a leading role. Also, Salima found a legitimate identity that allowed her to put aside some of the pressing issues of her past. When asked whether or not she had adopted Steve's religious views, Salima responded:

> I don't know. Actually, I think that for me it, it, it's something that I've always wondered about. . . . My parents aren't at all agnostic or against religion. It's not that at all. It's just that they made the choice to live their lives without religious practices. It's true that because of that, I asked myself a lot of questions when I was young. . . . And then, because my mother is mixed, I had an identity which wasn't obvious. On top of the fact that we were non-practicing, people often thought that I was French. So I've always had an identity. Well, my brothers, my sisters and I, we each have our own identity, exactly because we didn't have an obvious identity to start with. And so we each made our own. I often asked myself questions about religion. . . . It's a little complicated. After all, it's a choice to follow a religion. . . . But it's true that meeting him, and seeing that he had this faith which was so strong. Also it's true that my husband, his mother wasn't Jewish. So actually, he converted at 12 years old. It took him 7 years. So it was really very long, very difficult. I thought that it was really courageous for a child to have such a strong faith. This thing lasted 7 years. . . . It wasn't easy. So it's all of that which, which pushed me towards the choice that I made. It's a choice that I made for love above all. I mean, if I hadn't met him, I wouldn't have converted to Judaism, I think. It's a choice I made for love. Because I saw that, I felt that for him it was super, super important for his father, for his grandfather who passed away. It was very important that his children be Jewish and that they be raised in the religion. So, in some way, it's a subject that's always preoccupied me, but it's especially because it's important for him also that I did it. But I'm very happy that I did it.

As she recounted, Salima's childhood identity was ambiguous. Like Steve's mother, Salima's mother and grandmother were Christian. They were also mixed in terms of country of birth; Salima's father and maternal grandfather married Christian women born in France. Interestingly, Steve and Salima's decision to marry continues the family tradition of choosing partners from different religions. Part of the ease with which their relationship began and was accepted by their families could be due to this intergenerational history of mixed marriage.

The consonance between Steve and Salima's account is striking. Salima appears to have taken possession of the family history, borrowing some of the main features of Steve's narrative, such as his conversion and the wishes of Steve's father and grandfather. She emphasized that it was up to Steve to continue his family's Jewish tradition and the strength of his resolve to convert at such an early age. As she said, it was one of the factors that pushed her toward the choice that she made.

In a way, the decision to convert was simple; she made it for love or, rather, for the relationship. Indeed, one way of understanding the resonance of this story is that it was necessary for the relationship to go forward. There was an early agreement between both parties that the relationship could move forward only under these terms. Is this a workable possibility?

But it also shored up aspects of Salima's identity that she felt lacking. When asked if she experienced any negative consequences from her conversion, Salima said no and turned the question around:

> The positive consequence is that I feel a lot more legitimate in what I do, actually. I also feel that in some way I've chosen an identity. So, it's true that when you are the child of a mixed couple, that you sometimes ask yourself questions about your identity. Well, to choose your own and to go on to something else. Well, it's a relief. Because you have the feeling that the circle is closed. That's it, I can move on to something else. It's done.

Salima's sense of choosing an identity was experienced as a relief. She was able to stake a legitimate claim to being Jewish and, as the couple's story required, pass along to her children a clear Jewish identity. The circle is now closed and she can move beyond her youthful concerns with identity and on to other preoccupations.

Still, Salima's current identity is a complex and multiple one. She does not give up her old identity and replace it with a new one, but now that she has made a choice and converted to Judaism, she can better sense and live her Muslim identity:

I was born Muslim and converted to Judaism. I am totally conscious of what I am. I am totally conscious of my Muslim identity, even more now that I converted to Judaism than before—I am even more conscious of it now. I live it even better now than before, strangely enough. Because I made a choice, I made a definitive choice. So I live it a lot better now. I live with my identity better now that I made a choice, strangely enough.

Salima moved toward Steve's history and religion, but she did not lose her sense of her own past in the process. She doesn't experience her multiplicity as a source of conflict; rather, it strengthens her and adds to what she has to offer to others, most notably Steve and their family.

They have created a couple story that tolerates and appreciates the multiplicity and complexity of Salima's identity. Although Salima has moved further toward Steve, they seem to have found the right balance. Steve has also moved toward her identity and her family. For example, after Salima's conversion was completed, the couple married in the synagogue, but the couple had already completed several other marriage ceremonies, including a Muslim ceremony in North Africa. Interestingly, Steve converted to Islam in order to marry in Salima's tradition. The conversion was not one of faith, but it did please Salima's family, particularly her father.

Perhaps her sacrifices have been much greater. They have made a clear decision and have chosen the path set out by Steve's family. But he has made some movement toward her and has taken account of some aspects of her identity, her needs, and her family, facilitating a comfortable fit with the couple story.

Using the stories of Steve and Salima, then, I have shown how narratings provide the grounding for realities to be lived in. I have described the process as involving encountering, imagining, and resonating.

We encounter stories in our day-to-day experience, in a particular time and place. Salima encounters Steve's family story, the story of his Jewish identity and how it has been handed down from hand to hand, from person to person.

This story leads to new interpretations and new imaginings. Quite literally, they dream up a new life together. Could Salima fit into this narrative? Is it possible for Steve to maintain his Jewish identity and hopes for a Jewish family with Salima playing a part?

They imagine what this future might look like. Their discussions are frank and honest. What would their lives be like if they were together? What does each of them need? What can the other give?

This encounter and imagined future could have amounted to nothing at all. There is no inherent reason that this story should be a life-changing one. Steve and Salima could have decided not to continue, that the obstacles were too difficult to surmount, that they were not interested in each other because of their religion or for other reasons. But the story and being Jewish become the organizing principle of their life together. The story serves as a means for making interesting new interpretations of self and world. Becoming Jewish serves to shore up Salima's identity. She now has the sense that her religious identity is not ambiguous. It allows the couple to continue their relationship. In addition, this new self-definition and her relationship solve a number of problems for her and for their couple story.

ENDLESS SPIRALS

The dynamic interrelationship between encountering, imagining, and resonating bears a close resemblance to Ricoeur's (1984) three-fold mimesis, mapping nicely onto prefiguring (mimesis1), configuring (mimesis2), and reconfiguring (mimesis3). Ricoeur's theory is enlightening for understanding the movement from where meanings are encountered, in the pre-narrative potential of life itself, to the articulation of stories out of the "bits and pieces" (p. 74) of life and the effects that they engender in their reception.

Texts emerge out of life and have the capacity to reconfigure life. They circle back into one another. Most obviously, comprehending a narrative prepares the ground for new prefigurings. In such a way, subsequent narratings can follow in the footsteps of previous tellings. How texts are received influences the prefiguring potential for later narratings. By consequence, narratives tend to become sedimented in a particular style of composing or in a genre.

Although in Ricoeur's theory there is a sequential quality to prefiguring-configuring-reconfiguring, I see the relationship between encountering-imagining-resonating as more dynamic and packed in time. Ricoeur was principally dealing with literary and historical texts and, considering that material, the processes appear much more distinct.

Steve and Salima's account seems to be more orderly, and the elements of encountering, imagining, and resonating are more clearly demarcated. This could be an artifact of the interviews themselves—remember that Steve and Salima were interviewed individually—or it could indicate a more firmly established and polished couple story. Clement and Marine are obviously working through an accepted version of their past and the identity of each partner in the story of the couple. But the fact that this was a collective interview is also noteworthy. In Clement and Marine's interviews, we are given a clear window into the process of imagining together, which is alluded to in Steve and Salima's interviews but is not witnessed directly. Both are valuable and insightful. However, in everyday conversations, such as those of Clement and Marine, all three processes—encountering, imagining, and resonating—seem to play out almost simultaneously.

Still, Ricoeur (1984) noted that one could view the relationship between the three processes as a circle, where mimesis3 circles back into mimesis1, resonating into encountering. But, truly, although the relationship appears circular, we never end up in the same place where we started. "That the analysis is circular is indisputable. But that the circle is a vicious one can be refuted. In this regard, I would rather speak of an endless spiral that would carry the meditation past the same point a number of times, but at different altitudes" (p. 72). Mimesis1 is always a newly reconfigured prefiguring or, indeed, resonant encounters. In order to capture this sense of moving repeatedly through the same sequence but in a reformed manner, evocatively, Ricoeur writes that we should consider the process to be an endless spiral rather than a circle. In telling and reading, persons configure new ways of understanding experience, but such knowledge is constantly revised, perpetually turned back to the same starting point but, always changed, always "at different altitudes."

Following Ricoeur, we shouldn't view such meanings as an endpoint. Rather, they always have the opportunity to be reworked and reflected upon. Our knowledge about the self and the world is never a fixed and determined point, never set in stone and collected as another piece of what is true about life. Knowledge does not progress in a strict linear sense. For persons and researchers alike, the real story is continually, endlessly, open to contestation through the introduction of new information, alternate contexts, time, and other points of view.

But, as life goes forward, we never return to the same place. We spiral around back to what seems like the same place, needing once again to make sense of it all, but it is not exactly the same place that we once were. In the instant, we have changed and so has the world. We never begin all over again from scratch; rather, we take with us what we have learned in the interim. The spiral spins back, layered in with new experiences, new interpretations.

PART III

CHAPTER 6

Interpreting Interpretations

This chapter addresses the challenge of interpreting narratives. The problem is a central one in narrative psychology; it is a continuing source of contention and debate. I would prefer *not* to address method. However, there is a persistent need to address narrative methods of research, which continue to be a source of anxiety for many students and researchers studying narrative psychology. A clear and pragmatic discussion of the bases of narrative methods is missing from the literature. How does one go about the work of interpreting narratives? Is this interpretation the "right" one? How does one know that the research argument can be relied upon? Is it scientific?

I imagine that my discussion of narrative methods will not be the last statement in the debate. But in the following chapters, I clearly outline the practice of making sound interpretations in narrative research in the hope of guiding researchers in their inquiries and putting to rest some of the entrenched skepticism about the legitimacy of the narrative perspective so that we can get beyond method to the problems that our research endeavors to address. The need for understanding is considerable. And, after all, one doesn't become a narrative psychologist only to study methodology.

The challenge for narrative methods is to disclose the other's interpretations of life and world, in context, in such a way that these dynamics become accessible for our observation and understanding in order to develop theories about life experience that are grounded in the observations that we have made. In other words, our challenge is to put method and theory into a clear conversation with one another and to heed

Wittgenstein's (1953/1958) warning not to let "problem and method pass one another by" (p. 232). Method and theory develop together. Building sound theory requires sound methods of investigation and vice versa. In this sense, I hope that my observations on method will bring us to a deeper understanding of human lives.

INTERPRETATION IN THEORY

Narrative deals with the process of meaning making and, as Josselson (2004) writes, "Because meanings cannot be grasped directly and all meanings are essentially indeterminate in any unshakeable way, interpretation becomes necessary" (p. 3). Certainly, interpretation is a necessity in narrative research. But, in this respect, narrative is not different from other methods of analysis; every manner of investigating human beings, or the world for that matter, requires interpretation. The "problem" of interpretation for scientific knowledge is neither new nor limited to narrative psychology.

As Toulmin (1982) argued, all sciences, including the natural sciences, "are in the business of 'construing' reality" (p. 94). However, he writes,

> [i]t has too often, and too readily, been assumed that whatever needs to be interpreted in order to be understood will, to that extent, become a matter of taste or subjectivity; and, as a result, any claims to rationality and objectivity in the critical realms—whether moral or aesthetic, political or intellectual—have been too hastily surrendered. (p. 94)

The situation is problematic but not unworkable. Interpretation is everywhere, but psychologists can and should describe something beyond themselves. Psychology is not self-knowledge. It should strive to say something meaningful about the experience of others, about their reality. But how can psychologists, themselves immersed in interpretive practices, build vital and descriptive theories that reach beyond the perspective of the interpreter? Although Toulmin's critique applies to all of psychology, and beyond, in narrative research it has a particular salience.

In psychology, the idea of interpretation carries a negative connotation. Mainstream psychologists associate interpretation with subjectivity, and we have been taught that we need to defend against subjectivity in order to discover the hard, cold, objective truths about human beings.

By and large, mainstream psychology's response to the problem of researcher subjectivity has been to avoid it at all costs. Quantitative methods desire to create objective knowledge of what is generally and universally true about human beings. The researcher's subjectivity is considered an obstacle to be overcome in the pursuit of general knowledge. It is addressed as errors or fallacies that need to be corrected in order to reach more confident analyses (Wang, Watts, Anderson, & Little, 2013).

Methods of research have been developed in order to attempt to take the observer out of the observation, to quantify and, thereby, we suppose, make objective and valid our conclusions. As Gough and Madill (2012) point out, quantitative psychologists are not ignorant of subjectivity. The discovery of experimenter effects and demand characteristics (cf. Rosenthal, 1976; Orne, 1962) led to additional experimental controls, such as the double blind experiment, which are exemplary of the way that quantitative methods have addressed subjective biases. Another example is the measurement of inter-rater reliability in the coding of interview transcripts in order to achieve consensual interpretations. The lesson here: if you encounter your own subjectivity, make every attempt to root it out of the research process.

We might ask, even if subjectivity is always present, why shouldn't we ignore or get rid of it? There are many good reasons for answering "no" to this question. One that I find particularly convincing, as philosopher Thomas Nagel (1986) has argued, is that knowledge, by definition, embodies a particular perspective. Knowing is always grounded in the context of someone's subjective construal. It always comes from someplace, through my eyes or through yours.

Framing a knowledge claim, that someone knows or thinks something, as a point of view only makes explicit what is always already occurring. But, as Nagel (1986) insists, this doesn't mean that we should abandon objectivity as a goal; the subjective basis of knowledge does not derail our efforts to understand something beyond me. He argues that we must "transcend our particular viewpoint and develop an expanded consciousness that takes in the world more fully" (p. 5). In fact, a thoroughgoing recognition of the idea that knowledge comes from someplace may be very useful in allowing persons to stretch beyond singular and idiosyncratic formulations. In order to stretch beyond ourselves and to say something meaningful about the world, recognizing subjectivity, making it visible, and exposing it to critical investigation, or reflexivity, is a more productive strategy than ignoring the obvious.

Understanding is always subjective. It is always affected by the interpreter and their historical and social situation. Gadamer (1960/1993) begins from Heidegger's observation that understanding involves first projecting ourselves into a problem and making quick judgments about the nature of the problem. In other words, there is a fore-structure to understanding; we always bring ideas with us to new situations and are obliged to use these pre-judgments to make interpretations. Understanding requires pre-understandings—there is no blank slate. As we acquire more knowledge, we may revise our pre-judgments and come to know the object, person, or text in a new light. But, at least initially, what other options do we have but to rely on what we already know?

One of Gadamer's major insights is that all understanding involves prejudice, which he recasts as a basic aspect of knowledge. Prejudice is always part of the structure of understanding and is necessary to interpretation. This is one of the enigmas of every interpretive act. In order to understand, we must bring with us bias, which itself makes our understandings only partial. To put it in a pessimistic way, every understanding is always, and necessarily, subjective and partial and always, in some way, a misunderstanding. More optimistically, every understanding is only approximate, a placeholder of sorts and open to continuous revision and reinterpretation.

But we shouldn't view the project of understanding as hopeless. For Gadamer (1960/1993), although we can't stop ourselves from being biased—and indeed we need to begin with bias—we are not eternally trapped by prejudice. Understanding can build knowledge of real things in the world.

> A person trying to understand something will not resign himself from the start to relying on his own accidental fore-meanings, ignoring as consistently and stubbornly as possible the actual meaning of the text.... Rather, a person trying to understand a text is prepared for it to tell him something. But this kind of sensitivity involves neither "neutrality" with respect to content nor the extinction of one's self, but the foregrounding and appropriation of one's own fore-meanings and prejudices. The important thing is to be aware of one's own biases, so that the text can present itself in all its otherness and thus assert its own truth against one's own fore-meanings. (p. 269)

Gadamer's solution to the problem of bias isn't turning our backs to the fact that subjectivity exists. Rather, we are to recognize, analyze, and own our biases. To the best of our ability, we are to make them explicit and visible.

Part of the critical work of interpretation is to be aware of prejudice and to realize how interpretations are affected by who I am, the traditions that I am immersed in, and the attitudes that I possess. Shouldn't researchers ask: Why am I even interested in such a question? Why do I really want to study the question in this way? For Gadamer, we expose prejudice to let the phenomenon "assert its own truth"—as a challenge to our bias—in order to teach us something new and different beyond what we already know.

Owning prejudice is good advice for making any interpretation. But owning prejudice is no guarantee that the world, persons, or objects in the world will thereby assert themselves and show themselves to us. No matter how well we understand our bias, it will always be there. And all interpretations will carry along the accents and inflections of a particular subjective perspective. However, this doesn't negate the possibility for understanding, and there are ways of making sound arguments, even with our inescapable subjectivity firmly intact.

Another insight from Gadamer is, certainly, to be wary of methods and our methodological assumptions. Methods in psychology are part of the historical and traditional foreground, a kind of prejudice, which preforms the kinds of observations that we can make and the conclusions that we can reach. Breaking free of these pre-configurations is difficult, if not impossible. The methodological traditions in psychology have already constructed the kinds of questions that we can ask and the conclusions that can be drawn. What other knowledge do we have but socially derived categories? Can we ever get underneath or behind those constructions to find the "real" and the "true" (Gergen, 1985)?

An energized narrative perspective presents an immeasurable opportunity to reset the discipline and to investigate the essential psychological problems of interpretation and meaning making that are occluded by statistical and variable-centered analysis. Reversing figure and ground, a narrative perspective can document and make accessible to inquiry the dynamic process of human interpretation. But in order to get there we will need to take our leave of the traditional methodological assumptions that constrain psychological research and theorizing and break the variable mold.

NARRATIVE *AS* METHOD; NARRATIVE *AS* THEORY

Is narrative a method or a theory? Convincing arguments can be made in favor of either position. On the one hand, narrative is a useful framework for advancing more complex theories of human intention, experience, or interpretation. Narrative theory provides the key terms and concepts for understanding human psychology as a variety of interpretation in which persons manage memories and events from the past, present, and imagined future to create and perform meaning within discrete social and cultural contexts. In such a way, narrative theory is a powerful tool in describing central aspects of human psychology.

However, there is a certain way that one can take narrative theory as pure theory, independent of a method, that can be applied using diverse methods of inquiry, such as the survey, word count, experiment, or another variety of quantitative or qualitative approaches. In other words, it is possible to investigate a narrative theory using methods that appear to be incongruent with the close study of rich textual data. To a certain extent, theory can be, and sometimes is, divorced from method.

On the other hand, narrative methods are descriptive tools that provide researchers with a systematic means for examining how persons put words to use in life writing, interviews, conversations, blogs, and other forms of disclosure. From this perspective, narrative is a tool for closely attending to language in order to uncover aspects of meaning or linguistic structure. As a pure method, it does not imply any particular theoretical orientation to how narrative functions in people's lives. We are free to employ any theory that we like to explain what we uncover.

However, a third way of understanding the theory or method question is to suggest that narrative is neither one nor the other, but both. This is my position. In order to develop an innovative and robust perspective on human beings, narrative psychology requires a rational and scientific method of inquiry that is tied to an evolving theoretical framework for understanding human beings. Theory is nourished and supported by grounded observations of how persons talk about themselves, others, and the world in concrete situations. Methods serve to better describe the complexities of human nature in order to develop and refine synthetic theories that take into account the multiple influences on human intention, interpretation, and experience.

In a sense, one depends on the other. They are recursive. Ideally, narrative psychologists should aspire to a fit between theory and method. Theory addresses the realm of meaning and the use of meanings in human lives. Methods should direct attention to the phenomenon of interest and should view psychological processes as part of the interpretive context in which they exist. As will become evident, I believe that rich qualitative-narrative methods of study are most effective for constructing complex theories of human psychology.

Perhaps, this all sounds like common sense. But there is a trend to employing narrative theory in a reductive manner, a hypothesis-testing framework, in which narrative properties are solidified and analyzed as research variables. Numerous varieties of narrative research fall into this category, including some of the most prominent in the psychological literature.

Quantitative-narrative research employs narrative theory but breaks down aspects of narrating into the component parts of language (e.g., László, 2008; Pennebaker & Seagal, 1999) or thematic content (e.g., Haden & Hoffman, 2013; Lodi-Smith, Geise, Roberts, & Robins, 2009; McAdams, Reynolds, Lewis, Pattern, & Bowman, 2001). In my view, there is a real danger that the narrative perspective is being transformed into just another form of reductionist research in which "narrative" becomes yet another psychological variable to submit to statistical analysis. In making this move to reductive analysis, researchers are caught, once again, in the typical problems of variable-centered research that I described earlier. Rather than observing meanings and understanding how they are contextualized in persons and situations, they study correlations between variables, and just like other variable-centered approaches, we are uncertain about the underlying process at work. They miss the process, but also miss the person.

Still, I don't want to suggest that there is nothing redeeming about quantitative-narrative approaches. Some of them I find provocative and powerful—food for thought on persons and storytelling. Also, I appreciate that such quantitative approaches are successful in introducing concepts from narrative theory into mainstream psychology in an effective way.

My intention is not to police the borders of narrative psychology and sort research into different categories inside or outside of the narrative canon. Rather, it is to highlight what is gained, in focus, depth, and complexity, by tailoring narrative methods to the development of narrative theory and to offer strategies for getting there. I strongly believe that narrative psychology can produce sensitive, multicolored and multifaceted, nuanced and nonreductive portraits of sense making in action that allow for fine-grained theories of human lives that are, as I will argue, credible, trustworthy, and useful.

There are numerous examples of research in the psychological literature, but those that stand out are Freeman's (2010) exegesis of narrative foreclosure and narrative freedom in the reflections on past, present, and future of two artists, Samuel and Leah; Josselson's (2009) analysis of the changing evaluations of a single memory in repeated tellings and the meaning of this memory in the life of Maria as she moves through developmental time; Smith and Sparkes's (2008b) nuanced analysis of the constraints (and affordances) of socially shared resources and the physical body for how Jaime, a 40-year-old man with a devastating spinal cord injury, makes sense of self, life, and the future; Heavey's (2017) close and detailed analysis of both word and gesture in Adam's story of above-knee amputation and how he creates a body narrative that, despite of the loss of his lower leg, restores a sense of the whole and functioning body; Singer's (2001) sensitive account of Richard Markham's fragmented life story, his addiction to heroin, and his inability to sustain a coherent self-narrative that gives his life a direction and meaning. I would also include Lieblich, Zilber, and Tuval-Mashiach's (2008) analysis of balancing agency, communion, and serendipity in the life of a lesbian mother named Sara; Georgakopoulou's (2007) description of the identity narratives of Greek teenagers; and Lieblich (1993) and Bamberg (2004), whose work I discuss extensively in Chapter 8.

There are multiple benefits to developing narrative theory on the basis of narrative analysis. First, we are able to understand how psychological processes work in persons embedded in social and cultural worlds. Indeed, we are not dealing with how one variable is related to another variable, but we come closer to the complex and problematic role that interpretation plays in people's lives and social relationships. Second, we are better able to understand and account for the temporal movement of psychological processes. A person is not like a perfectly framed photograph sitting on a bookshelf, such as the one that I have of my grandfather. The photo provides the illusion of being fixed for all time. But I know that this is just one period in my grandfather's life. There were others. The snapshot is just an illusion, a momentary and incomplete artifact of the ongoing process that evolves and changes over periods of time. Finally, we have the sense that we are dealing with real persons, complex creatures who never quite match up to the abstract, fictional, average individual described in variable-centered analyses. Persons think and act in all kinds of peculiar ways that we could never predict. Even pinning them down for a moment and describing where they stand is difficult and incomplete. The narratives that they enact are part of their personal and social lifeworld and recall a particular place and time in their life.

Narrative methods should serve as a creative workspace for discovering and demonstrating how persons, along with others, make sense of life and make it present and real. To see this dynamic at work, researchers need to approach each interpretive action as a whole, as a part of a person's life or as part of a dynamic interaction. In the pages that follow, I endeavor to show a way forward toward this goal.

NOW WHAT?

Although narrative methods are quite diverse (Andrews, Squire, & Tamboukou, 2013; Clandinin, 2007; Holstein & Gubrium, 2012), they follow general analytic strategies that are based upon the principles of interpretation theory. The method is not in the collection of data; there is not one variety of "narrative" data. The range of interpretive actions is simply too broad to be accounted for with a single method of data collection. Narrative researchers can and should study interviews, talk in natural settings, letter writing, digital media, autobiography, diaries, works of art, and more. Others have written eloquently about how to collect narrative data (Chase, 2003; Josselson, 2013). Of course, certain observations may be more or less rich and more or less conducive to narrative analysis. But all of these observations can provide interesting data for studying how people make present understandings of self, others, and the world.

After careful observation and study, collecting interviews with individuals or groups, or writing copious field notes, carefully transcribing and rereading their data, narrative researchers find themselves in the same place—with an overwhelming amount of text. In my own life story interviews, the transcription of a single interview can amount to 30 to 50 pages of single-spaced typed text. In a "small" study of 10 interviews, the corpus of data could constitute a ream of paper.

Then, with a large stack of papers in hand, the question "now what?" appears. At this stage in the research process, no matter how well prepared our study, the question appears with some force. We ask ourselves, "What should I do with all of this data?" And, "How do I make sense of it all?"

In my opinion, this is the most interesting, and critical, step in the research process. Sure, we need to "interpret" the data. Data doesn't just interpret itself. And there are no tools that will decisively point the way to an interpretation.

Although there are textual programs that aid in the process of organizing narrative research, they can't replace the interpreter. Qualitative software programs such as Nudist, NVivo, Ethnograph, and Atlas can be useful in managing the enormous amount of text produced in interview- or conversation-based projects. But the software does not make the interpretation any more or less valid. Some narrative researchers fall into a quantitative mindset, believing that referencing technological tools will make their research appear more systematic and their interpretation more sound. It may sound more scientific, but it isn't.

To the contrary, these programs may constrain the ability of the interpreter to understand the data. By design, these technologies are biased toward particular methods of qualitative research such as grounded theory or content analysis, which examine themes across groups of persons. In effect, the software dissects textual data into thematic chunks, which can decontextualize themes from persons and discourage an understanding of who is speaking and the meaning of the telling in the person's life. The software may be at odds with the goal of understanding interpretive actions.

I wish I could say that there is something magical, packageable, even marketable, about the process of interpretation. But, ultimately, all that we are left with are the sound questions that frame our analysis, in addition to careful listening, wit, creativity, persistence, and good sense. There is no computer program that can replace the human interpreter.

The work of narrative scholars is to develop the human technology for carefully describing and interpreting lives, retaining the complexity of our existential situation and everyday life. The technology of narrative investigation is not a super- or artificial intelligence, but relies on familiar human capacities. Based upon a close reading of interviews, developing a way of thinking about the transcript, connecting with relevant literature and grounding theory in the text, it is the researcher's ability to see an interpretive action as part of a person's life, time in development, a conversation, a culture, which helps us to better understand its meaning.

We interpret research data in the same way that we interpret others in everyday life. It is a process of asking questions in order to see the wider and multiple contexts that speech depends upon, testing out and revising our convictions and making an argument. This is where the real power and energy of narrative work comes from—a complex understanding of meaning making practices in context.

For better and for worse, there is no formula, no rigid solutions or recipes to follow. In fact, I believe that there is, and should be, a *necessary vagueness* in narrative methods because each research question requires a tailor-made strategy to allow us access into the data. And the conclusions that we draw are, likewise, also developed through creative problem-solving; the results depend upon the researcher's capacity to insightfully organize the data.

This core inability to develop generally applicable, step-by-step, and necessary sequences is part of the critique of narrative methods; they are believed to be too artful and therefore not scientific. In this context, artfulness seems to imply arbitrariness in moving from evidence to conclusions. There is also an implicit contrast with statistical methods, which are, wrongly, believed to move directly from statistic to conclusion. But statistical methods also involve interpretive choices, which are artful, and could benefit from the same critical questioning to which we will submit narrative methods.

Although students are often looking for what they need to do to find the answers to research practice, there is no one-size-fits-all answer to narrative methods. In the final analysis, it may be a stretch to even call what I am offering a "method" of narrative analysis. Rather, these are strategies for engaging data, strategies for thinking about the data and disclosing meanings. In the following, I focus on strategies for narrative analysis and, in Chapter 7, I provide an illustrative analysis in order to make matters more concrete.

In order to understand interpretive actions, we need to understand them as part of other contexts. The "aha" moment of saying "now I understand" involves putting meanings into context in order to understand their connections to other realms. We see the place of this interpretive action in the context of who this person is, the social situation in which words are spoken, their place in historical time or cultural world, and so on. More complete understandings involve making multiple connections across domains and linking them together into a coherent framework that can be grounded in our observations and forcefully argued. Inquiry reaches inside the person and extends outward toward the social world, drawing these gestures together into one seamless movement. Understanding means making these connections to see speech as part of multiple interconnected contexts.

THE MOVEMENT OF UNDERSTANDING

Another reason that psychologists are skeptical of interpretation is because interpretation theory is typically associated with philosophy, not psychology, and, in particular, with a line of philosophy known as hermeneutics. The word "hermeneutics" has its origins in Greek mythology; Hermes was the messenger from the Gods to humans who "is associated with transmuting what is beyond human understanding into a form that human intelligence can grasp" (Palmer, 1969, p. 13). However, hermeneutics can be plainly stated as the theory and practice of interpretation. In contrast to our preconceived ideas of the term, hermeneutics is not speculative but can be, as I will argue, evidence based and pragmatic.

The modern study of hermeneutics began in Germany in the midnineteenth century, when Protestant theologians and philosophers began to approach the New Testament from a radical perspective, understanding the sacred text as the work of multiple authors whose culture, language, and life were critical matters for determining the possible meanings encoded in the Bible. Although the work of hermeneutics began in philological exegesis, Schleiermacher (1986), who was among the most important hermeneutic philosophers of his time, argued that the principles of hermeneutics could be applied widely to understand a variety of texts. Whether interpreting religious texts or simple actions in everyday life, the same principles of interpretation apply, and a general theory of hermeneutics is needed. Schleiermacher's writings can be read as practical observations and advice on how to approach texts and the pitfalls of making interpretations. Dilthey (1894/1976, 1989), Gadamer (1960/1993), Heidegger (1926/1962), Ricoeur (1981), Taylor (1971), and others build upon Schleiermacher's contention that interpretation theory is widely applicable to all varieties of actions and experiences (Palmer, 1969).

The hermeneutic tradition forms the basis for understanding persons as constantly engaged in the project of understanding the self and the world (Brockmeier & Meretoja, 2014) and the lives of others as texts to be described, contextualized, and understood. As Dilthey insisted in his comprehensive argument for the human sciences, mental life cannot be *explained* by borrowing the model of the physical sciences and atomizing mental life into component units. Rather, the close descriptive study and *understanding* of mental life must "deal with the living connections of reality experienced in the mind." As he famously wrote, "We explain nature but we understand mental life" (Dilthey, 1894/1976, p. 89).

Here my guiding metaphor is the hermeneutic circle. It has often been remarked that the shape of understanding follows a circle. "Complete knowledge always involves an apparent circle, that each part can be understood only out of the whole to which it belongs, and vice versa" (Schleiermacher, 1986, p. 113; originally published in 1819). This doesn't mean that reasoning is therefore circular, in the sense of being logically confused, or an act of sophistry, but rather that

1. Understanding always involves movement; we consider and revise our initial insights as we examine more information, moving back and forth, over the same material and ideas.

> A person who is trying to understand a text is always projecting. He projects a meaning for the text as a whole as soon as some initial meaning emerges in the text. Again, the initial meaning emerges only because he is reading the text with particular expectations in regard to a certain meaning ... which is constantly revised in terms of what emerges as penetrates into the meaning. ...

This constant process of new projection constitutes the movement of understanding and interpretation. (Gadamer, 1960/1993, p. 267)

2. Understanding is a process of asking questions in order to open a dialogue with the text. "*The hermeneutical task becomes of itself a questioning of things*" (Gadamer, 1960/1993, p. 269). Although questions always carry the imprint of a tradition and historical situation and other prejudices, we question ourselves and question the text in order to converse with it and arrive at a more adequate understanding. Gadamer argues that it is the "*priority of the question* in all knowledge and discourse that reveals something of an object. Discourse that is intended to reveal something requires that that thing be broken open by the question" (p. 363).
3. Understanding is never closed off; in a sense, we jump into the circle and begin our interpretation from some particular point of view and can always reconsider and think through the problem once again. There are no clear beginning or ending points. But, Heidegger (1926/1962) writes,

> [w]hat is decisive is not to get out of the circle but to come into it in the right way.... It is not to be reduced to the level of a vicious circle, or even of a circle which is merely tolerated. In the circle is hidden a positive possibility of the most primordial kind of knowing. To be sure, we genuinely take hold of this possibility only when, in our interpretation, we have understood that our first, last, and constant task is never to allow our fore-having, fore-sight, and fore-conception to be presented to us by the fancies of popular conceptions, but rather to make the scientific theme secure by working out these fore-structures in terms of the things themselves. (p. 195)

> Understanding always involves a hermeneutic engagement. We must enter into the circle and are constantly revising and revisiting prior understandings.

The narrative method of interpretation requires a process of engagement, close reading and consistent questioning in order to understand interpretive actions as part of the larger contexts in which they are produced and understood. This is the basis of hermeneutic thought. One reflexively considers oneself and expressions from various, and multiple, angles in order to try to understand what a text or telling means. How can an understanding of this person's past, their immediate social relationships, culture, history, and time help to understand the meaning of this particular interpretive action?

A distinction is required between the variety of observations that we make as interviewers or ethnographers and our treatment of those observations. Although there are multiple varieties of observations that narrative psychologists make, narrative methods of analysis share an interpretive, hermeneutic, method that applies equally to how persons understand the course of everyday life and to how researchers understand the persons that they study. In the study of human lives, the affinity between everyday hermeneutics and scientific hermeneutics is striking. There is strong continuity between the way that researchers go about the business of interpreting other lives and what laypersons do day in and day out, even researchers, in order to interpret their own lives. Cohler (1982) nicely summarized this idea when he wrote, "This interpretive approach to the study of the person parallels the approach usually used by persons in the successive interpretations or reconstructions of their own history as a personal narrative across the course of life" (p. 229). We take what we have learned from interpreting life—our own lives and those other lives that we have encountered through relationships and through the media—and apply it to the lives of the persons that we study.

There is a double movement in which researchers, themselves positioned in time and space, set out to interpret how others, also bounded by time and space, make sense of life and make present their interpretations—a "double hermeneutic." As Meretoja (2014b) writes, "narratives [I would add research interpretations] can be conceived of as having the structure of a 'double hermeneutic' in the sense that they are interpretations of experiences which are already interpretations" (p. 98). Narrative researchers are firmly inside the double hermeneutic, as Meretoja says, always "interpreting interpretations." The researcher's interpretation becomes a second interpretation, a second voice that is layered upon the voice of our participants. We tell the story of others' stories.

Narrative psychology is the science of interpreting interpretive actions, describing them, and theorizing about their meaning. Interpretive actions, as imperfect as they surely are, serve as our approximate attempt to understand how and why persons make present and ultimately make sense of life experience.

Interpretation provides narrative researchers with the means for understanding and describing the complex bases of human interpretation and experience. We are able to describe these processes in the actual context in which they occur and to theorize about the embedded nature of human meaning making.

Compared to other methods of study, in narrative research, interpretation is, perhaps, just a little more obvious and explicit. And narrative researchers are justified in making their world and subjectivity visible in their analyses.

Subjectivity is present in every interpretation, making it difficult to nail down a single interpretation. However, it is a mistake to conclude that because there is no "unshakeable" truth, that anything goes or that narrative is therefore doomed to be unsystematic or unscientific. In my opinion, narrative psychologists should recognize the scientific status of their work, but without turning narrative psychology into another variable-centered method. Narrative research should not reduce observations to quantitative terms. But narrative research is scientific as a grounded and well-reasoned investigation of how persons interpret life. Similar to quantitative methods, there are better and worse interpretations of data. There are analyses that are more or less skillful in their ability to observe and describe others, to develop interesting theories, and to back up theory with evidence.

The method moves in an inductive manner. But we always begin from somewhere. We might have—actually, we must have—preconceptions of what we will discover, but, as much as possible, narrative researchers allow the interpretive action to direct analysis. We closely attend to words or actions in order to understand them on their own terms. From these close examinations, we derive theories grounded in observation. We examine the adequacy of our theory, seeking out additional evidence that would help us to further develop and refine our conceptions. Finally, we form sound arguments that are grounded in observation and allow our colleagues to critique our evidence and interpretations.

The process is more like the inductive sciences, like archaeology or botany, than chemistry or physics. But this is not Freud's archaeology, digging deeper and deeper to find the unconscious motivations behind actions. Although some narrative researchers are concerned with the unconscious, they still must make a convincing argument about how what is observed reveals what is not expressed (Josselson, 2004). Narrative research is concerned with developing theories about what we take to be real-world processes.

The process of narrative analysis is more like finding a mysterious object while gardening in the backyard. It feels like a stone. The object is smooth and long. It seems to have an edge. Perhaps it is a blade. But, in order to understand the meaning, origins, and function of the object, we need to ask a host of questions about the stone: What is the shape of the object? What material is it made of? What markings does it have? How and where was it found? We might need to talk to our neighbors to see if they have found other such objects or know others who have, submit the object to a carbon dating test, go to the library to see if we could find similar documented discoveries, or even consult experts on stones in this part of the world. In short, our process of asking questions will lead us to construct theories about what the object must be and what it was used for. If my interpretation is successful, I will be able to construct a plausible argument about the stone that you would find reasonable and share.

But how do we know that *this* interpretation is *the* right or true interpretation? What happens when there are multiple interpretations? The object could be a blade or it could be something else, a bone of a large animal or money. Inductive methods do not lead to uncontestable truths; nor does any method, for that matter. Alternate accounts of interpretive actions can always be found. So, which is the "right" one?

On the one hand, there are no single interpretations that hold for all times and all places (not in physics and not in psychology). However, on the other hand, interpretations are not hopelessly diverse. There may be a wide range of possible interpretations, but there are only a few good ones that fit theory and account for direct evidence of the phenomenon.

In a classic analysis of the multiple interpretations for why Vincent van Gogh famously cut off his ear and gave it to a prostitute, Runyan (1982) lists 13 psychoanalytic interpretations that have been offered over the years, including emulating Jack the Ripper, inverted unacceptable homosexual impulses, and symbolically reuniting with his mother. As Runyan notes, there are many other interpretations—the list is not exhaustive. How do we make sense of them all? How do we sort through such diverse and conflicting interpretations, which are competing for the same explanatory space? Runyan asks, "Are all of them true, are some true and some false, or, perhaps, are none of them true?" (p. 42).

Runyan weighs the various explanations, arguing that some are indeed better than others and that there are accessible criteria for distinguishing between better and worse interpretations. Runyan (1982) uses this profusion of explanatory hypotheses in order to highlight the need for establishing principles of good interpretations. Such principles go beyond questioning the reliability of the data. In addition, the data must "be shown to have explanatory relevance or explanatory force in relation to the events in question" (p. 45). In a fierce critique of the more fanciful psychoanalytic explanations, Runyan admonishes, "It is not sufficient to suggest such possible symbolic equivalences; it is also necessary to provide possible reasons for believing that such representations were causally relevant to the actual course of events" (p. 46). He argues that

[e]xplanations and interpretations can be evaluated in light of criteria such as: (1) their logical soundness, (2) their comprehensiveness in accounting for a number of puzzling aspects of the events in question, (3) their survival of tests of attempted falsification, such as tests of derived predictions or retrodictions, (4) their consistency with the full range of available relevant evidence, (5) their support from above, or their consistency with more general knowledge about human functioning or about the person in question, and (6) their credibility relative to other explanatory hypotheses. (Runyan, 1982, p. 47)

Although some of Runyan's points reformulate the positivist view on science, we should still take these notions seriously. Narrative research is not an invitation to wild speculation—it is not just "anything goes." Inductive theories must describe the phenomenon at hand. But theories should also be logical, internally, and consistent with what we know about the world. They should be helpful and productive for understanding this particular case and human beings more generally. They should be plausible. They should account for the evidence. Theories should be able to withstand the test of time and future investigations in related areas. And they should prove useful when we start to talk about persons. Perhaps this is the true test of any theory—how useful is this interpretation for understanding the phenomenon?

Developing more complete and more complex accounts of human action, interpretation, and experience involves seeing interpretive actions from multiple angles simultaneously and using these insights to understand the expression itself. It means developing insightful theories, which work to better understand persons in context. As Freeman (2011) has argued, psychology can better achieve its scientific aims only through a faithfulness to the phenomenon under investigation which, paradoxically, necessitates those methods of descriptive inquiry characterized by humanistic methods so maligned for their unscientific approach. Narrative accounts that can "faithfully" (Freeman, 2011) describe and disclose the phenomenon and that can demonstrate the adequacy of their interpretations as tied with direct observational evidence are more complete accounts.

PERSONS (AND OTHER CONTEXTS)

It all begins with questions. Like all research, the process of narrative research should begin with curiosity, a problem that we would like to know more about or better understand. This curiosity is translated into a concrete research question that directs our data collection and is further refined for data analysis. In the metaphor of the hermeneutic circle, the research question provides our entry route into the circle and becomes the center of our analysis.

So, what do we want to know more about? What's interesting to know? As I have framed it, narrative psychology is focused on understanding interpretive actions. It is the interpretation of interpretations. The variety of questions most central to narrative psychology center on some aspect of how and why a person (or persons) understands herself and articulates her experience in these particular terms. Narrative is directed toward *how* and *why* persons make sense of life, experience, others, and the world in the way that they do.

In a particularly insightful chapter on the process of narrative research, "Learning to Listen," Chase (2003) instructs students to begin choosing interview projects by first selecting a group of people that they are interested in learning more about. But then, subtly, she directs them to significant questions:

> What are the experiences of such and such group of people? How do they give meaning to their experiences, their lives, their selves? What meanings do they develop? What cultural, ideological, and other social resources do they draw on or resist? How do they draw on or resist those social resources in making sense of their experiences? (p. 82)

Similarly, Josselson (2013) recommends structuring what she calls "Big Q" questions for qualitative interviews as "how" questions because "they are aimed at detailing process in order to obtain a better understanding of the theoretical questions" (p. 37). Research questions should be framed to invite rich elaborate reflections and detailed descriptions of events to help us visualize the experience of our interviewees with the goal of arriving at more comprehensive understandings of why (Chase, 2003).

Narrative psychologists ask research questions such as the following: How does a person with spinal cord injury, Jamie, understand his body after injury? (Smith & Sparkes, 2008b). "How do people" with recent brain injuries "construct their narratives when such essential memories are lacking?" (Medved, 2007, p. 605). How do older couples, with one member suffering from Alzheimer's disease, tell the story of their relationship? (Hydén, 2011). "How did meta- and public narratives associated with aging infiltrate" young athletes' "ontological narratives?" (Phoenix, 2011, p. 118).

Research questions are starting points. My focus is somewhat later down the road, on the analytic phase and on what we do with the data after they have been collected. In the process of moving from data collection to analysis, our understanding of the research question is fine tuned and may be quite different from where we began. It may be only a part of the original question that now interests us; or, perhaps, a wholly new question has caught our attention that we now want to submit to analysis.

At the beginning of the analytic phase, we will ask more and more questions, opening up our understanding of the phenomenon to multilayered points of view. As part of the analysis, Chase asks students to choose a portion of one of their interviews for the group to listen to together. In their preparation, and as a group, she asks them to consider:

> What is this person doing or communicating (especially if that is different from what he or she is saying)?
>
> How does the interaction between you and the interviewee facilitate or hinder his or her story or ideas?
>
> What do you think is important or particularly interesting about this passage?
>
> What social factors (for example, social structures, ideologies, or social processes) help you to understand what is going on here? (p. 92)

I am going to suggest something of the same order. Though my questions are slightly (but not wholly) different, the spirit is identical. How do we understand an interpretive action? The answer, of course, is—ask *more* questions.

WHAT AND HOW?

Of course, first questions should address the action itself: What was said or done? How was it said? What did we observe? How can we describe the phenomenon in question?

The descriptive sense of "what" was said or done and "how" it was said provides the focus for analysis. But I don't want to imply a realist or objectivist notion of making observations. From the beginning, the data, as an object of inquiry, are always thoroughly constructed (Riessman, 2008). We are always forced to make choices. What should we study? What kinds of questions should we ask? What is important to know? Who should be present in the interview? Who should ask the questions? What should we pay attention to? Even, when do we turn on the tape recorder and when do we turn it off? Or, should we videotape to include gesture and body posture?

Even the act of transcription itself configures the data (Gee, 1999). What are the conventions that we use to transcribe? How do we organize speech and gesture into the written word? Which details are salient? Do we transcribe for pauses in the data? Where do we put quotation marks and periods, and how do we parse speech into meaningful units? And, finally, what aspects of the transcript do we focus on? Should we concentrate on the content of what was said, or one of the many variants of the structure of how it was said?

Here our inquiry focuses on constructing an object of inquiry and then engaging the object that we have built. What is the phenomenon that we seek to understand? What is the interpretive action? What happens? Who speaks or acts? What language is used? Does it have a beginning, middle, and end? Is it more partial and fragmented? How are the structural aspects of what is said organized? How was it said? Is the language used esthete or colloquial? Is the language performed with affect and energy, or is it flat? Is it tentative or authoritative? Is the interpretive action a single speech turn? Is there is a single speaker or are there multiple contributors?

I don't want to diminish the complexity of the task of describing an interpretive action or the legitimate variety of ways of constructing narrative objects of study. The choices that researchers make in framing the subject matter of the analysis are innumerable and crucial. But this is not yet the heart of the matter.

Understanding the "what" or "how" of an interpretive action necessitates that we layer other contexts into our interpretation. In this section, I build upon my theoretical analysis of the functions of narrative in order to describe a method of interpretation suited to developing narrative theory. In Chapters 4 and 5, I argued that narrative functions, such as making present and making it so, are actions with temporal and spatial characteristics. Into this analysis, I now add a third consideration—persons—and return to my contention that psychological processes are always embodied in personal, and interpersonal, experience.

Lieblich, Tuval-Mashiach, and Zilber (1998) argue that narrative research can be characterized along two different dimensions: holistic versus categorical, and content versus form. On the one hand, researchers focus either on whole lives and take a more contextual approach to life stories (holistic), or they concentrate on portions of transcriptions (categorical). On the other hand, researchers focus either on the themes or meanings of "what" is said (content), or they concentrate on the structural aspects of "how" it is said (form). Logically, Lieblich et al. (1998) argue that the combination of these two dimensions leads to four varieties of narrative research: holistic-content, holistic-form, categorical-content, and categorical-form. The approach that I advocate is resolutely holistic, keeping the person in focus as we move through analysis, but I include questions of "what" (content) and "how" (form), as well as what I take to be unsurpassable questions of context, "when" and "where," that are etched into every interpretive action. This isn't merely an aesthetic choice, but represents an opening into understanding psychological phenomena as personal and social processes.

In order to interpret an interpretive action, I argue that, at a minimum, we need to account for the person, space, and time. At the least, we need to ask the following: (1) By whom? (2) Where? and (3) When? An adequate interpretation of an interpretive action requires answering "who" said or did "what," and "how," "where," and "when," in order to begin an argument for "why."

These three questions can be thought about as points along a hermeneutic circle for understanding an interpretive action. The movement goes back and forth between questions of who, where, and when.

Questions are developed *less* in regard to the representation of who, where, and when as found in the interpretive action and *more* on how current, and previous, contexts have produced this interpretive action. In other words, I am not advocating coding markers of developmental and historical time within an interpretive action, such as "I was born after 9/11" as an end in itself. Although this is critical information to document and use in our analysis, researchers should concentrate on how contexts produce texts or, better yet, how text and context mutually produce one another. How is this interpretive action shaped by historical time? How does being born after 9/11 affect the telling? How does this perspective shape what is told?

WHO?

I fully recognize that starting with persons is a choice. There is no ontological reason to leap into the circle with persons, rather than the interactional situations in which persons always find themselves. Other researchers might rightly begin with the "wheres" or "whens" of interpretive actions. But, as Gubrium and Holstein (2009) point out, "regardless of which starting point we choose, the interplay of the components oblige us to eventually shift analytic gears to bring into view how each component plays out in relation to the other" (p. 28). This is the essence of the hermeneutic circle.

However, from my point of view, the idea of the person is key to describing and understanding the interpretation of life experience and the logical place to begin a narrative investigation of psychological phenomena.

But, why persons? What's so special about the idea of the person that it merits a privileged position in narrative psychology? One of my primary objectives in this book is to describe what a narrative perspective can offer the discipline of psychology for understanding of persons. As I argued in the Introduction and Chapters 1 and 2, contemporary psychology makes a devastating error by approaching psychological processes as distinct from the person and his or her experience and thought process. A narrative perspective should serve as a corrective force by disclosing the dynamic way that persons come to imagine and inhabit worlds of their own device. And, it all comes together in the embodied experience of persons and how they, in concert with others, make sense of themselves and the world.

Although narrative studies are diverse in how they approach their research, I believe that some consideration of personhood is essential in order to understand interpretive actions. There are varying degrees or depths of understanding the person that might be appropriate for a particular analysis. The question of "who" is most prominent in psychobiographical studies (Schultz, 2005) and holistic investigations of life stories (Josselson, 2007; McAdams, 2011; Singer, 2001). But, in order to understand the meaning of any particular interpretive action, we need to layer in basic notions of who spoke or acted.

Who is this person speaking? What aspects of her life made this interpretive action possible? What unique experiences have shaped her words? What is her typical character/stance toward the world and others? What kind of impression is this person trying to make? Given what we know about this person, what was their motivation in saying or doing this?

Distinguishing the person from their social world is a difficult task indeed. I am not arguing that researchers should consider the person as separate—above, beyond, and outside of the here and now of their interpretations or the multiple contexts, biological, relational, cultural, in which persons dwell. In fact, I am advocating the opposite. I am arguing that persons are an integrative center of action, awareness, and experience. Persons are contexts in themselves for understanding interpretive actions. A consideration of the distinctive aspects of the person's life, history, voice, motives, and experiences within time and within space brings critical insights to light about the meaning and function of narrating. When we write persons out of our analysis, we miss an opportunity to fully understand an interpretive action.

WHERE AND WHEN?

The person is not the only relevant context, and the exploration of even the simplest utterance requires a consideration of multiple contexts and levels of analysis—most importantly, where and when. One way of dealing with these multiple contexts is to put them in conversation with one another. We are never just dealing with a who—as if the person is out of context of the when and where. Who, when, and where go together to form a more complete picture of an interpretive action, that is, where and when a person does something. If we begin from who, there are two lines of questioning that are especially salient: who-where and who-when.

Who-Where?

Persons are never really alone. Even in our most private moments, we carry with us the rhythms and cadences of previous interactions (Bakhtin, 1981; Gergen, 2009). Interpretations are creative responses to ongoing dialogues that we participate in. The dialogue is situated in a given setting that is populated with others and is ongoing. It existed before we even came onto the scene. We arrive and need to figure out what the conversation is all about and find our place in it.

A description of the "where" of interpretive actions, rightly, should be as complex as our description of the "who." We should be concerned with not only the present conversation at hand, but also the echoes of culture that make their way into the conversational setting. The idea of "where" includes both of these moments, the immediate and distant contexts.

Interpretations are actions carried out by particular persons, along with others, in a definite context, a specific and grounded situation with its own dynamics. The nature of the conversation that we find ourselves in, the frame or purpose and ground rules for the conversation, the other actors who are present, and how we are positioned in terms of not only our identity but also relationships of power, privilege, and authority are all critical aspects of the meaning of this interpretive action.

Layering the "where" into our analytic project means taking into account how immediate social forces are imminent in every interpretation, and taking seriously the notion that interpretations are always joint productions, co-narratives, in a particular "where" that requires our close attention and interpretation (see Chapter 4). In order to understand this telling, we need to find its place within the ongoing conversations in which it is embedded. Interpretations are part of the "local context" (Phoenix, 2013) where "narrative environments" are built from the ground up in the unfolding interaction between persons in a concrete social setting (Holstein & Gubrium, 2004) and in which speakers draw upon linguistic resources in order to situate themselves, others, and the past (Koven, 2012). Narrative investigations of where, in this sense of the situatedness of interpretive actions, are most prominent not only in small story research (Bamberg, 2004, 2006; see Chapter 8 for a more extensive discussion), but also in the closely associated fields of discourse analysis and discursive psychology. Where is the talk taking place—in a research setting, a school or business, a home? What is the frame of the conversation? What is tellable here? How is the talk constructed? Why are we talking? What happened prior to this conversation? Who else is present and talking (or not talking)? Why are they there? What are their motivations? What are the roles and positions of the actors (and observers)? Who has the authority to speak or to silence others?

However, there is a second sense of the space of the conversation. This is the idea that conversations are part of ongoing dialogues that extend outside the present and immediate circumstances. The language that we use and what it means can only be made sense of through our knowledge of what these words have meant in other dialogues. The current conversation is part of other previous conversations, in which we have played a part personally or not, and which become part of our complex, and multivocal, self-understanding (Hermans & Dimaggio, 2007). In other words, interpretations take place within a definite cultural horizon. Part of the work of analysis is to understand how interpretive actions use the terms and meanings of particular figured worlds (Holland, Lachicotte, Skinner, & Cain, 1998) and how persons engage cultural resources in order to make sense of their lives (Cain, 1991; Hammack, 2008; Hammack & Cohler, 2009). What is the cultural horizon in which persons are speaking? How do persons engage cultural figurations in order to understand themselves, others, and the world?

Who-When?

In a sense, "when" goes along with "who" and "where." Persons are always in time, developmental and historical. People and spaces are always temporalized, historical creations with a distinct look and feel.

Certainly, how persons make interpretations is influenced by emotional, social, and intellectual reasons—which are developmental. As persons age and their lives change, they bring new and different resources to narrating the past and the self. Children interpret themselves and the world differently from adolescents, young adults, and so on. And developmental periods introduce new challenges and preoccupations that must be reconciled in our self-understandings (Schiff, 2014). Childhood is the time for figuring out how to tell stories with others and the language of the self in our given community (Miller, Chez, & Olivarez, 2014), adolescence for crafting a coherent narrative (Habermas & Hatiboğlu, 2014), emerging adulthood for placing the self in a cultural and historical horizon (Hammack & Toolis, 2014), middle age for the challenge of dealing with fading youth and the prospect of death (McAdams, 2014), and old age for reviewing our past or choosing to immerse ourselves in present concerns (Lieblich, 2014).

Persons are caught up in time and are only able to see their lives from the perspective of the present. As life changes, we need to engage our personal history anew. The past is always a *presently understood past*, which rewrites how we interpret previous events (Cohler, 1982).

As we move through our life course, we understand our past, present, and future in new ways. Each moment carries with it a presently constructed notion of self and world, in which we reconstruct the meaning of the past, where we are in the life course, and possibilities for the future (Freeman, 2010; Ricoeur, 1980). Interpretations are part of developmental time and change in character as persons age, gain new life experience, and take on new challenges. But, also, the personal sense of the life course is always inflected with cultural and historical ideas—the life course is a historically evolving concept, and persons measure themselves against changing normative goals and time tables (Hammack & Toolis, 2014; Neugarten, 1979/1996). How do interpretive actions express developmental concerns? How are they rewritten with the passage of time?

Likewise, space is temporally inflected. There are prior, concurrent, and projected conversational contexts, which configure the character of this conversational moment. Stories and meanings are carried forward, referred to, and repeated in new contexts, or are left behind.

Persons participate in particular systems of meaning about self, body, emotions, sexuality, social relationships, life, and so on, which vary between cultures but also change over time within cultures (Chauncey, 1994; Cohler, 2007). Persons encounter these ideas in their sociocultural world as resources for self-understanding—for telling a personal narrative. Culture is not static or pristine but is constantly in the process of being reworked and re-evaluated (Hobsbawm & Ranger, 1983; Sahlins, 1985). The meeting point between culture and time is history, in which different epochs develop and favor enormously different vocabularies, selves, and attitudes toward life.

Finally, developmental and historical time intersect. As persons develop and their lives change, history affects them differently (Elder, 1974/1999). For example, as Erik Erikson (1968/1994) observed, adolescents are characteristically more in tune with the spirit of the day, taking its beliefs as explicit understandings for their identities.

WHY?

Understanding the "why" of an interpretive action is the central objective of narrative research. The goal is to provide a sound and reasoned account for the "why" of this interpretive action. Why did this person say this? What purpose does it serve? What is the function of this speech action? What does it mean? What does this action accomplish? Why did people engage in talk/action/expression of this sort and in this way? Why say it at all? Why talk? What's the use of it?

Framing the goal of interpretation in this manner moves us closer to a functional description of narrating. The "why" is the function of the interpretive action. To what end is this interpretive action?

Undoubtedly, "why" is the most difficult question because it is not descriptive or concrete in the sense of our other questions. We can, more or less, effectively describe what, how, who, where, and when interpretations are made. But why is another step beyond. Theoretically, a detailed description of the context of an interpretive action, opening up our analysis to questioning, should help to make progress in understanding whys. But understanding why necessitates using the data in a different way and making our own interpretations and conclusions about the data as a whole.

The question of why is not wholly foreign to narrative analysis. For example, Labov (1972; Labov & Waletzky, 1967/1997) argues that fully developed oral narratives include evaluations in which the narrator reflects upon the meaning of why a story is told. As Hyvärinen (2013) points out, Labov's model included structural and linguistic indicators for understanding the function of personal experience narratives. Evaluative clauses provide clues to the point of telling a narrative. In the first iteration of the model, Labov and Waletzky (1967/1997) argued that evaluations were clauses external to the complicating action of the narrative. In other words, people stop telling the story in order to comment on why they are telling it. In later work, Labov (1972) argued that evaluations are also embedded, linguistically marked, in the referential content of the narrative. In other words, speakers provided clues about what the story means in the way that they tell about it. By closely studying the structure of such narratives, one can find aspects of narratives that are evaluative and that help guide us to the narrator's point in storytelling.

Structural or linguistic markers can provide useful clues to the point or purpose of narrating. However, an excessive reliance on the structural aspects of a text can limit our ability to imagine alternate interpretations. Still, these are only clues; they do not reveal the whole picture and must be submitted to the same process of questioning that I have outlined to find a place in an argument for their meaning.

The interpretation of narratives requires the "folding in" or "layering in" of context in an effort to understand this interpretive action as a facet of, or in reference to, multiple contexts. As we fold more and more context into the interpretation, we begin to see it as a complex and real event, a process or dynamic, articulated by a person and taking place in space and time. We move around and around the hermeneutic circle until we begin to understand the meaning of this interpretive action, what shapes it, and how it functions, for this person, in this social and temporal context.

But the movement isn't only circular. After a period of questioning, we begin to turn our observations into a concrete story about the data—in the effort to construct a sound argument that takes into account what we have learned about this interpretive action through our questioning and the data itself. For the moment, I am concerned with the process of questioning the data, opening up the meaning of interpretive actions to multiple points of view. In Chapter 9, I address making arguments from the data.

CHAPTER 7

Interpreting Ben's Survival

Rather than leave the discussion in the abstract, I return to my interview with Ben, whom I briefly introduced in Chapter 4. In this chapter, however, I want to present a reading of the interview in light of the three questions that outline the hermeneutic circle of understanding an interpretive action: that is, who, where, and when.

Ben was one of 20 Holocaust survivors living in the Midwestern United States whom I interviewed in the mid-1990s. I began this project with two main research questions: (1) How do survivors of the concentration camps interpret the meaning of the Holocaust? In other words, how do they understand why the Holocaust happened? and (2) How do survivors interpret their own survival? How do they explain why they lived while so many others died?

These are the "Big Q" questions that guided my interviews (Josselson, 2013). I developed a detailed interview guide in order to help my interviewees tell narratives and rich reflections that would help me understand how they think about these two questions. A central part of the analysis focused on their Holocaust experience in the ghettos and camps. But, in order to allow survivors the space for reflection, I decided to begin with their current life experience and how they are doing now, rather than following the usual route that oral history projects take of directing the interview to life before the war, the Holocaust, and life after the war. I also added questions asking survivors to reflect upon why the Holocaust happened and why they survived. The interview guide served as what Amia Lieblich (cited in Josselson,

2013) calls "pocket questions," meticulously prepared to address the subjects that I wanted to include and to imagine various ways of approaching these subjects, but out of sight in the interview situation. The goal was to have a conversation. I was there to listen—not to mechanically reproduce question prompts. Questions were offered, sometimes in different ways, to keep the conversation moving toward the goals of understanding how survivors narrate their survival and the Holocaust.

My analysis of Ben's story of survival is based upon an extensive interview, which lasted close to 3 hours. In the interview, Ben describes his experience during the Holocaust, but also reflects on his present life, family relationships, career, religious beliefs, psychological state, views on the world, politics, emigrating to America, his thoughts on Israel, and so on. The tone of the interview is sometimes emotional, at others moments vindictive or humorous, and at others reflective. In short, it was a powerful interview—I am enormously grateful that Ben shared such an intimate experience with me.

But, first, I want to further specify my question. Indeed, how can we interpret how Ben interprets his survival? If you haven't noticed, we are squarely inside the double hermeneutic.

Understanding Ben, or anyone else for that matter, would be no small feat. Somewhat tongue in cheek, Toulmin (2001) suggests that "seen from a truly impartial standpoint," Ricouer's *"hermeneutics of suspicion* must surely be balanced by an equally strong *hermeneutics of self-doubt"* (p. 96). But the point is well taken; researchers should be critical of their assumptions and conclusions, and their power to make interpretations about what others think, feel, or experience. I am humbled by the task. In the end, what I can offer is a way of approaching Ben's interpretations as part of his life, experience, the world, and give them more descriptive color and richness.

WHAT IS THE OBJECT?

What do I want to understand? In a sense, it is the entire interview, where Ben's survival is constantly at issue; it is a recurrent theme that runs through the whole of the text.

Although his descriptions of life before and after the Holocaust remain more schematic, either recounting habitual actions that he engaged in or overarching reflections on matters such as his psychological state, his account of what happens during the war, when he says, "that's where, that's where the story starts," when Ben is almost 16 years old and the war has just begun, are highly narrative in structure. Many times, they are full-blown narratives in structure, displaying many of the elements that Labov and Waletzky (1967/1997) described (orientation, an abstract, complicating action, evaluation, coda, resolution). They are little episodes, concise pictures of another world and the events that happened over there, usually told in serial fashion, with the next story directly arising from the previous one. During the interview, I said very little.

Ben's account is filled with danger, violence, and narrow escapes, where life and death hang in the balance. In the course of telling these experiences, sometimes, Ben breaks from the sequence of recounting events, complicating actions, in order to offer an evaluation (Labov & Waletsky, 1967/1997) and reflect, however briefly, on why he wasn't killed. Also, toward the end of the interview, I ask him directly, "So tell me, Mr. H., I am interested how or why you think that you ended up here today. Why you survived, why you are here to talk to me and other people aren't." Ben answers:

I said why. Because, first thing it was luck, something it was luck with me. Because I wanted to be killed. Nobody wanted to kill me. (laughter) So that's luck. Maybe it's a purpose, that's why I believe a little bit in God because maybe that's a purpose I was here to do the things I did and nobody knows about it. You are the only one. I didn't have it on the video. What I told you is not on the video what I did for people in this country, what I did in Germany after the war. How I helped the sick . . . I did all the things I knew who had money, I went to them and I said you got to help this one and this one and they respected me for it and we did all these things and just like that nobody knows about it. Not to Rabbi X., I didn't talk to no one, not on the videotape, I didn't tell anyone about all these things that I did. That's a purpose why I'm alive, you see why God let me live. To help these people. To put these people in business, even in this country. After the war, and in the war. Until today, (taps the table) till I die it is the same thing. If anybody needs anything within my power, I'll do it. I always did it in business. I had a business, people came in, not even Jews, not only Jews, even people came in from Korea or from other countries. Americans that which they were starting college, they couldn't afford my shoes. So I never forget, kids came in, a few kids came in and I looked at them and they loved my merchandise, I had a good name. I was one of the tops. OK, I'm not going to brag but I have to tell you [I] was number one, second to none. So, I could see the kids, they going to college, worn out sleeves, no. And they like my. So, I say you know what I'll tell you what I'll do, take what you like, you can pay me whenever you can. If you become a doctor, you pay me. If you become a lawyer, you gonna pay me someday but one thing I want you to remember, I said to them, if someone comes to you if you are a doctor and cannot afford to pay, do the same thing what I did to you. That's all I want from you. Until today I know some of them which they kept their promise. This was an attorney, but he became a doctor. Only do the things. I didn't want no money from them. If they were able to pay, become a doctor you'll pay me out. Whatever you can do. Take it, I know you need it, you go to college, you're going to be a doctor, you're going to be a lawyer whatever. Only time remember, that's all I want from you, remember what I did to you, you do to (inaudible). That's all I'm asking. . . . (pause) See, nobody knows about it.

Ben "wanted to be killed" but "nobody wanted to kill [him]." Beginning with his words, "maybe that's a purpose," Ben recounts a series of actions that he did after the war, helping others and only asking that those he helped return the favor by helping others. "That's a purpose why I'm alive, you see why God let me live." Finally, it is important to note that these are actions for which Ben did not seek recognition. "See, nobody knows about it."

On the face of it, luck and purpose appear to go in opposite directions. Purpose conveys the idea that there is a divine plan, while luck implies the randomness of our fate. Ben's summary interpretations, "luck" and "purpose," are also found in other passages in the interview, embedded as evaluations in the narratives themselves.

In order to further specify what I want to understand, I present three narratives where Ben's survival is at issue. Similar to the preceding quote, luck and purpose are used as evaluations of the narrative being told, but the narratives enrich our understanding of Ben's interpretation of survival. In each narrative, I italicize the external evaluations, where the sequence of complicating actions is interrupted in order to comment on the story and serve as clues to understanding the narrative. But they are far from the whole picture of the purpose or meaning of Ben's survival.

The first narrative takes place when Ben was working with a small group of skilled workers building the infrastructure for the Krakow Plaszow concentration camp. The second and third stories are from later in the war, when Ben is incarcerated in the Krakow Plaszow camp that he helped to build.

The first narrative takes place early in Ben's incarceration, when he has more freedom of movement to leave his work group. The borders are more permeable and Ben takes advantage of this relative freedom. Ben "saves" his brother by helping him to escape from his camp and join Ben's group of skilled workers, who, at the time, were better protected. Indeed, there are several narratives in which Ben is watching over and defending others, his brother in particular, but not only his brother. In the interview, Ben tells three stories about when his brother's life is in danger, but Ben is there to shield him from danger and "saves" his brother. I present two of Ben's narratives of saving his brother. In the following, Ben told about how he bribed his brother out of the camp.

> And I took the watch (from his father) and I took some leather with me and I went in the street, down the middle, without a band that I am a Jew, just like that. *I wasn't afraid of anybody.* I came to that camp, to that camp where he was and there was Ukrainians with the long black coats all over here, *I was scared cause I knew those people you cannot trust.* So I says to him, I have here for you, I got leather, and I got a watch, now my brother's here, he's going to march out to work, here, in another half an hour or so, if you look away, this is all yours. So he agreed with me. *That's luck too, not because, because sometimes they use to take away everything and then shoot you too. I could've killed him, I could've killed me, but I took the chance, I'd nothing to lose.* So sure enough, marching out my brother, marching out, I don't know, 30, 40 kids. So I handed over to this, to this, Ukrainian and he looked the other way and I got my brother and there was a kid *who's smart,* he grabbed the arm of my brother and I took 'em both. Took 'em both and took them to the camp to that I was in. *That was luck. That was really luck.*

The narrative is evaluated as "luck," but there are other evaluations, including self-descriptive evaluations such as "I wasn't afraid of anybody" and "I'd nothing to lose." The mix of Ben's interpretations presents some problems. How does he understand his survival? Is it luck, or is it purpose, or both, or is it something else? Still, Ben's self-described agency, almost bravado in the face of death, is not merely a footnote in his account of survival. There is a way of reading the transcript that puts Ben's agency front and center.

The following narratives are instances of serial storytelling, where one recounting leads directly to a second recounting. Both stories take place in Krakow Plaszow. Both take place later in the war and are told later in the interview. Once again, external evaluations are italicized. Here is the first:

> Again once they caught me, *I don't remember what it was I stole, maybe some potatoes,* I was cooking potatoes or something, *I don't remember what it was,* and they

took me, *it was a long time ago, I cannot remember everything, as the older you get, you forget things.* The chief of the police was (name). *It sound to me a little bit at home, I listened to (name) but a kid you know I didn't pay attention.* He was chief of the police, *also a good looking guy. . . .* And they took me to the police station *and I was afraid I'm going to die now.* So when they took me to the police station, so there was, the guys who didn't know me, didn't know my name at all, *but luck of mine, somehow God was watching over me.* (inaudible) with boots like, looked like a real Gestapo, comes in with his cane, takes a look at the list and sees my name, "H. who is Ben H.?" I says, "I am." "What are you doing here, what did you do?" I says, "I don't know, I must of stole a potato (inaudible)." "Get the hell out of here we don't want you here." (laughter) Now I found out he was (name) and my family, they were, they were partners once. His mother used to be, used to work for my family or somehow connected with the family you see and he knew (inaudible).

The story, like many others that Ben tells, is filled with danger, suspense, and surprise. The ending is completely unpredictable. At least, it is only because we know that Ben did, in fact, survive that there must have been some way out of the situation. But exactly how the narrative will end seems to descend out of the blue. It isn't a rational ending, but is almost magical. We both laughed at the Gestapo's words, "Get the hell out of here we don't want you here." An old connection from his home just happens to be police chief in the camp, recognizes his name, and kicks him out. Life, indeed, is stranger than fiction.

One should note that Ben could have evaluated the narrative otherwise. There is more than luck or purpose at play: the aid of someone else, an explanation that, at other points in the interview, he steadfastly rejects.

A minute or two later in the interview, Ben evaluates the story again, saying, "So anyways this happened again, so I was saved again." Still, his evaluation, "but luck of mine, somehow God was watching over me" is an intriguing, if ambiguous, conflation. He seems to be saying that he was lucky to have God on his side, but is it the randomness of fate or the chosenness of divine intervention that should be emphasized?

Here is one final narrative that emphasizes Ben's agency. It is told directly after the story of his escape from police headquarters at Krakow Plaszow. The setting is just outside of Amon Goetz's villa.

So I'll tell you why because once I had night shift and we worked, his villa was up there on the hill and we worked down there not far away, he could look out and see what we were doing, that close. Again my brother was sitting, *you know he was tired, so he probably sat down at night,* it must have been 1, 2 o'clock, 1 o'clock, 2 o'clock at night, nightshift, and one of the guys over there were playing cards probably came out to smoke a cigarette or something. So he came out and he saw that someone's sitting, he came down, didn't know from nothing, all of the sudden I see that he's coming down, *I really got scared. I didn't know what was . . .* then I noticed that my brother's sitting. He's coming down and takes the revolver out, he's already taking his revolver and he's gonna take out. *And you know what I did, you wouldn't believe this what I did.* I jumped right over and throw his gun out from his hand. *I wasn't afraid for nothing.* Then I says to him, "you cannot shoot this man, I told him to sit down. He worked so hard, you know what he did, look what he did," I said. "You're not going to shoot him, he is the best worker here." And I kicked him in his tuchas, my brother, and he just went like that, you're OK.

BRIAN: (laughter) That's what the German did?
BEN: Yeah. *So I saved him again, my brother. Cause I didn't. I said if they're going to shoot him, shoot me too, what can they do? Killing that's all they can do.*

At the moment, we have three seemly contradictory interpretations evidenced in Ben's words. Ben sees his survival as luck or divine intervention, but he also portrays his own actions as forceful in determining the continued survival of himself and others. It is interesting to note that, on the one hand, when talking about luck or purpose, these are evaluations of the stories but are also found in larger reflections on his survival. On the other hand, agency is displayed mostly in the stories themselves, not in larger reflections, and they are not extensively evaluated or elaborated upon in the same fashion. Agency is developed in the stories that Ben tells and how he tells them. In other words, purpose or luck is told, and agency, mostly, is shown.

However, let's make things just a little bit more complicated and more representative of what actually transpired during the interview. Purpose, luck, and agency are explanations that attribute some variety of meaning or cause to his experiences, even if they are poorly understood. There is another movement in the conversation that says something like "reject all explanations," it is incomprehensible. I should be careful here in attributing the rejection of understanding to Ben's survival. He never explicitly links these ideas directly to his own survival, but this is his major interpretation of the Holocaust.

What they did to people. It's unbelievable what I saw my own eyes. Unbelievable, I don't believe myself, already. I started to think, is that a dream was that a dream or what? It haunts me all my life, at night like I said twice, three times a week . . . I dream what's happening, what's going on.

The memories not only have a dream-like quality, but also reappear in his current dreams.

A second example appears in the transcript after telling the bulk of the stories during the war. During the tape break, Ben mentioned that he only told some of the stories but left a lot out. I ask:

BRIAN: So you were saying you had a little bit left of your story?
BEN: There is a lot left, you cannot predict everything. It's impossible for me to tell you all of the things of all these years. I'm just giving you short part. Because it is impossible. I don't believe myself if this is true what I went through, what I've seen.
BRIAN: Why do you say that?
BEN: Because it's impossible. It's something unbelievable, taking people, you know half dead, still alive and bury them. The way they murdered and killed them, it's impossible.

I have given a rich and complex description of how Ben interprets his survival. Let me just take a second to put some of the strands together into some kind of order. The diversity of, potentially, contradicting interpretations is tough to manage. Rather than giving a single interpretation, Ben gives us multiple ones. Normally, we expect some coherence in explanations or at least that the explanations fit together in some constellation. We could chalk up the contradictions to the aftereffects of the trauma of the Holocaust—the power of the experience has split apart the normal configuration of his personality. The experience does still haunt him, even in his dreams. But I don't believe that this mix of interpretations is necessarily linked to trauma. Rather, as I see it, multiple interpretations are perfectly normal. When we pay close attention to what people tell us about their lives, they are much more inconsistent in their interpretations of self and world than we might expect (Schiff & Cohler, 2001).

But how do we, interpreting Ben, make sense of it all? To return to the analytic question, how do we interpret Ben's interpretations of survival? How does an understanding of the contextual questions (who, where, and when) help us to understand why Ben interprets his survival in these various ways?

Or, better yet, who is the Ben made present in the interview setting? And, heading toward the center of my analysis, how does knowing who Ben is help us to better understand how he interprets his survival?

I have already presented evidence from the interview in which Ben describes himself as generous with the money that he made in business, helping others to get their start, and with his time. And he does this, and much more, without asking for anything in return. He is a protector of others—literally putting his life on the line in order to protect others from death. There are numerous other examples within the interview that support this assertion.

Ben presents himself as special in, at least, two senses. He is special not only in his generous and protective actions, but also because, unlike others persons who help, these actions are carried out as goods in themselves—he is not seeking any recognition for his deeds. But he also possesses a unique perspective on the events, a special knowledge, even as they unfold around him. For example, at the beginning of his incarceration, Ben escapes and warns the people in his shtetl of the disaster about to unfold, knowing full well that this is the beginning of the destruction of the Jewish people, but like Moshe the Beadle in Weisel's *Night* (1960/1982), his fantastic stories are not to be believed. Another example is that Ben was incarcerated in the Krakow Plaszow camp, which was made famous by Thomas Keneally's (1982) book *Schindler's Ark* and Steven Spielberg's film rendition of Keneally's journalistic account, *Schindler's List* (1993). (The interview takes place after the book's publication and the film's release, after both had become icons of the Holocaust narrative.) Although Ben saw Schindler and is sometimes classified as one of Schindler's Jews, he rejects this categorization, saying, "Whoever had money went to Schindler, but I couldn't afford it so I had to go to that other murderer (Goetz)." Ben tells a narrative about meeting Keneally.

> My daughter came in says dad, I want you to. A Canadian is here, which he wrote a book from Schindler's List. I want you to meet and talk to him, I have pictures for him. So I said OK if you want me to go I'll go. So after his speech I went and congratulated him and told him I read your book, I said 90% of your book is all the truth. All of these details that he wrote in that book it's exactly as it was. A little mixed up, because I was there, I've seen it. But it was almost exactly like it was. "But the beginning" I says "you wrote a beautiful book, but the beginning you didn't have." I says "I know." "I wish he would have. I would have known you, I would have come to you and asked the beginning."

In this example, he possesses a kind of special knowledge or special insight. In short, one way of reading Ben's account is that he is, in some way, special and distinct.

Finally, a last matter of who Ben is in the interview is related to his interpretation of survival. There is a continuous, firm connection with his family, which finds expression in both his generosity and his, if equivocal, dedication to God and religion.

Ben views his care for the other as following in the family tradition modeled by his parents. Ben's mother cared for the sick and gave food to those who needed, like Ben, without asking for anything in return. But Ben's identification with his father is even more critical in this regard. I asked Ben to provide me with more insight about why he was so protective:

BRIAN: There were many points in the story where you talked about saving people or your father asking you to save somebody or pulling your brother out and saving him. I was wondering, what inspired you? What was going through your mind at that time?

BEN: Promise, I promised my father, that's the first thing that's my first responsibility. It was responsibility of me as an older brother. . . . But that was my responsibility, I promised my parents that I'm gonna save my brother. Even now until today, the same thing, if he needs any advice, he calls me and I give it to him. I'm obligated. Not obligated, it's my responsibility, to you know. It's my younger brother to older brother to do it. The promise is the first thing, the second is my responsibility as a brother. It's tradition from our family. It's in our blood. My father was the same way, you could take the pants off my father in the middle of the street, that's how good he was. Good hearted person, I'm the same way. It runs in the family. So, that's how it is. I do for. Not only for my brother, I do for other people. I brought sick people to this country, sick people. They would never come without me. I put people in business and I never wanted a thank you from no one. . . . Everybody I knew. Today nobody knows me. . . . When I was in business, I'd connections, anything I wanted, I could accomplish . . . I don't want a thank you, I don't want anybody to know anything. And, that's the way I am I don't want no thank you, I don't ask for thank you. But, that's in my blood. That's in my blood always since a child.

In the preceding passage, he links this spirit of generosity and responsibility directly to his father and directly to his upbringing. He has kept his promise to be responsible for others in the same way that his family acted before the war.

Another promise kept to his family is religious. Even though Ben has "a case with God," he does not abandon the family's belief system. When asked about his religious beliefs, Ben responds, "Well, I have to believe there is something. The world is not by itself run. There is a God." But his answer is more nuanced than just a simple yes. He continues:

> BEN: Now to go too deep in the Bible it does not allow a Jew to go too deep to study. Why or how or what if there is a God or not. I believe there is a God. But I talk to a lot of Rabbis and they cannot answer me my question.
>
> BRIAN: What is the question?
>
> BEN: My question is to them is a father, a father, if he loves his children, would he murder them? Would he allow something like that to happen? No matter, no matter, if the father, kids are no good or whatever, have the children, they're innocent, just kids, did they sin? They cannot answer that question, nobody no one can answer me that question. But tradition, I have to do how my father was, my grandfather and my grandfather from generation to generation. I have to keep up to believe in God. There is a God. I was straight. I've seen it. So I have to go *dor ve dor* [Hebrew for generation to generation]. I have to go generation to generation. Some others do differently, that's different, but this is the way we are, my wife and myself. Sure we believe in God. I have a case with God. To tell you too, I have a case, a good case. I would like he should explain me why?

Ben does, indeed, have "a good case" with God. His question—"a father, if he loves his children, would he murder them?"—is haunting and disturbing. But, in citing the family tradition and the set of beliefs that have been passed down from generation to generation, as he cites in Hebrew, and now from Ben to his children and grandchildren, Ben keeps the window open to God: "I have to keep up to believe in God" and "I've seen it."

Ben's interpretations of purpose, luck, and agency can be understood as the expression of who he is in the context of the interview. The bag isn't so mixed after all; each of these interpretations represents an aspect of his personal history, family, and identity. His specialness and his connection with his family of origin help to understand the mix between agency and purpose. They go together; maybe his actions did have a purpose.

But what about the awkwardness between luck and agency? Understanding who Ben is can only get us part of the way there. In order to move toward a more complete and complex understanding, we need to add in more context: where and when he makes these interpretations.

BEN IN TIME AND SPACE

Although the interview was collected in 1996, I am now writing about Ben almost 20 years afterward. It is fascinating that the text has stayed, objectively, the same. The first few words seem to bring an entire world into being, and the last few words bring that world to an abrupt close. I want to hear more but I am suddenly cut away. The voice on the tape cassette comes through loud and clear. I recognize Ben, and the sound of his voice brings back a flood of memories of what, for me, was a pivotal experience in my research.

The textual object apparently remains the same, or at least on the face of it, but I have changed. I am no longer a graduate student, no longer the young man whom Ben saw in the interview. But I also see more clearly the outlines of the historical period when we spoke together—allowing me to understand his words not as timeless but as grounded. Indeed, in our imagination, we have to see Ben's interpretations as situated in a particular space and time, a particular there and then.

Where Is Ben?

Ben is telling his life story in an intimate setting where I am the only one present. Ben's wife is at home and greeted me at the door, but quickly retired to another part of the house. After he hears his voice rising in the interview, Ben shuts the door so his wife will not be disturbed by our conversation. We are alone.

I am an important part of the context of the telling. The where of the interview directly concerns my presence. My interaction with Ben, how I framed the interview, the variety of questions that I ask or don't ask, have, in some way, contributed to the production of the story that Ben tells and why he tells it. But I am not the only audience. Like many survivors, Ben views the interview as a way of communicating with family and future generations. Indeed, with Ben's permission, I made a copy of the interview and gave one to his daughter and grandchildren. And Ben hopes that I will tell his story to others. The interpretations were offered somewhere, and someone is being addressed.

However, larger cultural understandings are also at play. Ben knows what kind of interview I am asking for. Or at least he thinks that he knows. The interview is framed as an interview with a Holocaust survivor from the camps. And, in 1996, there were many oral history projects on Holocaust survivors occupied with this variety of work, including the massive archival project launched by Steven Spielberg, *Survivors of the Shoah*. Many of the survivors whom I interviewed had already given other interviews, sometimes multiple interviews. In Ben's case, he has given one, a "short video" that he refers to several times in the interview and distinguishes from our conversation, which contains additional information. "You are the only one. I didn't have it on the video. What I told you is not on the video."

As I have already described, I attempted to structure the conversation somewhat differently, starting with current life rather than before the war, to allow survivors the space to reflect upon their experiences. My questions are extraordinarily sparse. During the interview, I speak very little. The rare moments that I do intervene are to ask for clarifications, reflect back Ben's interpretations, or to help him find words that don't come to mind readily. There are no back-and-forth exchanges in the transcript, as we saw especially clearly in our discussion of Marine and Clement in Chapter 5. The cultural frame of what it means for survivors to give their stories seems to direct the bulk of the interview. Ben has a "story" to tell about the camps, which unfolds smoothly and forcefully into the conversation. There is very little negotiation to figure out what is tellable in this context. From the beginning talk about his psychological health, aging, and his business, the Holocaust "story" seems to take over.

Still, there is some evidence, marked in the interview, that displays how Ben looks at me and how he is tailoring his interpretations to what he thinks I would like to hear or should hear.

In 1996, I was in my late twenties, and Ben was 73, almost 50 years my senior. Although it is not marked in the transcript, I had the sense that Ben saw me like one of his grandsons, whom he does discuss at length during the interview. After the tape recorder was turned off, he also asked me whether or not I knew one of his grandsons and said that we would like each other.

But, in fact, we do have two relations in common. First, Ben did know my great-uncle and great-aunt before they died. Before the interview, I did not know of their acquaintance. But, after Ben tells me what business he was in, I ask him if he knew my great-uncle, by marriage, who was also a Polish survivor and was in a related business. It is possible that this connection reinforced the grandson transference that I sensed, but it certainly does mark me as being an insider in the Jewish, and survivor, community. Second, and more important, I was introduced to Ben through a rabbi whom we both knew, who gave me Ben's phone number. Explaining how he feels at the end of the interview and why he spoke with me, Ben says,

> Because of Rabbi X., he told me me you are a nice young man, OK I'll do this. I couldn't refuse, but otherwise I wouldn't. . . . Rabbi X. told you to call me and I respect him.

In retrospect, I think that a good deal of the intimacy found in the conversation is attributable to being "like" his grandsons and to our connection with Rabbi X. I was a "nice young man," even a nice Jewish boy, who could be trusted with his story and who was the kind of person that Ben should help.

Not only does Ben have special knowledge of the Holocaust, but at several points in the transcript, he communicates that I am being given special, private, knowledge in the context of the interview. The transcript contains several markers that the stories are being told just to me: "I never told this to anyone, you are the first one, which you are going to hear about it." "You are the only one." "See, nobody knows about it."

Ben's interpretations of purpose and luck and his agentic self-portrayals need to be viewed within the context of this intimacy. In another, more public, context, there's no way of knowing which interpretations he would make present.

Putting luck in the mix of interpretations is readily understandable in the context of telling the story to another person(s). Interpersonally, saying that one's survival is due to agency is self-serving and, potentially, egotistical. Remember, Ben doesn't often make this assertion explicitly, but rather he shows his agency in the narratives that he tells and how he tells them. Given our common religious background, purpose might make sense. But purpose, too, can be read as having equally negative connotations. It is difficult to maintain the purpose of one's own survival while so many others—including, as Ben emphasizes, innocent children—died. Interpersonally, in the conversational context, the notion of luck works to assuage some of the implications of purpose and agency. Whether or not Ben actually believes that luck was a factor, or purpose or agency for that matter, luck works in the interaction to level down the idea that there could be a reason for one's survival. Luck, like incomprehensibility, works against explanations of purpose and agency.

Finally, we should address the larger cultural context in which Ben tells his story. Indeed, he is telling it in the United States and in English. In a sense, he has lived the American dream, rising from the ashes of the Holocaust in order to begin a family, a business, a life, and, like many survivors, he was very successful in these endeavors (Helmreich, 1992).

From one perspective, the plot line of his life story follows the pattern of a redemptive narrative that is highly developed in American culture (McAdams, 2006). At times, his narrative follows a "generative script" in which the person is distinguished by early advantage, specialness, and lives through a difficult experience but the suffering is overcome. The person feels a sense of "chosen-ness" for greater projects and a desire to help others (McAdams, 2006). Ben's interpretation of purpose to help others fits very nicely in the cultural context of the American "rhetoric of chosen-ness" (McAdams, 2006) and could be viewed as a highly appropriate interpretation in the American context.

However, like other survivors, redemption is not the only possibility. He seems to turn back and forth between finding purpose in the past and finding meaninglessness or a sense of contamination (McAdams, 2006).

Developmental and Historical Time

Ben's interpretation of his survival could also be a part of the developmental context of old age. At 73, Ben was at the beginning stages of old age, but he does appear to have gone through, or to be going through, the process of a life review. Based upon his reading of Erikson, Butler (1963) theorized that a life review is part of the normal developmental process in old age, where reminiscing has the function of revisiting past experience and accepting the past in order to achieve a sense of integrity. Butler believed that engaging with the past in a life review had diverse consequences, including an increased risk of suicide in old age, but that a life review also could lead to increased life satisfaction and wisdom. Here are some representative quotes from the interview that suggest that Ben is, or has, engaged in reviewing the past:

> As older you get as well as all of us, I spoke with the doctor. I says how come it's getting worse and worse? He says because it takes years, until, to develop until now. You are really going to feel it. He was right. He was right. It's getting worse

as a person gets older, you know it's getting worse, because the whole thing you know comes back to you.

But when a person gets older, he starts thinking, he goes back. What he did, what he accomplished in his life. What happened 50, 60 years ago. So . . . But I can't complain, I doing well, as long as I'm well, my wife is well, nobody is perfect, everybody has something.

Like I said before, I don't want to repeat myself, when you get older you start thinking, my God, my God what happened?

A life review might not be a necessary part of aging well, but for persons with troubled pasts, the life review might provide a pathway to finding well-being in old age (Lieblich, 2014; Wink & Schiff, 2002). Ben states that he is engaged with the past, especially the Holocaust, which he comes back to time and again with his wife and friends.

In the end, Brian, we always come back to the Holocaust. There is never a time when we discuss anything, whatever it is, not to come back to end with the Holocaust.

The loss of family, community, the severity of the experience, in my estimation, make it unlikely that Ben could ever really come to terms with the Holocaust and find acceptance and integrity in the sense that Erikson (1968/1994) meant as "the acceptance of one's one and only life cycle . . . as something that had to be . . . and an acceptance of the fact that one's life is one's own responsibility" (p. 139). But we could view Ben's reflections on purpose and demonstrations of agency as the result of the process of engaging and reflecting upon the past as an attempt to find meaning.

Finally, we need to see Ben's interpretations of survival as a matter of the historical period in which he is speaking. In 1996, Ben is speaking from a distinct historical perspective in our understanding the Holocaust and survivors. Soon after the war, the Holocaust and the Jewish victims of Nazi crimes were hardly spoken about or spoken to. What we now know as the Holocaust was not yet thought of as a distinct phenomenon from the events of the war. If the victims were referred to at all, they were most commonly called displaced persons or former concentration camp prisoners. Survivor was not a category available for understanding. Often, the victims were viewed negatively in the United States and Israel, and only spoke about their experiences with each other (Novick, 1999). After the Eichmann trial in Jerusalem in 1961, when the testimony of victims was given center stage as evidence for the crimes of the Nazi regime against humanity and the

Jewish people, this image begin to change and the notion of survivor began to appear (Wieviorka, 1989). By the 1990s, this negative image of survivors is reversed. Peter Novick (1999) wrote:

> In recent years "Holocaust survivor" has become an honorific term, evoking not just sympathy but admiration, and even awe. Survivors are thought of and customarily described as exemplars of courage, fortitude, and wisdom derived from their suffering. (p. 68)

Even the fact that I am listening to Ben, including my belief that his experiences should be heard, is part and parcel of this historical horizon in which survivor stories are worthy tales for study and consideration. And, by consequence, Ben's interpretation of survival, as purposeful and agentic, only becomes tellable to me (Norrick, 2007) by virtue of this historical context. Indeed, it is tellable not only as a story of luck, but also one of purpose and action.

FROM QUESTIONS TO ARGUMENTS

At the beginning stages of narrative analysis, then, I have advocated questioning and exploration, opening up the analysis to seeing interpretive actions from multiple points of view. Asking the questions of who, where, and when produced a wide variety of ways of thinking about Ben's interpretation of survival. Of course, some of my interpretations are better than others; some are more plausible and more directly supported by the data. But, in the first stages of analysis, we are interested in asking questions. Here, the metaphor is circular. But it's not all circles all the way down. Straight lines are possible. An argument should, ideally, come out of this stage of questioning.

Grounded in evidence, we try to piece together a convincing account of interpretive actions, which is based upon the process of questioning and closely attending to the data. Our questions should have produced some insights into the meaning of the interpretive action. Now, we have the opportunity to test them out. We begin to try out interpretations that respond to our questions and that lead us to some reasonable conclusions about the function of this interpretive act. The structure of this response takes the form of a reasoned argument of why.

Although elusive, a well-reasoned argument that connects a purpose to an interpretive act is possible. Analysis articulates a case for what narrating does, how it does it, and to what end. Arguing for a purpose is a theoretical move, when we begin to structure an argument about what this interpretive action means. It is the job of the interpreter to make explicit exactly how they do so. The argument might not be universal and timeless, but it should be interesting and portable—insightful when applied to other circumstances and other studies.

In regard to Ben, we can't see his interpretation of survival as merely a personal fact. Although there are important reasons that he presents about why his survival is purposeful, which can be found in who Ben is, the situation of telling, culture, development, and history impose their own requirements on what can be and should be told, and by whom. Ben's status as an American survivor in the 1990s allows him to claim purpose, agency, and personal redemption, but, perhaps, not for too long or too forcefully. Luck and the incomprehensibility of the events work to downplay what could be taken as conceit and to discourage all-inclusive explanations.

The next two chapters further develop this interpretive perspective on narrative analysis. In Chapter 8, I provide concrete examples of how questions of who, when, and where are applied in narrative research across one of the major divisions in the field between big and small stories. In Chapter 9, I introduce a theory of argumentation for making claims about the meaning or purpose of interpretive actions and for critically evaluating research in psychology, both quantitative and qualitative.

CHAPTER 8

Interpretation in Practice

In what follows, I contrast two approaches to the study of narratives: Amia Lieblich's (1993) research on Russian immigrants to Israel, which principally focuses on the life story of a single person, Natasha, and Michael Bamberg's (2004) research on masculine identity formation, which principally focuses on a small unit of conversation told in the context of a group discussion with adolescent boys about girls. The contrast between these two approaches highlights some of the basic tensions concerning what constitutes narrative data and analysis. However, I will argue that these differences in the construction of the data mask substantial commonalities in their interpretive strategies.

Lieblich starts from the person; Bamberg starts from the situation. Each choice presents its own problems and challenges to understanding interpretive actions. Although Lieblich's research does make some attempt to include aspects of the conversational context, the interview situation remains relatively underdeveloped. Lieblich details the meaning of immigration and growing up for Natasha. Natasha's personal striving, motivations, and unique life experiences are revealed with color and depth. We have a sense of her character and how her unique life situation has led to particular interpretations. Bamberg's research is firmly directed at the level of the situation of talk, with very little attention given to the subjective experiences of those persons involved in the conversation. We have a strong sense of how narratives are part of a social context in which identity is part of the conversation's social work. In some ways, these are the strengths and limitations of the data that they have constructed at the out-set. Start with persons, and one sees the "who" of the telling. Start with situations, and one sees the "where" of the telling.

But I will not end my discussion deadlocked between two incommensu-rable positions. After briefly describing what each does well—indeed, they are among the best examples of narrative research that I can think of—I will make some suggestions about where I think that both can make their accounts, interpretively, more complete and fully fleshed out. This is no easy task as, once again, both studies are among the most compelling and well executed in narrative (or in psychology, for that matter).

My suggestion is that each can learn from one another. Although aca-demics are eager to separate the world into sharp contrasts in order to form controversies and debates, I see a common approach to narrative analysis in which persons can be seen as making present identities within ongoing talk and in which situations can be seen as composed of persons with their own histories, development, character, and motivations. In short, both can benefit from understanding interpretive actions more fully as a part of per-son's lives, interactions, culture, and time—in other words, to more fully address the questions of who, where, and when.

In a way, I am taking a stance in the debate as Michael Bamberg, Mark Freeman, and Alexandra Georgakopoulou (Bamberg, 2006; Bamberg & Georgakopoulou, 2008; Freeman, 2006; Georgakopoulou, 2007) have framed it, between "big story" and "small story" approaches to narrative. The emphasis on big stories is on the expression of personal meaning. Big stories begin from the person and attempt to come as close as pos-sible to how persons interpret the past and make sense of their lives. Big story researchers take as their data life story conversations, typically from interviews, oral histories, or autobiographies, in which a person recounts the stories and reflections that give their lives significance and meaning. Freeman argues that big story research opens a space, in some ways sepa-rate from our day-to-day lives, in which persons are given the opportunity to construct general interpretations of the past and identity.

The emphasis of small stories is on the social context of narrative and how conversations produce identities. Bamberg and Georgakopoulou argue that researchers have paid overwhelming attention to fully devel-oped narrative accounts, such as Labovian personal experience narratives, and have virtually ignored narratives as they unfold in actual conversa-tions, which are often small, contain minimal complicating action, and are jointly produced. According to small story researchers, the context of big stories is artificial, rarely occurring in everyday life. Narrative expressions are more naturally partial and tentative, part of a concrete conversation.

Furthermore, once small stories are understood in their appropriate context, they are abundant in meaning.

The notion of "small stories" has expanded our understanding of what narrative is and does. There is great value in looking at narratives as part of our daily lives and conversations. However, I don't believe that the binary of small/big is very useful. The distinction in the size of the story does not merit a new and separate mode of interpretation. Although the debate treats big and small stories as incommensurable approaches, they are in fact quite compatible and should inform one another. Big stories demand that we consider the more intimate aspects of a person's life and see their expressions as part of life's course, while small stories demand that we consider the social context of talk—life as it unfolds in conversation. Both are right in the sense that we need to consider even more context in our interpretations.

The distinction erodes if we consider narrating as the expression of the way that life is interpreted. As I have argued, narrating is an interpretive action that unfolds in time and space. Isn't this what is happening in stories, big and small? Not only do they critique each other, but, potentially, they enrich one another. In big story conversations, the social dynamics of talk are always part of the text produced. In small stories, persons are always speakers and a necessary unit of interpretation. The problem is to see how. How do we put the social in the personal and the personal in the social? Interestingly, both agree on the importance of the temporal and make explicit reference to it. Both deal with the "when." Big stories emphasize the "who" and "when," and small stories the "where" and "when." The trick is to treat all three in the same analysis.

WHO IS NATASHA?

Amia Lieblich's (1993) "Looking at Change: Natasha 21, New Immigrant from Russia to Israel" is an excellent example of narrative research and a model for investigation. In the chapter, Lieblich investigates the life story of a Soviet immigrant, Natasha, who has recently moved to Israel with her parents and brother. Natasha leaves Moldavia in the midst of young adulthood, during her third year in the university. In Israel, she attends the Hebrew University of Jerusalem, where Lieblich meets her as a participant in a research study on Soviet immigrants.

The interpretation that Lieblich gives of Natasha's life story is driven, mainly, by an interest in developmental theory and how narrative can help to better understand developmental change. Specifically, Lieblich is concerned with processes of identity change and transition in youth, but also how immigration complicates identity development. In the course of her immigration, Natasha undergoes what Lieblich terms a "dual transition." Natasha is making the transition to Israeli social and cultural life in the midst of the normative developmental transformation from adolescence to adulthood. In other words, her move and the requirements of adapting to Israeli social mores are complicated by her transition into adult life. The two arrive together, at the same moment, and are layered upon one another. One of the most provocative and useful theoretical assertions that Lieblich makes is the necessary balance between a sense of continuity and change in healthy psychological adjustment.

Lieblich's evidence is drawn from conversations that she had with Natasha and her reflections on conversations with other young Soviet immigrants to Israel. But the data that she presents in this chapter come exclusively from her conversations with Natasha. The chapter is filled with lengthy quotes taken from these in-depth interviews. Lieblich notes that each of the students in the study was interviewed at least twice, and often the interviews lasted 4 hours. But, from the chapter, the reader can surmise that Lieblich and Natasha met several times and developed a close confidence atypical of researcher–participant relationships.

One of the few weaknesses of the research is that Lieblich does not elaborate on exactly how she derived her insights on developmental theory. There is no record of how Lieblich arrived at the conclusions that she did. Were there multiple readings of the transcripts? Was her theory developed from reading the corpus of interviews from the entire research study, or just those of Natasha? In addition, Lieblich does not provide an extensive discussion on how her insights on Natasha apply to the group as a whole. Lieblich does note a variety of different paths through the transition, with some students moving much faster toward an Israeli identity. She writes, "in comparison to these cases, however, Natasha is—to my mind— changing more moderately and profoundly at the same time" (p. 124). Still, are Natasha's identity shifts unique in some important respects? Why did she choose Natasha and not some other participant?

The text defies conventional scientific writing in psychology. It is not divided into the standard format of a literature review, methods section, and results. Theory, previous literature, and observation are treated together simultaneously in the main body of the text. The chapter reads like a short story or case study in which the main plot line is the story of Natasha's transition. Natasha has a compelling life story and is highly articulate in her reflections. Lieblich skillfully uses the material. The artfulness of the narrative, writing and structuring the plot line, is an important aspect of the chapter itself.

The chapter follows the developmental trajectory of Natasha's life, briefly from her childhood, her painful early experiences with love at age 13, her early university studies in Russian language and literature, the rise of Moldavian nationalism, her parent's decision to leave Moldavia, and her emotional departure. Lieblich describes Natasha's account of arriving in Israel as "euphoric" and "idealized." In Natasha's words,

> My impression was that everything in this country is pretty, and the people so nice. . . . In the morning I saw the view, it was all so green and beautiful. I had always dreamt of living near the seashore, and here I saw the Mediterranean from my cousin's window. Oh, and I remember just as we descended the airplane the delightful smell of orange groves, it was everywhere. For the first month I ate oranges all the time, until I couldn't stand the taste anymore. (pp. 102–103)

As Lieblich comments, "the oranges memory obviously stands for the return to reality, with its promises and disappointments, and the growing awareness of what Natasha left behind and lost" (p. 103). I would be more measured in my interpretation of the hidden meaning behind the memory, but certainly loss is a major part of Natasha's narrative, and Lieblich documents an array of losses in Natasha's understanding of her identity and place in the world. With immigration, Natasha's parents, skilled professionals, must resign themselves to menial labor. She has lost friendships and social status—and is still in the process of mourning for these losses. In Israel, there is a shift in parental authority and status as Natasha is more competent in Hebrew and is given more freedom to make decisions about her social life and dating. She loses a clear sense of the norms of gender roles and expectations and career aspirations.

The chapter makes a strong impact, in part, from the artfulness of Lieblich's choices in telling Natasha's narrative. But the real strength of this research is Lieblich's use of evidence in describing critical aspects of Natasha's experience, interpretations of herself, and the psychological strategies that she develops in confronting this double transition. The chapter is much more than an artful telling of a life. Indeed, the artfulness of the narrative betrays the fact that Lieblich's account is in fact a meticulously documented description of Natasha's identity transition. For example, in their first meetings, Lieblich recounts Natasha's reluctance to change in her "typical reactions" to Lieblich's suggestions for practical solutions to daily problems.

"I'm fine, please don't worry about me," and: "If I take this step—the situation might get worse." Here I detected for the first time the reluctance to change in the midst of changing, or her holding on to the stability that was available during the general turmoil she was experiencing inside and outside. Take the following example:

I: Perhaps you should ask to be moved to the dormitories here on Mount Scopus; I could help you in that.

She: Oh, no. I have a nice roommate, an Israeli girl, and I can speak a little Hebrew with her. If I move up here, who knows who will be my roommate.

Only much later did I find out that her relationship with that roommate was quite unsatisfactory. (p. 95)

The preceding quote is illustrative of Lieblich's investigative style of making grounded interpretations that question what is being said, how it is said, and why. What does this quote say about Natasha? Lieblich is using it as the basis of establishing an important fact about Natasha when we, and Lieblich, first encounter her. She seems to be clinging for stability as her world rapidly changes, even if the status quo is unsatisfactory. Lieblich gives the reader the evidence from the interview, which establishes the basis for her assertion.

It is also important to highlight the way that Lieblich writes herself into the situation of story creation, the story realm (Young, 1986, 2004), where the reader is given the opportunity to imagine the received account as part of a process of production, in which Lieblich is intimately involved. We don't imagine Natasha alone—as if a story could unfold without a listener—rather, we see Natasha's account as jointly produced in the interview situation. Lieblich also writes herself into the analysis by highlighting how she arrives at conclusions: "Here I detected for the first time" and "Only much later did I find out." The use of the first person voice further reveals how knowledge about Natasha is derived, but also calls attention to the fragility of the claim—all knowledge is partial but, Lieblich seems to be saying, this is how I know what I know. And, even, this is why I now doubt the account that Natasha told me.

Quotes are used to further the story of Natasha's experience and interpretations of her identity; also, critically, the quotes ground observations so that readers find meaningful evidence of the processes described. In other words, the quotes are used as a means of validation (Mishler, 1990). They provide the substantive evidence for following Lieblich's argument and judging the adequacy of her interpretations.

Like a good film or short story, Lieblich's narrative has elements of suspense and surprise (Sternberg, 1992). How will this story turn out? Where will we leave Natasha? The character herself changes over the course of time. When Lieblich first introduces Natasha, she describes her as "a colorless and subdued young woman. She seemed to be skinny and pale, her black eyes enormously sad, her smile polite and somewhat shaky" (p. 94). But, at the end of the chapter, Natasha is no longer a "person in hiding" as Lieblich first saw her, but she is starting to make new choices about her future, exploring and holding open for new possibilities in career, relationships, and values. She also displays more ease with herself and her life in Israel. Lieblich documents the many ways that Natasha's attitudes and life have transformed. Natasha is more secure in her relationship with her boyfriend. She has a new relationship with her parents and a new course of study and career goals.

But, interestingly, despite a host of evident changes, Natasha resists the notion that she has changed. "Although numerous changes took place in Natasha during the first year of her life in Israel, it remained important for Natasha to claim repeatedly that she actually did not change, or changed very little" (p. 119). After quoting Natasha's words, "I am still my old self. In Russian they call me a 'digger'—I think and reflect too much about myself and about all that is happening around me," Lieblich writes, "To rescue her sense of continuity, Natasha is speaking here about traits she has long recognized in herself, such as her depressive moods and need to be accepted, that have probably been accentuated, but not produced, by the immigration process" (pp. 123–124). According to Lieblich's observations, in the face of profound shifts in identity, Natasha's self-story works to buttress her sense of selfsameness.

But why focus only on one person? How can we develop a scientific understanding of identity transitions on the basis of a single case? Following Josselson (2006), how can we build general knowledge from narrative research? I agree that more should be done in order to understand how Natasha's experience relates to the experiences of other youth, and to immigrant lives in the psychological literature at large. From a statistical perspective, we might want to know about how typical such interpretations are. However, statistical approaches are not able to arrive at a complex understanding of the dynamic process of identity development that Lieblich investigates so eloquently.

Indeed, for me, one of the critical insights to be drawn from the chapter is that the thematic content of interviews only makes sense when put into the context of the person. In other words, Natasha's quotes are legible only as her words and only as seen through the lens of her evolving story. We understand how Natasha makes sense of her transition because we see this process as part of Natasha's personal story. Taking her thoughts outside of her other reflections and who Natasha is does violence to them.

We could well imagine a second approach, such as grounded theory, to this same data set, which would code themes across the whole group of interviews, of which Natasha is just one interview (Charmaz, 2006). But I believe that our understanding of identity transitions would be the poorer for it. The chapter provides a nuanced understanding of identity in transition exactly because we are presented with a detailed understanding of Natasha's life and how her experiences of immigration and identity fit into this larger framework. The context of the person, the who of the narrative, is critical.

The focus of analysis is principally on Natasha herself. Indeed, Natasha is the main character in the story that Lieblich tells. We learn a lot about how she reflects upon herself, the world, and the past. Her voice is present and clear. Lieblich's main concern is with the experience of immigration and Natasha's transition to life in Israel, the inner story of this transition, the meanings that Natasha constructs in the course of her transition—the interpretations that she makes, and why she makes them.

However, Natasha is not the only character in the story. There are other characters in the taleworld (parents, friends, boyfriends, etc.), and Lieblich herself is located as a principal actor in the storyrealm. Indeed, the chapter begins with a description of Lieblich's life, where she is writing from, on sabbatical in Berkeley, California, and some of the challenges Lieblich experiences living in a new culture. This analytic move is an interesting one that opens a discussion about the role of the researcher in the creation of knowledge. How does Lieblich's identity influence her understanding of Natasha? In fact, given the focus on Natasha's inner story of transition, Lieblich is quite successful in bringing out her own role in the conversations as an interviewer and interpreter of Natasha's life story.

Lieblich uses the first person "I" to give her impressions and to voice possible interpretations. Lieblich marks problems with her data, the limitations of her interpretations, and she frames interpretations as her own. At other moments in the chapter, Lieblich includes interview exchanges between herself and Natasha. In one exchange, Natasha openly contests Lieblich's interpretation. "I suggest that perhaps she has higher status in her family because she has made more progress into Israeli society than any of them, but she rejects my explanation. 'I don't think so,' she says, 'they still don't see me as an independent adult'" (p. 122). We are given a feeling for the kind of interactions that went on in the scene of talk, and some aspects of how this knowledge was created from the interview context and the reflections of the interviewer/researcher. Of course, one could, and maybe should, go further into the analysis of the interview situation. But it is noteworthy that this discussion does take place at all.

Michael Bamberg's (2004) "Form and Functions of Slut Bashing in Male Identity Constructions in 15-Year-Olds" presents us with an excellent contrast to Lieblich, and an excellent opportunity to consider whether or not there is a common narrative method of interpretation. My object here is to give an account of the interpretive strategy of Bamberg's research in order to put his approach in conversation with Lieblich's. Despite the obvious differences in style, I believe that there are deep commonalities in the variety of questions and interpretive reasoning.

Like Lieblich, Bamberg is also interested in the process of identity formation in youth. However, the data are constructed in a completely different fashion. Rather than focusing on extensive interviews with a single person or a group of persons, Bamberg's research object is a 3½ minute excerpt of a group interview with five male 15-year-olds and a moderator.

The time frame is much shorter, providing little details about the persons who are talking. In a similar vein, Bamberg never says who the moderator is, but it is clear that the moderator role is played by Bamberg himself. This is my major critique of the article. Bamberg never adequately treats the persons who motivate the situation. I understand that this is not the focus of the article. Rather, Bamberg is interested in the identity implications of the situation, how persons position themselves within a scene of talk, and what we can glean about how identities are enacted in such conversational performances and the consequences of such enactments. But, given another set of actors, we would have had a different set of meanings. I will say more about this later.

The data might be "small," but the theoretical aspirations are not. Bamberg masterfully uses this small segment of speech to argue a theory of identity construction. Identity is "emergent" in conversational contexts:

> Starting from the assumption that self and identity are not givens, as sitting on a shelf to be picked and plugged into communicative situations, but rather, that they are constantly under revision and interactively renegotiated.... Detailed descriptions of the moments of revising and renegotiating selves and identities lay open the emergence, the coming-into-being, of identities as contextual and draft-like processes. (p. 334)

Bamberg brings together how identity work is accomplished in concrete situations (bottom-up) with how persons come to be positioned in and inhabit larger cultural and discursive identities (top-down). Bamberg begins from the premise that interactions in the course of everyday life are the primary site for negotiating and inhabiting identity positions, which then have relevance beyond any particular conversation. He emphasizes not only that personal agency is inherent in the process, but also that within interactions strong social forces are in play that constrain choice, negotiating and sometimes imposing alignments that have durable consequences.

Bamberg argues that we can situate the process of identity formation by describing three levels of positioning, which are evident in conversation:

1. In level 1, interpretation focuses on the content of what is told. What is happening in the taleworld? How do the characters and personages relate to each other there? What is the action of the stories being recounted? He asks: "How are the characters depicted, and what is the story about (its theme)?" (p. 336).

2. In level 2, interpretation focuses on positions of actors in the situation of talk, or, in other words, the storyrealm (Young, 1986, 2004). What is the role of the actors in telling stories? How do persons work together? What is their relationship to one another? "It is at this level . . . that we ask why a story is told at a particular point in the interaction or, more specifically, why the narrator claims the floor at this particular point in the conversation to tell the story. What is he or she trying to accomplish interactively with the story?" (p. 336).

3. Finally, level 3 puts together the positions taken in what is told and the interaction itself to make larger identity claims about who the person is. Bamberg writes:

> By talking *about* others and arranging them in narrative space and time (level 1) and by talking *to* others in the here and now (level 2), narrators engage in the creation of "a sense of (them as) selves." In other words, narrators transcend the level of story contents and the interactional level of "How I want to be viewed by you, the audience" and (most often implicitly) address the question "Who am I?" (p. 336).

In other words, larger identity claims are built up from our stories of ourselves and others in what we tell and how we position ourselves in relation to those stories and others in direct face-to-face conversation. We become selves, which can, potentially, be carried over from situation to situation, through this process of storytelling, negotiation, and alignment. The theory is powerful and convincing.

Like Lieblich, Bamberg grounds his theoretical claim in the close observation and analysis of the transcribed interview, in which positioning levels 1 and 2 are meticulously documented and connected to level 3. The strength of the article comes from establishing a clear evidentiary link between theory and observation, firmly grounding theory in the data itself. Bamberg's analysis of the interview text is a detailed exploration of each of these three levels.

Compared to Lieblich, the data are less densely packed with long reflections or a single person recounting well-structured narratives. The transcript contains multiple speakers who speak over one another and confirm and question what is said. Speaking turns are short. Indeed, the data look like everyday conversation. But, as Bamberg argues, there are two narratives in the transcript: one the story of a young girl who the boys say had sex, and another about the letter she wrote. They are "minimal narratives" (Labov, 1972) without much elaboration or complicating action. But Bamberg convincingly argues that what is said in the stories and interactively established around the stories are crucial in understanding identity formation. These minimal narratives found in the transcript are similar to other interpretive actions that occur over and over again in our day-to-day lives.

Bamberg pays close attention to how participants work together to negotiate the conversation, what is said, how it is said, and by whom, in order to describe the way that meanings are built up in joint storytelling. The two main narrators, Ted and Fred, work together in order to divulge the critical details of the story of a girl in their class who "had a lot of sex with boys" and who "earned the reputation of being . . . a slut" (p. 339). The young girl then wrote a letter "to another child in our class" saying that she might be pregnant and how she would get rid of the baby, which was circulated in the class. Ted and Fred evaluate the girl's motives by stating that "she wanted everyone to read" and "that she also did for attention" (p. 339), but also dismiss her as someone not even worthy of their concern: "I mean I know it may sound mean to say this but we couldn't really care less about her anyway" (p. 340).

At level 1, Bamberg's analysis is a thick reading of the interview and consists of exploring the taleworld of events and expanding on the meaning of "what" is told. In the dialogue, the boys characterize the girl as an active agent in the construction of her reputation as something that she earned and, in fact, desired. She is portrayed as solicitous, in need of attention, and childish in her solutions to terminate the pregnancy. The boys "effectively characterize the female protagonist as not only irresolute and irresponsible, but also stupid" (p. 342). Bamberg's second reading of the text, at level 2, draws out the conversational dynamics of how Ted, Fred, and the moderator work together to negotiate what is told. In a sense, we are dealing with the "where," the social context that animates this particular kind of storytelling. In the situation of telling, Ted and Fred work together to take the floor and lead the conversation, which is on the topic of girls, to one particular girl and to provide a moral reading of her behavior. Bamberg argues that Ted and Fred, as the main contributors, establish a group voice, a "we," even though most of the other participants are silent, which aligns them together in order to teach the moderator something about their understanding of girls in general and this girl in particular. Bamberg writes:

> Ted, supported by Fred, "teaches" the adult moderator who *we*, as young boys—in contrast to *this* girl—are: smart, rational, in control of our minds and actions, stable, well adjusted. In sum, we are responsible, *young adults* who make their decisions on the basis of commonly shared, adult-like standards. (p. 344)

In their work at describing happenings in the world, level 1, and how they align in the storytelling realm of conversation, level 2, Bamberg argues that the boys come to inhabit larger identity positions, in level 3—that of occupying a "male position."

For Bamberg, the critical elements are "where" such details are told, that is, the social space of the tellings, and "when," that is, the developmental time in life of these adolescent boys. It is the intersection between where the stories are told in social space, together with the when of developmental time, that explains the how and why of these narratives. The boys position themselves as males, and a certain kind of mature men, in relation to, and in contrast to, the behavior of the irrational, immature, attention-seeking girl depicted in the action of the narrative. These identities are worked out and expressed in the conversation. Indeed, the boys claim the identity of mature men, just like the moderator, in the context of the dialogue—identities that should be useful in later talk.

DOES SIZE MATTER?

Although there are clearly differences in approach, style, and emphasis, there are basic similarities between Lieblich's and Bamberg's interpretive strategies. Both ask questions about the meaning of their data in reference to who said what, how they said it, and in the context of when and where. And they both are ultimately concerned with questions about the meaning, or the why, of this interpretive action. There are substantial commonalities between their approaches that warrant a general theory of narrative interpretation. Rather than breaking the narrative perspective into two competing branches, we can speak about a single hermeneutic approach of questioning data in order to reach theoretical insights.

In terms of who, Lieblich concentrates on the personal aspects of identity formation, while Bamberg is more concerned with the social aspects. In a sense, Lieblich is investigating an "I" and Bamberg a "We." The difference is important and, once again, points us to how each researcher constructs the data itself. Lieblich focuses on the personal aspects that make up reflections in extensive interviews with a single person, while Bamberg focuses on the social aspects that make up performances in conversation with multiple speakers.

Both researchers make evidence-based arguments about the purpose and meaning of talk for identity. Lieblich's conception of the relationship between talk and identity is more straightforward. She uses in-depth interviews as a kind of representation of Natasha's reflections. She studies them as evidence about how Natasha understands herself. Although Bamberg also uses the data as a representation of identity, Bamberg's view of the data can be rightly considered generative. Talk produces identities in the moment. Identity emerges and is confirmed through conversation. For Bamberg, the notion that talk can be viewed as merely a representation of inner reflections would be problematic.

In terms of the debate, Lieblich's research could be characterized as "big" story research and Bamberg's is self-consciously "small." But is this distinction a critical one? I don't believe that it is, especially when we consider the analytic concerns of both "big" and "small" story researchers. Both approaches are interested in describing the interpretive process of poetically making self and making world. The distinction only becomes important when we talk about the kind of data that each prefers, but this difference is only superficial. Indeed, the narrative perspective benefits in methodological acumen and theoretical richness by recognizing the way "big" and "small" story approaches complement one another.

Given Bamberg's data, there is less freedom, and interest, in describing the personal motivations of speakers and how their life experience and family history can be understood as aspects of their identity performance. But wouldn't it be useful to know more about Ted and Fred and how their lives, family histories, and personalities have shaped how and why they participate in this dialogue? An interesting question to ask would be, exactly, *"who"* are Ted and Fred? Not all the boys participated in the same way, and this group has a different character because of their presence and participation, or lack thereof. Likewise, given Lieblich's data, there is less freedom, and interest, in understanding how Natasha's choices have been shaped by her participation and positioning in conversations, with Lieblich and others. But wouldn't it be useful to know more about how Natasha's reflections echo social positions negotiated in the interview and previous interactions, and which aspects of social identity are incorporated into her self-understanding?

Of course, one can't research everything. Interpretations are limited, partial, capable of illuminating only certain aspects of human experience. And perfection is not possible. But these questions challenge us to reconsider the line separating persons and interactions, separating the "who" and the "where." They underscore the potential benefit of folding more context into our interpretations and, additionally, how the contributions of small story and big story research can inform each another. Indeed, small story research could benefit from the inclusion of more aspects of personal identity in asking questions about data. Big story research could benefit from a more detailed consideration of the interactional settings and their impact on identity and the data itself.

The difference between small and big story research is not as simple as context-sensitive versus context-neutral interpretations. Indeed, there is one important area of the conversational context that Lieblich develops in much more detail than Bamberg. This is the contribution of the researcher's subjectivity in making interpretations of the data. Bamberg does consider how a 50-year-old male interviewer plays a role in the positions that the boys inhabit within the interview situation. But he does not consider how his own subjective biases have led him to interpret the data in the way that he does. I am not sure how Bamberg would react to the criticism that his research could benefit from more reflexive insight into his biases in the interpretation of the data. Although not explicitly stated, Lieblich is working from a feminist tradition in which self-conscious consideration of one's biases and point of view, reflexivity, is a necessary step in the research process.

The temporal nature of the data is important in both interpretations. Both studies are based upon the premise that youth is a time of forming and reforming identities. In a sense, each captures the temporal aspects of development over the life course of a person. Lieblich's interviews were conducted over time—longitudinally. So, we are able to consider how Natasha's self-reflections change and evolve. Bamberg's data are a slice in time, but are explicitly contextualized in terms of other conversations and the development of masculine identity in adolescence.

Developmental time is a central item in the interpretive lens, but historical time is less prominent. Lieblich gives us a feeling for historical time by situating Natasha in the wave of Soviet immigration to Israel in the 1980s and 1990s. She also includes Natasha's reflections on how Soviet immigrants are viewed in Israeli society and how Natasha makes sense of these social stereotypes and compares herself with them. This information is important to know. But we might like more detail connecting how historical attitudes toward Soviet immigrants played a role in Natasha's identity construction. Bamberg clearly considers ideas about gender and masculinity a sociocultural construction. Indeed, one of the main objectives of the study is to describe how larger discourses are taken up by social actors. But more attention could be paid to the historical construction of masculinity, which in this case allows for the positioning of female sexuality as morally distasteful and condemnable. We might be curious about how contemporary American constructions of masculinity influence the ability of young boys to bond together around themes that portray women as inferior.

In fleshing out an account of how and why is identity formed, both Lieblich and Bamberg are asking common questions of who, when, and where. It is this process of asking questions about our data and validating them in observations that characterizes narrative interpretation. This is what makes both studies such excellent exemplars (Mishler, 1990) of narrative research. But does this make it a "science?"

CHAPTER 9
Reasoned Interpretations

The interpretive view of psychological science that I am advocating is skeptical about universal claims for psychological knowledge. Knowledge doesn't accumulate or progress in a step-by-step, straightforward, manner. It is not evolutionary, but changing and contested. There are fits and starts, radical upheavals, encampments, sedimented facts in esoteric knowledge communities, fads, and cycles in what is new, hot, or fashionable. The movement of knowledge is anything but orderly.

Psychologists tend to think that we are building up a picture of how people are in general—even universally. Of course, this at times can be true. But, the great majority of the time, we are dealing with phenomena that are highly contextualized, sociocultural, historical, and changing. No doubt, this is one of the main reasons why articles in psychology have such a notoriously short shelf life—after about 10 years we consider research findings out of date.

The reception of knowledge is always subject to the hermeneutic circle; knowledge is always evaluated by a community that uses it and finds it valuable—or not. Provocatively, Meretoja (2014b) writes that interpreted interpretations, from the "double hermeneutic," are further interpreted in their reception, application and use—a "triple hermeneutic."

There is no external vantage point from which we can judge and record timeless truths. But this shouldn't be our aspiration. Rather, as an interpretive science, we are invested in the trustworthiness and usefulness of knowledge claims in reference to a particular question and community. In other words, knowledge becomes knowledge because it is demonstrated in the accepted terms of a knowledge community that finds a claim insightful and valuable, at least in the meantime, and uses it for further exploration (Gergen, 1994).

Framing the research argument as a hermeneutic enterprise calls attention to the interpretive, and creative, activity involved in the social construction of psychological knowledge. It would be incorrect to bracket off qualitative, in distinction to quantitative, research as *the* hermeneutic approach. Both are interpretive construals of reality that form and re-form the world from a particular perspective, and both should be subject to the same kind of critical scrutiny and engagement. And, of course, there are more skillful, forceful, and compelling arguments.

Although there may be no escape from the hermeneutic circle, not everything is circular. At least, some straight lines are possible. There are entrance routes into problems and exit strategies that pragmatically, if only temporarily, formulate knowledge claims for further interpretation and debate. In Chapter 6, I detailed an entrance route into narrative analysis through the questioning of who, where, and when. In this chapter, I turn to exit strategies for making arguments from psychological research.

I want to suggest a common framework for making interpretive practices visible and productive, in both quantitative and qualitative research, with the goal of making our research more "faithful to the phenomena one seeks to explore" (Freeman, 2011, p. 391). But I will primarily address how narrative research can produce reasonable and scientific knowledge claims. The framework focuses on the research argument and its reception by a scholarly audience.

ARGUING INTERPRETATIONS

As in other domains of inquiry, understandings take shape and are articulated in a research argument. Researchers ask questions that address specific intellectual or practical problems. They carry out investigations designed to address these problems. However, when it comes to building a theory from the data, we construct an argument—an argument for the *why*. The argument is developed in a claim, which is justified in logical reasons and grounded in sufficient evidence. Ultimately, the argument must either make sense in terms of our premises about what we already know to be true within a specific horizon of meaning, or attempt to change the terms of the debate. For Toulmin (1958/2008, 2001), this is the general form for making sound arguments that is found not only in psychology or the social sciences, but everywhere.

Arguments in the human sciences do not follow the strict mathematical model of the natural sciences. Not only is such a model dubious scientifically, but it is also empty of the fleshy complexity that dominates everyday life. It is hard to imagine a statistical equation or numerical expression that could properly characterize the richness of the experience of life and how and why persons act, feel, or think the way that they do. Rather, "the description, and explanation, of social behavior must employ the same conceptual framework as the social agents themselves" (von Wright, 1971, p. 28). As such, arguments in the human sciences are bound up in the everyday language of those very persons whom we seek to understand. In a sense, our arguments need to account for complexity, in the terms lived and experienced by the persons we study, because those are the only conditions that make their lived experience describable and understandable. But how can we use these terms to build knowledge?

In *Return to Reason*, Toulmin (2001) contrasts two approaches to argumentation: one that is abstract, logical, and rational (formal arguments), and another that is concrete, situational, and reasoned (substantive arguments). Since the seventeenth century, the style of formal arguments, to develop timeless, logical, and generally applicable proofs about the world, has been viewed as the ideal model of inquiry in the natural and physical sciences; it also has been fetishized and imitated in the social and human sciences. Although, as Toulmin (2001) documents, the ideal of pure rationality never really worked in practice, not even in physics, "certain methods of inquiry and subjects were seen as philosophically serious or 'rational' in a way that others were not" (p. 15).

Toulmin argues for a third way, a balanced approach, that combines features of substantive and formal arguments. "Rhetoric and Logic—the situational and the intellectual—are inseparable in practice" (p. 21).

> If we concentrate our attention exclusively on the propositions that figure in an argument, while ignoring the situation in which it is presented, we can be described as viewing the argument from the strict standpoint of Rationality. If we focus exclusively on the devices that make an argument persuasive, by contrast, the best that can be said about a case is that we present it as reasonably as we can: *only if we can balance concern for the substance of an argument with a style that is convincing but not too pressing can we be credited with a Reasonableness that combines intellectual force in content with a moderation in manner.* (p. 21, my italics)

This moderate approach, sensitive to the substance and form of arguments, is what makes Toulmin's model so appealing. In addition, Toulmin's perspective (1) provides the scaffolding for scientific arguments that use natural, everyday, language; (2) is highly contextual, able to take into account the multiple concrete expressions of human experience; (3) makes visible the logical and evidentiary bases of interpretations; (4) establishes sound practices for making interpretations and critiquing them; and (5) holds, at least in the case of substantive arguments, interpretations to a standard of certainty that is more tailored to the open-endedness of life. Rather than certainty for all times and places, arguments "put a conclusion 'beyond a reasonable doubt' and establish the 'strongest possible presumption' on its behalf" (p. 19).

Toulmin's (1958/2008) choice of expressions is intentionally legalistic. And the legal realm provides fertile ground for a different metaphor of the way that logic is practiced not only in everyday life, but also in science. "Logic is concerned with the soundness of the claims we make—with the solidity of the grounds we produce to support them, the firmness of the backing we provide for them—or, to change the metaphor, with the sort of *case* we present in defence of our claims" (p. 7). We should "*collage* in the words 'grounds' and 'backing' and take as our model the discipline of jurisprudence." And to reverse the terms of the debate: "Logic (we may say) is generalized jurisprudence" (p. 7).

In directly tying arguments to jurisprudence, Toulmin effectively puts front and center the social sphere where arguments can have direct consequences on the lives of persons as individuals and social bodies. Also, the legal system is less inclined to be preoccupied with matters of ultimate Truth about the nature of the world. A case is at stake, and so are persons' lives. Certainly, truth is also at stake. But truth pertains to the local matters of what the evidence can reasonably account for, rather than establishing laws about all human beings or the status of the universe. The law tries to find practical solutions to real-world problems. Jurisprudence is implicated in applying laws, determining reasonable presuppositions of guilt or innocence, adjudicating rights, benefits, and justice. In other words, the law is concerned with the same issues of interpretation that are omnipresent in our daily lives and with codifying these principles.

Following Toulmin, I see research arguments as practical, and reasonable, solutions to real-world problems. Research arguments make a case, premised on a claim that follows from convincing reasons, which are grounded in evidence and warranted by the conventions for reasoning in a particular community. I introduce a way of considering the product of psychological research, including quantitative and qualitative research and everything in between, as a structured argument that is read and evaluated by a community of others. Toulmin's theory is especially productive because it offers an alternative, pragmatic view of knowledge, not as the progressive building of universal truths about the world, but as the very human activity of argument, dialogue, and debate. Although the exact form that particular arguments take is variable, there are common characteristics in well-reasoned arguments, which can serve as the basis for critically engaging research claims.

If research questions are beginnings, claims are destinations. They are what we want our audience to be convinced of at the end of our investigation. Our claim is the centerpiece of our argument, the centerpiece of our interpretation—what we would like the reader to take away from our study. In quantitative research, the claim is often worded in the language of the hypothesis to be tested and findings that are supported by statistical inference. But, in practice, the hypothesis amounts to a claim. In general, negative findings are not published in our research journals.

To be sure, one central portion of the argument responds to the specific research question that we are studying. But a second, often implied, aspect of the argument is the argument for the argument itself. As Cronbach (1988) termed it, there is a validity argument, which must "*link concepts, evidence, social and personal consequences and values*" (p. 4). At the same time that we are making an argument for our claim, we are also making a validity argument, which argues that the reader should take our argument seriously as sound, convincing, and trustworthy. How is the research argument structured to justify conclusions? Although the validity argument is the bedrock of all research, it is often ignored as an already established fact. But it isn't.

One of the main avenues for justifying research arguments is through opening the interpretive process to scrutiny. Indeed, there is enormous value in making visible the interpretive process and opening it up to further analysis. Reckoning with interpretation in psychological research doesn't diminish the scientific value of the enterprise. On the contrary, it enhances it. This is equally true for qualitative and quantitative research. Both stand to benefit from an open and critical examination of how and why our research arguments are so constructed.

In an important paper, Yanchar, Gantt, and Clay (2005) call for a *critical methodology* in order to stimulate innovation and progress in psychological theory. From the perspective of a critical methodology, research should always be open to question and critique. "The need to challenge existing standards of theory testing and methodological practice is continuous, because there is no transhistorical standard for evaluating, or necessary conclusion, to scientific investigation" (p. 38). Methods are "a flexible set of research techniques" that describe "a *contextual and evolving theory of inquiry* within a research program" in which "research strategies ... conform to the subtleties of specific questions" (p. 35). Methods are not to be taken at face value. Researchers should be conscious and explicit about the reasons for their methodological choices, suiting them directly to the question of interest and making their choices open to evaluation and criticism. In other words, methods are an integral part of the validity argument and always require backing. Or, as Yanchar et al. (2005) write, "the traditional scientific projects of theory development, model building, theory testing and other attempts at description or explanation would be viewed as processes of *argument construction*" (p. 38).

Although interpretation is often recognized as being integral to qualitative approaches, practitioners of experimental and correlational research tend to favor the detached language and style of the natural sciences in describing their practices and findings. Qualitative approaches often include extensive justifications for their choice of method and why it is appropriate to this particular question; in contrast, quantitative approaches do not make this logic explicit. It is taken for granted that the application of statistical methods yield correct results (Slife & Williams, 1995; Yanchar, Gantt, & Clay, 2005). Still, in both cases, the role of interpretation is underappreciated and theoretically underdeveloped.

A focus on research arguments also opens psychological research to innovative methods of inquiry. Although quantitative and qualitative research are often taken as representing two mutually exclusive approaches, both are (1) credible choices for the study of particular questions, (2) potentially systematic modes of inquiry, and (3) interpretive arguments subject to the general principles of argumentation.

I want to highlight three points that are central to the reasoning and reception of research arguments: credibility, validation, and usefulness. Then, in the following section, I will show how they work in a specific case of narrative research, my study on Palestinian students with Israeli citizenship at the Hebrew University of Jerusalem. Finally, I end with a reflection on the scientific status of narrative psychology.

Credibility

Credibility speaks to the soundness of one's research question and the logic of one's study to address this question. The issue isn't exclusively one of rigor. Rather, as critical methodology (Yanchar et al., 2005) would have it, how well suited is the study to describing the phenomenon at hand? How well do the methods disclose the phenomenon and make it open to inquiry and insight (Freeman, 2011)? There should be a credible, and visible, interpretive link between the question posed and the way that we design to investigate it.

Although I am principally concerned with the product of research, this is far from the beginning of the research argument. From the very first moments when researchers are imagining the contours of a project, deciding what they will study and defining a question, the research is already layered with interpretive choices. What is important to know? Is this a worthwhile question to investigate? What questions are interesting to ask?

How we frame our study into a question, how our question addresses the larger intellectual problem at stake, the way we go about making observations, the analysis of our observations, and how we tie the analysis back to the questions posed are all elements of the argument and should be subject to scrutiny. In making a research argument, we are essentially saying, this is a sound way to approach this particular question. And, given the way that I have gone about studying it, I hope that you, the reader, find my approach credible.

Questions already suggest a direction for making observations and can be subtly reframed in order to steer the research into a particular methodological framework. There is a large difference between "how do persons negotiate an identity?" and "what identity status predicts healthy adjustment?" and between "how many Canadians identify themselves as First Peoples?" and "what does it mean to be a member of the First Peoples?" They should lead to different choices for study.

A larger variety of questions are amenable to scientific inquiry than is currently recognized in the mainstream. Psychologists can and should study the big questions about human experience and meaning making. The discipline of psychology should be more open to approaches that offer challenging ways of conceptualizing psychological phenomena. Furthermore, innovative methods can be legitimate modes of inquiry that lead to useful knowledge. And they can do so in a way that is credible—true to the object of study.

The friction between qualitative and quantitative research quickly recedes when we start to focus on the questions posed and the most credible strategies for finding answers to those questions. The pathways should be clear and direct. Researchers should carry a full compendium of methodological tools that are tailor made to particular varieties of questions.

Although psychologists often begin with a method and then design a question—we shouldn't. Pragmatically, depending on the question, we should determine the best available option. "What is important to know?" should always precede "how do I go about studying it?" Researchers should begin with their curiosity and their good sense about what questions are burning to be asked. As Yanchar and colleagues suggest, researchers should practice committed openness to innovation in their research programs: "the development of contextual and evolving theories of inquiry would need to occur within specific programs of research and be sensitive to the unique questions and challenges that arise therein" (Yanchar, Gantt, & Clay, 2005, p. 39).

Validation

A second central concern is *validation*. Here, I am following Mishler (1990), who frames "validation as the process(es) through which we make claims for and evaluate the 'trustworthiness' of reported observations, interpretations, and generalizations" (p. 419). Mishler's definition implies the critical evaluation of the whole research argument. I will focus more narrowly on the interpretation of evidence in terms of the claim. How trustworthy should we judge this interpretation of the data?

For Mishler (1990), validation is process oriented, flexible in its use, and geared toward particular arguments, including "the range of ongoing activities through which claims are made and appraised rather than on static properties of instruments and scores" (p. 419). In other words, there are "'no rules' for assessing validity" (p. 418), no one-size-fits-all prescriptions that we can follow; rather, validation is based on the specific case at hand. "Investigators, of course, follow accepted procedures in the their domains of inquiry" which "are modified by pragmatic considerations" (p. 418).

Finally, validation is ultimately a social enterprise. As Polkinghorne (1983) argues, "the acceptance of a knowledge claim finally stands within the community to whom the researcher will present his or her results for acceptance" (p. 4). For Mishler, readers deem a study as trustworthy enough to be used in their own work. It is also readers who deem the knowledge useful—a point that I return to in a moment.

Critiquing several distinct exemplars of qualitative research, Mishler (1990) arrives at a promising conception of the validation of interpretations. He offers his own work, concluding,

> The view of validation that I have advanced suggests that the questions to be asked about my study, and of any study within any research tradition, are: What are the warrants for my claims? Could other investigators make a reasonable

judgment of their adequacy? Would they be able to determine how my findings and interpretations were "produced" and, on that basis, decide whether they were trustworthy enough to be relied upon for their own work? I believe that these questions have affirmative answers. The primary reason is the visibility of the work: of the data in the form of the texts used in the analysis ... of the methods that transformed the texts into findings; and of the direct linkages shown between data, findings, and interpretation. (p. 429)

In sum, validation is based on a reasoned argument, making direct and visible interpretations, backed up by the evidence and the reception of that argument by a community of readers.

One way of enhancing the visibility, and validity, of the research argument is through the researcher's reflexive criticism of the research process (Gough & Madill, 2012). As Riessman (2015) argues, researchers should reflexively evaluate the way that social, personal, and political positions produce the data and their understanding of the data, questioning as follows:

How has the setting influenced what we, as well as what participants, can do and say? How does the setting insinuate its way into the texture of interaction? What about the resources we bring to the encounters, compared to those our participants may call on in these settings? (p. 234)

In the service of transparency, qualitative researchers sometimes employ a "double voice," as we saw in Amia Lieblich's analysis of Natasha's life story in Chapter 8, allowing readers access into the interpretive process that is driving conclusions in the research argument. But the practiced use of a "reflexive scientific attitude" could also be successfully, and fruitfully, integrated into quantitative research (Gough & Madill, 2012). For all research, "the task is to account for our situated selves in a scholarly product, thereby lending the research credibility and validity" (Riessman, 2015, p. 233).

Usefulness

Finally, *usefulness* speaks to the value or impact that others in an interpretive community attach to our research enterprise. What do the findings mean to them? How can they be productively used in understanding other questions and framing other research arguments? How insightful is the research argument judged? Of course, the most devastating question that any research argument faces is "why is this interesting?"

The notion of usefulness emphasizes the hermeneutic value of the research in the social construction of knowledge because it is always and only a community of readers who can answer the "why is this interesting" question. Research arguments, inherently, don't have more or less value, but they are given value through the esteem of one's colleagues and peers. Credibility and trustworthiness may enhance the appraised value of a research argument, but so does the perceived authority and distinction of the author. In each case, however, it is the public readers, responding to the argument, who are definitive in making a judgment about the value of the findings as knowledge.

There is no formula that could possibly measure the impact of a research argument like the ill-conceived system of advancement and prestige that scholars in the United Kingdom are currently subjected to. Although it is fanciful to think that impact can be measured quantitatively, I can't help but like the word. Research arguments have impact because scholars find them exciting, insightful, applicable, and transportable to other contexts of their choosing.

But impact does not progress in a step-by-step fashion, building knowledge one orderly step at a time. It doesn't strictly follow rational or logical rules. Here, the process is creative and, once again, hermeneutic. It is more akin to the construction of knowledge in our everyday lives. As I argued in Chapter 5, knowledge spreads because meanings resonate and are reimagined for other purposes and other domains. Knowledge is more about "what I can make of it?" than "is it true?"

IDENTITY STORIES OF PALESTINIAN STUDENTS

I want to turn from a theoretical exposition on research arguments to a concrete application. My purpose is not to give a complete and polished analysis. Rather, it is to use the ideas of credibility, validation, and usefulness in the framework of narrative research and to discuss how they could be addressed.

My research on Palestinian students with Israeli citizenship at the Hebrew University of Jerusalem is ongoing, with 24 interviews completed during 2012–2016; some of the interviews are longitudinal. An earlier group of students was interviewed in 1997–1998 (Schiff, 2002).

The project itself stems from a long-standing interest in complex identities and, specifically, my guiding research question: How do persons negotiate between multiple competing identity possibilities? This is a question that I have come back to time and again over the years in different research projects (Schiff, 2002; Schiff & O'Neill, 2007; Schiff, Toulemonde, & Porto, 2012).

Admittedly, the question is a big one. It is process oriented and concerned with the dynamics of reflecting on life in the context of developmental time, history, and culture. One of the primary contexts that I am interested in is the role of relationships in identity formation.

Although there are credible alternatives to studying a question of this kind, such as focus groups, experience-sampling method, or diary writing, I chose to study it through in-depth conversations with students individually. Indeed, as I will show, the interviews were rich and insightful into the process of negotiating complex identities.

The group of 24 students included 19 women and 5 men and both Muslims and Christians. The interview was designed as a dialogue to investigate reflections and stories about identity—who they are now and how they arrived at these self-understandings.

Although an interview guide was prepared with questions on identity, relationships, life at the university, Jerusalem, dating, and family, interviews were intended as unstructured conversations. Questions were asked naturally in the flow of the conversation. I conducted all interviews myself, in English, and each lasted about 1.5 hours.

After transcription, I used a whole-life method of analysis, in which each interview is treated as a case (Lieblich, Tuval-Mashiach, & Zilber, 1998). I attempt to understand each case on its own terms. How does this person respond to my question?

Multiple cases are compared, and different interpretations of each case are tested (Rosenwald, 1988). Although I am interested in commonalities, my primary focus, as my question suggests, is how each person negotiates his or her way between multiple possibilities. As I have argued, this also makes sense analytically, keeping the "who" in focus while considering the "where" and "when." Thus, the analytic frame keeps the person's voice intact and tries to understand, person by person, how identity is told in words.

The method is not without its problems—the first of which is my influence on the interview situation and subsequent interpretations. Strangely enough, I bring myself everywhere I go: a psychologist, a university professor, a man in his forties, an American living in Paris. My idealistic aspirations for peace, equality, and respect leak out. The interviews are in English and thus select students who can speak fluently and by consequence are more familiar with, and perhaps more friendly to, Anglophone-Western culture. The interviews took place on the Hebrew University of Jerusalem's campus, in a faculty office; in other words, I am associated in some way with the university and have professor's status. The interviews are also framed by my statements about the purpose of the conversations as a way of learning about the identities of Palestinian students. All of this context is written into the here and now of the interview situation and finds its way into the conversation and analysis.

Still, there is the problem of retrospective bias. How do I know that these stories conform to the objective reality of what actually happened to the interviewees? But, of course, this is exactly what I am interested in, the subjectively understood and presently recounted identity.

Also, there is the problem of performance. How do I know that they aren't just putting on a show? But identity is always performed in a concrete here and now.

I would argue that these conversations, longer and more extensive perhaps, are really not all that different from the conversations that people have with friends, family, or with their diary. All of this is to say that, when asking this basic question about identity formation, there is a credible argument for the fit between my question and what I did in order to study it.

What did I learn from this study? How do persons negotiate between multiple competing identity possibilities? I will offer some preliminary claims based upon the data that I have collected thus far, but similar claims can be found in Schiff (2002):

1. In my sample, students often experience a sense of "between-ness." Being between Western, Israeli, Arab, and Palestinian identities— neither one, another, or all of the above.
2. The identities of my interviewees were much more tentative, incomplete, situational, and fragmented—much less coherent than we might expect.
3. Finally, others, as remembered and recounted in talk, form the contours of identity stories, with experienced closeness or distance to others reflecting belongings to larger identities.

The claims are related. But I will focus, mostly, on the last one on recounted relationships and identity stories. Addressing the issue of validation, I hope to show the interpretive line from evidence to claim, with enough visibility such that others might find my claim reasonable. Although I am dealing with a larger claim, I am going to be more circumscribed and discuss a single interview of the 24—with Lana.

LANA'S IDENTITY STORY

Lana is originally from a Muslim village in the North, but moved to Jerusalem to study at the Hebrew University 4 years before our first meeting. As she recounts, she identifies as Palestinian and believes her experience coming to Jerusalem has clarified this identity. But coming to Jerusalem has also accentuated a sense of affinity with Israeli culture and a particular alternative subculture of Israeli youth that she, perhaps sardonically, calls "hipsters." Coming to Jerusalem has also led to increased social distance with Palestinian youth.

I will follow the thread of the interview from the opening minutes of the conversation, after framing the purpose of the interview and signing the informed consent. Lana seems to notice that I am inviting her to take the lead. She takes my invitation and jumps in and asks me:

LANA: Do you have organized questions?
BRIAN: It's a conversation, but you can jump in. How do you think about—if you would meet somebody.
LANA: This is very hard because the thing of identity has been occupying me since I got to Jerusalem. I grew up in a village in the North. Eighteen years I was only there. I did not move. I did not live like out of the village. And I didn't really think of this. My father never talked to me about identity. So at some point when I was 18, I was really furious that he never talked to me about Palestinians, Israelis, and so although he is a very patriotic person himself, he is a communist and he told me: "I knew that when you grow up, you will find the answers yourself," but it was not a very good thing that he did that because the more I knew things and the more I tried to acquire the experiences myself, it became harder and harder for me because there is no black and white in life. (. . .) Then I came to Jerusalem and I started to feel the conflict more and I became more attached to my identity as an Arab person, as a Palestinian. That was on the national level. But on the social level I found that I might be an outcast for behaviors that I have, for, I don't know, ways of life that are not really norms in the Arab lives.

Lana says that she had no preparation from her family for thinking about her political identity, which, she alludes, may contribute to the state of crisis that she finds herself in right now.

Coming to Jerusalem, Lana becomes more attached to a Palestinian identity, which she calls her "national" identity in contrast to her "social" identity that is outside the accepted "norms in Arab lives." However, the division is too simple to describe her. For Lana, there is no clean separation between the national and the social. She feels an "outcast" from Arab society, yet doesn't fit completely into the Israeli Jewish world.

Lana continues and elaborates on what she means by "outcast":

> I should have also mentioned that I don't have friends from my village. And even in high school I usually tried just to shut up when we were having discussions about all kinds of stuff because I knew that there would be a mark on me if I opened my mouth and said my honest opinion. (. . .) I remember once I was in 11th grade and I said that I have no problem to go home and to get a ride from a male mate of mine in his car. And someone said, "We are not living in Europe." And that was like the last time I. Since then I said. That's it. I just have to keep my mouth shut.

On this occasion and others, Lana states that she doesn't have friends in the village. In the preceding quote, Lana highlights her distance from the people in the village—even before the university. It is a strange position, to belong to a group that you don't feel like you belong in—an outcast, in which heartfelt opinions and expressions are silenced.

The turmoil in her identity has been intensifying. The transcript continues:

> And I have been living in Jerusalem for 4 years. And I went through a lot of conflicts with myself as well regarding my identity, with the people I should hang out with. And again it's becoming harder and harder each year because. (. . .) I don't know. There is some, how do you say this? I'm kind of torn between the two. I have Jewish friends and I have Arab friends. I have more Jewish friends than I have Arab friends. And sometimes it's just on the surface that with Arab friends it's easier for me to express myself language-wise, you know, same slang, same things we grew up on. But with my Jewish friends I'm more comfortable with. I don't know, drinking alcohol, smoking. It's more. If I'm hanging out with Jewish friends and I'm drinking, I'm not concerned about whether someone is going to say a word about me. But when it comes to Arabs. They are not really friends, you know, Arab people that I hang out with sometimes. It concerns me, but it is still there. And sometimes my Israeli friends make me feel that there are no blocks, there are no barriers between us, but sometimes it's still there on some levels.

In this passage and others, Lana describes a superficial closeness with Arabs. She describes a feeling of being criticized by Arab students for behaviors that come with her alternative lifestyle (smoking, drinking, dress, free thinking) that Lana considers not only normal but an authentic part of herself. Interestingly, there is a problem of authenticity; as she says, Arabs are not "really" friends. She expresses a deeper and more natural, but incomplete, intimacy with Jewish friends.

In reference to Lana's words "blocks" or "barriers" in the previous quote, I ask, "What is still there?" She responds:

> Here is a very first story. I dated a guy from December to February, I think, but he was an extremely left-wing person, you know, a socialist and all this shit. And at some point during the relationship it just came to me that it's all only because it's cool to have an Arab girlfriend. I broke up with him in February, but since then I still have the scar (. . .) So I can't tell you that I feel I 100% belong when I'm with, I don't know, Israeli people, Israeli places. But with Arab people it's also difficult because I know that I'm not really accepted.

Lana often feels "in between" and is searching for an authentic sense of who she really is, what she believes in, her place in the world. The relational world plays a key role in her self-construction. Lana feels closer to Jews than to Arabs. She shares with them attitudes toward life, parents, the world, dress. Indeed, on the day that we met, Lana was wearing headphones, stylish jean shorts, and an open top exposing her shoulders.

But Lana doesn't feel that she belongs "100%." There are experiences in her relationships with Israeli Jews that hold her back from full belonging and assimilating. She labels them "blocks" or "barriers." For instance, she breaks up with her boyfriend because she realizes that "it's all only because it's cool to have an Arab girlfriend."

Lana is concerned about not being loved for who she really is as a person—being treated as a kind or type of person, a stereotype. In other words, she doesn't really belong. She believes that her ex-boyfriend's motives were inauthentic.

Because Lana's relationship with Israeli Jews is so close and she is able to blend so seamlessly, the barriers are subtle. Later in the interview, she says:

> LANA: When I hang out with people that I love these people, but I'm aware also of the fact that they were in the army. And it also tears me from the inside because this, I don't know, this lovely girl that I'm hanging out with. She used to be on. I don't know. A check

point or something. Tormented. I may not be aware to this, but she maybe she tormented some. I don't know, some people that I belong with. And it's not about my national definition because I know what my definition is. . . . But these daily experiences, this tiny stuff.

BRIAN: Does it come up though conversation? Is it something that you know?

LANA: Sometimes we talk about it as a cultural thing, like they say, "When we were in the army, we used to blah blah blah." Like nicknames they had or, I don't know, people started smoking in the army or gained weight in the army. And I don't really stick on that because I know it's a part of their lives and I just go on. But still at the end of the day I think of it and I say. Fuck! First of all, I wasn't there. We don't really share these life experiences. And second they were in a system that I loathe, it's a system that I really object to and not only because it's Israeli, I think all armies should be just destroyed, no matter where . . . I mean sometimes they also share jokes about the army and I laugh and everything and then between me and myself I think that. But on the other hand these people accept me better than (Arabs).

With all the complexities of her identity, the question is, can Lana authentically be her true self? Lana doesn't feel like she belongs completely to any world. There is always something holding her back.

For the most part, Lana feels comfortable with her free-thinking, leftist Jewish friends and a desire to be part of their world. But there are barriers.

On the Palestinian side, Lana feels distant from Arab youth at the university. She doesn't hang out with them and questions their motives in their own roles/identities, even Arab hipsters. She comments, "Each of them is going to head back to his village, get married with a girl his mother picked for him." Their commitment to the free-spirited lifestyle of a "hipster" is only temporary and artificial. They are only putting on a show.

She has fashioned what I think of as a "Jerusalem" identity, which is largely associated with the hipster lifestyle and mostly in the company of Israeli Jews. But it is difficult for Lana to maintain this Jerusalem identity in all situations—especially with her family. It is difficult to maintain who she is in Jerusalem when she is back in the village, back with her family.

This lack of consistency has emotional costs. Her mother calls her a "free spirit" and laments having a daughter like her. She knows that her parents are "not really satisfied with the way I choose to live my life." She thinks they know about her drinking and smoking, but there is much more about her life that they don't know. They don't know the extent of her relationships with Israeli Jews. They don't know that she has had Jewish boyfriends or that she works as a waitress in the city center. It "breaks [her] heart" that she can't interact openly with her parents, like her Jewish friends do.

She tells one revealing story about getting her nose pierced and why she removed her nose ring.

> Two months ago I had a piercing here. And it was only for one month because then I went home and it was a Holocaust when they saw the piercing. And my father just told me, "There are things that are not acceptable. In Jerusalem do whatever you want as long as it does not affect us. I never ask you what you do there. But if you are coming to visit or to live or whatever, you will have to respect this place and the rules of this place." And I tried to defend myself and I said that I feel that this year I have become more aware of things that I'm growing up and I'm studying more. So he said, "I know, I know all of this. But still there are things that aren't acceptable."

The use of the word "Holocaust" is shocking. I don't read the word as making a political statement but as attempting to describe the intensity of her parents' reaction. Although she does her best to keep the world of Jerusalem and the world of the village separate, they do intrude on each other. Indeed, Lana's Jerusalem identity is not as free as it seems, but is anchored, if only partially, by the village and her relationship with her family.

I have presented ample quotes and rich descriptions that make clear the claims about how Palestinian students at the Hebrew University negotiate multiple possible identities (at least in the life story of Lana): (1) students often experience a sense of "between-ness," (2) identity stories were more tentative and less coherent than we might expect, and (3) relationships shape the plot line of identity stories.

As Lana's interview shows, she describes how social relationships tether persons to identities. At least, persons make their collective belonging cohere with their current relationships. Lana's incomplete closeness to Israeli Jewish youth and distance from Arabs entails a feeling of being "in between" Palestinian and Israeli worlds. Although Lana clearly is Palestinian, she is becoming more "normalized" (her word) into mainstream Israeli culture. Her assimilation is checked by subtle perceived rebukes by Israeli Jews, which seem to erect barriers to full belonging. Also, her relationship with her parents appears to provide a kind of anchor. Indeed, it is hard to imagine Lana giving up her Palestinian identity without completely giving up her parents.

Of course, we would want more than a single case. But such larger pictures of psychological processes can be fruitfully built from the ground up by looking at one person at a time. What I hope that I have shown is that, although we are always interpreting interpretations, there are ways of moving forward that are both credible and trustworthy—even in those methods considered the *most* interpretive. Qualitative—like quantitative—research must make a convincing research argument. And convincing arguments are always closely tied to what has been observed, the evidence, providing a check on the applicability and validity of interpretive assertions.

Does the interpretation fit the evidence? The job of the interpreter is to make these descriptions and connections explicit and visible, and the job of the reader is to evaluate their trustworthiness. In the end, that is what we are left with: the trust that the reader places in the credibility and validity of claims.

A couple of words on the concept of usefulness in my analysis of Lana's interview: Although it is not the job of the author of a research argument to determine the usefulness of a study, I can make several suggestions about how this research *could be* valuable for other researchers. First, quantitative studies of Palestinian identity often measure identity labels, allowing participants to choose one, or more, of a variety of labels, and study the percentage of the population that endorses one label or another. Smooha (1999, 2005) has studied identity labels in the Arab population in Israel since the 1970s. Smooha has been able to document a change in identity preferences over this long period of time. Historically, the Arabs living inside the borders of Israel proper, inside the "green line," were more likely to self-identity as Arab, Israeli, or Arab-Israeli, but in recent years, the trend has been toward identities that include "Israel" as a part of the definition. For instance, in a 2004 nationwide representative sample, 45% of those surveyed chose a label that included some variation of "Palestinian" and "Israeli," such as "Palestinian Arab in Israel," while only 8.6% chose simply "Palestinian" (Smooha, 2005). Smooha (1999, 2005) interprets this change as an increasing "Israelization" of the Arab population. Using large samples across the population, merely documenting such a change is fascinating. But what does it mean? Based upon his own surveys with youth, Rouhana (1997) argues that the label "Palestinian in Israel" denotes an increasing separation between the Palestinian national identity and the Israeli civic identity. As my presentation of Lana's life story showed, percentages of identity labels across populations cannot capture the complexity of what belonging or not belonging means. The identity label approach exaggerates the ability to be just one thing, all the time, in every situation—even if we can check more than one box, the assumption is that we are all of those categories at once. It also assumes that we know what that label means to the person. I believe that my research is useful because it shows the ways in which identity labels are insufficient to describe how persons actually think about their identity. Persons can have a multiplicity of conflicting interests and belongings, which complicate any easy categorization. Furthermore, as the case of Lana shows, such identifications are often situational, geographic, and partial.

Still, readers may find my discussion of Lana as useful for thinking about narrative identity or relational theory—or, better still, as a model for doing narrative analysis and arguing for credibility and validation in their own analyses.

Now that I have made my argument, the question isn't so much, "do I find my research claim useful?" but rather, "do you?" How translatable is it to your thinking? Is it valuable? These are the questions that you, the reader, now need to decide.

But, of course, the question of usefulness is not answered by a single reader. Research arguments are read by communities of readers, such as groups of scholars or students in a class, and are processed together. After we become practiced members of a community of readers, we have internalized the voices of others and can also anticipate what their various positions will likely be, even when they are not directly present. Still, we find arguments through other arguments, which reference and support or refute the original argument. In other words, we hear from others that this is an argument that we need to pay attention to (or not), and we do (or don't).

NARRATIVE SCIENCE

As I have argued, narrative analysis is a pragmatic activity of asking questions about the data, developing provisional responses, and then making an argument, which is tied to the data itself. Although there are no steadfast rules about how narrative research should proceed, there are better and worse research arguments. I don't like the label "best practices" in narrative analysis because the formulation sounds too sure of itself and limiting. I can well imagine new and innovative approaches to narrative that add to or challenge the idea of "best practices."

Still, because I am advocating for a wider engagement with the discipline of psychology to reorient narrative from the margins to the center of the discipline, some precision in terms is necessary. As a basis for a narrative perspective in psychology, we need some explicit sense of what determines adequate research. So, what are the rules of the game? What should we look for in distinguishing high quality from poor research? What are the tools for criticizing narrative research?

I think that Gergen (2014) is on the right track in arguing for "highly general criteria, minimally specifying the kinds of activities honored within the broad spectrum of qualitative inquiry" (p. 57). Although credibility, validation, and usefulness include, but extend beyond, narrative or qualitative research, they also provide some of the terms for engaging and criticizing the quality of narrative research:

1. Credible interpretations make clear, visible, and explicit connections between question and method of study and between data and theory.
2. Trustworthy interpretations are validated with the conscientious and meticulous use of rich data that demonstrate for the reader how the phenomenon under discussion is apparent in the data itself, in other words, between what was said (and how) and our argument for why. Data should be able to demonstrate, in detail, whatever interpretation we are trying to make.
3. As best as possible, researchers should practice a *"reflexive scientific attitude"* (Gough & Madill, 2012) through the constant questioning of themselves, their methods of study, and the data itself and to make these observations, when appropriate, visible in their analysis.
4. And, specific to narrative research, adequate interpretations of narrative data are able to account for at least the basic elements for understanding interpretive actions of who, where, and when. What does this expression mean in terms of the life of this person in space and time?

Certainly, every domain of research has its own problems and questions that it deems pertinent, as well as specific definitions of what constitutes reasons or evidence. Disciplines and subdisciplines also have their unique style, genre, language, and conventions, which, skillfully employed, can enhance the prestige and value of scholarship. Despite these differences, research boils down to how well researchers have supported their claim with reasons and evidence. This is true for all varieties of psychological research, narrative and otherwise. At the very least, such general criteria should help us in critiquing the merits of research arguments.

The most frequent argument against narrative psychology does not question the value of a close understanding of persons or the usefulness of attention to the dynamics of psychological processes. Rather, most critiques challenge narrative psychology's status as science. In psychology, narrativists are considered closer to literary theorists and philosophers, whose research may be interesting but, according to this perspective, should not be conceived as scientific and should not be accorded the same status within the canon of scientific psychology. Such arguments are typically made verbally, after a talk is given or a paper is read, and are rarely put into print. Perhaps the narrative perspective is still too marginal in psychology to merit the effort that it would take to mount a sustained critique.

True enough, narrative research does not conform to mainstream research practices, which require quantified data that are statistically analyzed, typically, within a hypothesis-testing framework but entail posing questions from rich data and building inductive theories on the basis of observations. However, I would like to argue that narrative research is science—or, better, that it can be scientific. Science is central to what we do. But the problem is that the definition of what counts as scientific psychology is far too narrow. Kvale (1994) argues:

> Neither textbooks on social science methodology nor dictionaries of the English language provide any unequivocal and generally accepted definition of science. It is thus difficult to unequivocally characterize qualitative research as scientific or unscientific. . . . The characterization of qualitative research as scientific or unscientific will then depend upon which definition of science is used. (p. 150)

We need to ask, what do we mean by "science"?

Contemporary psychology's formula for producing scientific results is, by and large, based upon the adoption of a particular method that requires a variable-centered model. But quantification alone does not produce a science. It doesn't make the practice unscientific either. Depending on the question and the variety of knowledge that we seek, this formula could produce results that we would consider credible, trustworthy, and useful. But reductionism is not the *sine qua non* of science. More than anything, the formula is neutral. It is a way of seeing the world, which is useful for answering certain kinds of questions.

Reductionism is not the "scientific method." The term "scientific method," if anything, is open to numerous significances. As Slife and Williams (1995) point out, "[t]here is no such thing as *the* scientific method. There are as many scientific methods as there are scientists doing research" (p. 169). Even in the natural sciences, there is more than one scientific method. As Feyerabend (1976) has argued, the advancement of knowledge requires an opening up, not a closing off, of the scientific method and must include novel frameworks. Still, Slife and Williams (1995) continue, "[t]here are, however, some commonalities among scientists in the sort of methods they use, so it is possible to study their methods and talk about what qualifies as science" (p. 169).

What is common, or should be common, is a commitment to observing, describing, and understanding phenomena and, perhaps above all, a commitment to a resolutely critical stance of the entire enterprise and of knowledge itself. As Polkinghorne (1983) points out, the etymological roots of "the word method is thus 'a going after' or 'a pursuit.' In the case of science, it is a pursuit of knowledge" (p. 4). Science is more rightly conceived as an attitude than a specific method, an orientation toward the project of knowing, where researchers pose questions about features of the world in order to make phenomena visible and accessible to insight and understanding. As Slife and Williams (1995), correctly, and simply, put it, "[s]cience might best be understood as a language with which or through which people try to understand the world" (p. 195).

What makes research scientific is not the choice of method, or the measures, but the specific attitude toward inquiry. A scientific attitude requires a deliberate approach to describing the world and discovering something beyond my personal, and admittedly narrow, conception that can be agreed upon by like-minded others engaged in related pursuits. The toolkit is flexible and pragmatic, open to the contingencies of what we would like to know. "Going after" knowledge sometimes requires logical construction or deconstruction and sometimes empirical observation, gathering more information, and it sometimes requires quantification and sometimes the qualitative exploration of meaning—it depends. But, in each and every case, the scientific attitude is skeptical, critical, and attempts to recognize the limits of its own capacity to reveal the world. Such a definition of science is open to multiple methods and perspectives.

By its very nature, the narrative perspective does not follow the rules of reductionism. We are not interested in producing a numeric formula that will help us to predict human behavior. Rather, the result is a description, itself to be formulated in everyday language, that aspires to better understand fundamental psychological problems of how persons interpret themselves, the world, and others. To reach a fuller understanding of human psychology, we must uncover the dynamic connections that motivate interpretations. It is not enough for psychologists to know that this variable is related to these other variables and under what conditions. The fundamental problem of how persons interpret experience cannot be seriously approached using variable-centered methods. In order to get to this level of detail, we need to observe interpretive actions, to carefully listen to others and let them tell us about their experiences, memories, and reflections. We need to get to know the other up close and in detail. And, to do so, research-ers need to pay attention to what persons say and do.

Critics argue that narrative is too subjective to be scientific. Researchers inevitably use their knowledge and life experience to make interpretations. It is true that narrative research relies on the researcher's skillful inter-pretation of evidence. However, this criticism is equally applicable to all research, qualitative and quantitative alike. But, it is a charge that is often aimed at narrative research. Although it is impossible to put aside preju-dice in order to get the one or true story—if there even is one—narrative emphasizes investigation of the other's perspective and world, not the researcher's.

Of course the method is imperfect. Narrative methods are subjective. And it is impossible to truly know another person's mind, or even our own for that matter. But what I hope that I have shown is that, although sub-jectivity is always present, narrative research is not subject to the whims of the researcher. In other words, narrative research is a reasonable pursuit. Interpretation is never free from the constraints of reality or evidence. I have put the notion of "data" in the center of the research arguments as the reference point in all interpretations. Arguments are always closely tied to what has been observed in the data itself, providing a check on the applicability and validity of theoretical assertions. Does the theory fit with the data? The job of the interpreter is to make these descriptions and con-nections explicit and accessible in the research argument.

A narrative approach allows researchers to make scientific observations and construct theories about these fundamental problems. Imperfect as our tools are, they are the best that we have. Given that our objective is to understand human beings, they are, perhaps, the best tools that we can hope for.

Conclusion

Unity in Psychology?

This book is about narrative in two senses: it concerns both narrative *in* psychology and the narrative *of* psychology. Of course, the two are interrelated. In my view, narrative *in* psychology substantially transforms the narrative *of* psychology. We wind up with a different discipline at the end—a psychology that is more descriptive, more sensitive, and better attuned to understanding the focal problems of human lives.

I have argued that a fundamental part of the human project, and a proper focus of scientific psychology, is the project of meaning making. As Charles Taylor (1985) put it:

> We can say that the human animal not only finds himself impelled from time to time to interpret himself and his goals, but that he is always already in some interpretation, *constituted as human by this fact*. To be human is to be already engaged in living an answer to the question, an interpretation of oneself and one's aspirations. (p. 75, my italics)

Psychology must be able to come to terms with the fact that from the very first moments of our life, and even before we are born, we are always already concerned with figuring out what things mean, what life is all about. We try to figure out: Where am I? What is this world? Who are you? What is an I? Who am I? How are we related? Where do I end and you begin? What do you want from me? What's going on here? What is my place in life? And the work is never finished. Even provisional answers just lead to more and more questions.

Substantially, figuring out what it all means, what life is all about, necessitates engaging with narrative. The activity of narrating is the central way that persons involve themselves in the project of meaning making and come to know something like a self, a world, others. The challenge for narrative psychology is to describe this process of engagement, how narrative works to create meanings, how an understanding of narrative interpretation can help us to better describe the complex and problematic lives that we lead, and how narrative can help us to address the basic problems of psychological and social being, health and distress, peace and conflict. This is the work that is in front of us. It is critical work concerned with the fundamental problems of human psychology. The challenge is enormous.

Narrative is an integral part of psychology's story. This is the argument of the book. In this concluding chapter, I want to ask, if we accept that narrative is a central problem for the discipline, where do such ideas fit in the discipline as a whole? How does narrative relate to other aspects of psychology? What does this do to psychology? What does psychology become?

NARRATIVE, QUALITATIVE, OR MIXED?

I have argued that it is impossible to neatly separate theory and method, but rather theory and method nurture, define, and configure one another. Methods, themselves, are theoretical stances that harbor assumptions about the world, framing observations and leading to theory development and refinement. In essence, we choose to examine how persons talk about themselves and the world because we already assume that some process or action is happening there, in interpretive activity, that we need to pay attention to. Something important is going on here—so, listen carefully.

The analytic approach that I developed treats interpretive actions qualitatively. In other words, we are interested in observing, with trained sensitivity, and describing, in detail, the "whats" and "hows" of meaning making in order to understand the "whys." From a bird's-eye view, I positioned the narrative perspective on the qualitative side of the so-called quantitative-qualitative divide. And, in my view, narrative psychology shares a great deal with critical qualitative approaches such as action research, discursive psychology, and phenomenological psychology.

But, of course, life is never so black and white as to permit such easy distinctions. Qualitative and quantitative break down upon closer examination, and the celebrated wall between qualitative and quantitative data turns out to be a rather porous membrane. So-called qualitative data can be easily transformed into quantitative data. Interviews can be coded, even for themes, and assigned the simplest of numbers, for instance, a dummy variable (0 or 1) that denotes the presence or absence of a theme and then can be submitted to statistical analysis in the same manner as other variables from survey or experimental data. This is the strategy of content analysis in the social sciences, but also language-based approaches to narrative (Campbell & Pennebaker, 2003; László, 2008; Pennebaker & Seagal, 1999). We can quantify qualitative data. Likewise, so-called quantitative data can be treated qualitatively, for instance, looking for patterns of meaning in the answers of self-report questions. Aided by weighting items across a large number of numerical responses, this is the strategy of factor analytic techniques in personality research. We can give a qualitative reading to quantitative data. When purely considering method, qualitative and quantitative are not wholly distinct, but blend into one another.

There are no perfect data, no perfect concepts, and no perfect methods to study those concepts; every attempt to investigate the world is, by definition, incomplete and inadequate. Certainly, there are better and worse approaches and, as Campbell and Fiske (1959) argued, when we compare variables, measured differently, but assessing the same theoretical construct, with each other and with additional variables measuring other concepts, we can begin to understand how well our constructs validly stack up against one another. The spirit behind Campbell and Fiske's multi-trait multi-method model isn't merely that more is better. Rather, thoughtful and conscientious use of multiple methods is helpful in establishing a validity argument.

In Campbell and Fiske's model, the methods were variable-centered, quantitative, but clearly their intention was to bring concepts and methods into conversation with one another. In qualitative inquiry there is also a rich tradition of research that draws upon multiple qualitative methods in the same research study: triangulation (Denzin, 2010). There is continuity between Campbell and Fiske's comparative approach, which calls into question the accuracy and validity of any particular measure, and qualitative approaches triangulating interpretations to research questions and a movement in the social sciences toward "mixed methods." Personally, I have a lot of sympathy for the *methodological eclecticism* advocated by mixed-method proponents (Teddlie & Tashakkori, 2010), where questions take precedence over any particular method.

However, in prioritizing method, are we merely raising yet another methodolotry? Rather than just a quantitative approach, from the perspective of mixed methods, now we are encouraged to combine research traditions, as an ideal for research, in the same research argument. Although Teddlie and Tashakkori (2010) make it clear that "[t]he best method for any given study in the human sciences may be purely QUAL or purely QUAN, rather than mixed" (p. 9), there is a parallel between the old view, which said you must use only one method, quantitative and reductive, and the mixed-methods view, which says you should use both qualitative and quantitative methods. Although a mixed-methods eclecticism is preferable to dogmatic reductionism, and there are many good reasons for selecting mixed qualitative and quantitative approaches to the same research question, mixed methods are no guarantee to a better understanding of the phenomenon. There is no assurance that using both qualitative and quantitative methods will lead to any more insight than using only one.

However, there is common ground between mixed methods and narrative psychology. Both argue that there is more than one credible approach to psychological knowledge and that we need to be more critical and more reflexive about our choices of study in line with what we want to know about the world and can reasonably argue. In this way, both argue against the methodological straightjacket imposed upon contemporary psychology, which says that there is only one way of studying psychology, only one legitimate scientific method.

Where we differ is on the need for theory to direct our investigation. Mixed methods argue that research can be theory-free or theory-neutral. One of the key debates in the literature on mixed methods is on the search for a guiding ontology, often pointing to philosophical pragmatism (Biesta, 2010; Johnson & Onwuegbuzie, 2004; Johnson, Onwuegbuzie, & Turner, 2007). Although there's nothing wrong with pragmatism, ontology is not an add-on to methods. Investigations begin with theoretical assumptions about a particular phenomenon, which should be clear to the researcher. Indeed, in order to make a credible argument, there should be a clear line between our understanding of the problem and how we go about our inquiry. "What are the reasons for doing mixed methods research?" is a question that can only be answered on the basis of some theory about the phenomenon.

Choosing to work from a narrative perspective represents an option, among others, and should be based upon an informed and deliberate decision to study the process of making meaning and to approach fundamental questions about interpretation in human lives. I believe that I have convincingly argued for a reasonable alternative to doing psychology, which is attuned to how persons, in context, make sense.

Still, a narrative perspective isn't *just* another qualitative method to be placed alongside other qualitative methods of data collection (such as narrative interviewing or ethnography) or data analysis (such as grounded theory or discourse analysis). It is a way of thinking about psychology, coherent in its aims and practices, that holds the following assumptions:

1. Persons are active in the process of trying to make sense of themselves, others, and the world;
2. Persons and their interpretive actions are grounded in relational, cultural, historical, and developmental contexts;
3. Within these contexts, interpretive actions have a variety of functions, and they serve the purpose of making meaning.

The method of narrative analysis that I developed in previous chapters, interpreting interpretations hermeneutically and formulating sound arguments on the basis of this investigation, is well suited to the theoretical investigation of how and why persons make self and make life.

Throughout this book, I have self-consciously used the expression "the narrative perspective" because this new psychology argues for a revised ontological and epistemological foundation. Its basic problems are those of meaning making and consequently interpretation and narrative. Its methodology is the comparative study of lives. Its goal is the descriptive and theoretical project of understanding how persons make sense of themselves, others, and the world in time and space. Certainly, narrative concepts can be studied in other ways. There are no intellectual copyrights to the term "narrative"—nor should there be. But examining the fundamental psychological problem of human meaning making, in all of its complexity, requires a theoretically informed narrative perspective that is able to descriptively grapple with the phenomenon at hand.

SYNTHETIC PSYCHOLOGY

Psychology commonly defines itself around the core ideas of science, thought, and action (or some variant thereof, such as the science of mind, cognition, and behavior). The definition is exceedingly broad and is construed in numerous ways. At the current moment, the discipline is segmented into various groupings. The American Psychological Association (APA) boasts 54 "Divisions." In 1988, scientifically oriented psychologists split off entirely from the APA to form a new organization, the Association for Psychological Science (APS), formerly the American Psychological Society (Association for Psychological Science, n.d.). Although these interest groups converse across the divisions, psychology does have distinct factions that act, in many ways, like small disciplines in their own right. They have their own operating assumptions, theories, languages, preferred questions, and legitimate methods of study. The list changes, but the groupings are often referred to as perspectives or points of view, rather than paradigms, in apparent deference to Kuhn's distinction between the mature natural sciences, which possess shared paradigms, and the immature social sciences, which are pre-paradigmatic. The list of perspectives goes something like this: biological, behaviorist/social learning, cognitive, evolutionary, social, cultural, trait, psychoanalytic. I could continue, and others would give a different list, but that's not the critical point.

Curiously, the discipline has taken to heart only one small part of Kuhn's (1962/1970) highly influential *The Structure of Scientific Revolutions*. Since the publication of Kuhn's book, over 50 years ago, psychologists have lamented the status Kuhn gives to the social sciences as pre-paradigmatic, while at the same time virtually ignoring Kuhn's larger critique of scientific knowledge as a social enterprise in which communities configure the facts of observation and discovery (Driver-Linn, 2003). Indeed, Kuhn is often regarded as a critical voice in unseating the logical positivist view on science as the rational, and steady, uncovering of verifiable facts about the world.

On the face of it, these differences are not inherently problematic. "Fragmentation" could be understood as "multiplicity," "pluralism," "hybridity," or just "difference," which all have a positive valence, emphasizing the value of more than one point of view (Kirschner, 2006). We might also view the process of exchange and debate, or even critique and conflict, as essential signs of the health and growth of a discipline.

However, some psychologists argue that the discipline is split apart by incommensurable ontological and epistemological differences, and that this fragmentation represents a loss of valuable resources, is unproductive in building a coherent body of knowledge, and will lead to the dissolution or division of the discipline (Gardner, 2005). An entire literature on fragmentation and unity has taken shape, mostly in the past 20 years, after the split between the APA and the APS, with various positions on the need for unity and proposals for unifying psychology. But, as Yanchar and Slife (1997) pointed out, there isn't even any unity on the value of unity or solutions for unifying psychology.

In a sense, psychology has always been fragmented. This is nothing new. From the very beginning, the discipline was an agglomeration of various philosophical groupings, experimentalists, and practitioners, uneasily mixed together as recently minted psychologists.

But, at the current moment, fragmentation is taken to be a problem that calls into question the discipline itself. How can psychology call itself a science if it does not have a unified theoretical and methodological basis? How can it be a science when subject matter, questions, and terminologies are unique to particular communities of psychologists? And when sharing and accumulating scientific knowledge are questionable?

These are hard questions. But framing the problem as one between unity and fragmentation does imply a particular spin on the ultimate goals and purpose of a scientific psychology. In previous chapters, I offered a pragmatic account of psychological science as the deliberate activity of going after knowledge and framing knowledge claims in the form of a reasonable argument. But, of course, that is not the only way of conceptualizing science. Another, more expansive, vision—that of logical positivism—understands the purpose of scientific inquiry as uncovering the universal logic and laws about the nature of the universe and, as part of that universe, mind and action. Although even once committed logical positivists have long since declared its death (Meehl, 1985), this is hardly the case. The ideas are so ingrained and so pervasive that they are barely noticed.

Fragmentation is problematic, only or perhaps mostly, from the perspective of logical positivism, where the goal is for enduring, and objectively true, explanatory systems for all times and places, most commonly referred to as the discovery of "covering laws" (Hempel, 1962). The notion that different takes on psychological reality are possible, and even desirable, calls the premise of "one science" and "one psychology" into question.

Indeed, unity contains these hidden theoretical implications. It implies a philosophy of science intent on generalizations of what is universally true about all human beings, or an admonition that psychology should steadfastly be moving in that direction. As inspiring as the dream is, we should be skeptical of the premature conclusions and boundaries imposed upon what can rightly be called psychological science.

Unity implies a firm belief in the unity of knowledge and that through investigation we can disclose the eternal hidden truths, or laws, about the world, from the natural world to the social and cultural world. Biologist Edward O. Wilson (1998) gives clear voice to the idea of scientific unity in his influential program of consilience, which seeks to synthesize scientific knowledge "across the great branches of learning" (p. 7). He asks, "Given that human action comprises events of physical causation, why should the social sciences and humanities be impervious to concilience with the natural sciences?" (p. 9). For Wilson, consilience is "not yet science" but it is a belief system, a metaphysics:

> Science offers the boldest metaphysics of the age. It is a thoroughly human construct, driven by the faith that if we dream, press to discover, explain, and dream again, thereby plunging repeatedly into new terrain, the world will somehow come clearer and we will grasp the true strangeness of the universe. And the strangeness will all prove to be connected and make sense. (pp. 10–11)

Does science require us to believe in the one, universal, all-encompassing, version of truth or knowledge? Does it require our faith in such a metaphysics? From my point of view, it is a strange, but revealing, juxtaposition to consider science as metaphysics. As Kirschner (2006) points out, the search for the one true science bears some striking resemblances with the belief in the one true god. Unification has some affinities with intellectual monotheism in which *belief* is a principal operator.

In psychology, various propositions have been made for a unified psychology. Some, such as Henriques and Rychlak, for example, attempt to map out the overarching conceptual topography of psychology and to make some suggestions about the relationship between the various elements.

Henriques (2008) rejects Wilson's metaphysical assumptions and Wilson's more extreme positions about the ability of theories and methods of the physical and natural sciences to cannibalize other disciplines, such as psychology, but simultaneously endorses Wilson's overall goals and spirit of integration. Henriques' conceptualization of psychology includes four fundamental levels of complexity (matter, life, mind, and culture) and their corresponding classes of objects, domains of existence, theoretical perspectives, and so on. The Tree of Knowledge system, or the ToK, as Henriques (2004, 2008, 2013) likes to call it, attempts to connect together levels of analysis in psychology and show how they are related by various "joint points" from one level of analysis to the next—in other words, how life emerges from matter, mind from life, and culture from mind. Henriques (2004) takes as his model "the modern synthesis" in biology, "the theoretical merger of Darwin's theory of natural selection and genetics" as "the clearest example of a joint point ... because it provides the framework for understanding how complex, self-replicating organic molecules were ultimately transformed into organisms" (p. 1209). For Henriques, in psychology, the joint points are Skinnerian behaviorism (mind from life), which he labels behavioral investment theory (BIT), and

Freudian psychoanalysis (culture from mind), which he labels the justification hypothesis.

Rychlak (1993) focuses on the theoretical groundings for psychological explanations, which he sees as diverse, but complementary. He describes four separate theoretical grounds, or "assumptive frameworks," that guide psychological thinking. According to Rychlak, we can, alternatively, view psychological processes as (1) *physikos*, grounding psychological explanations in the terms of inanimate material processes; (2) *bios*, also grounding explanations in physical processes, but animate ones, such as genetics and organic systems; (3) *socius*, grounding explanations in social groups, culture, and history; or (4) *logos*, grounding at the level of thinking and the "cognitive organizations that we call meaning" (p. 937).

Rychlak argues that all four are legitimate in their own right as explanations of psychological processes. The four assumptive frameworks are not necessarily, reducible to one another—*bios* cannot subsume *socius*—nor should one framework be privileged over another. In a sense, Rychlak's contribution to the debate on unity is to propose non-reducible, non-consilient, theoretical positions, while calling on psychologists to recognize the value of explanatory systems other than their own. "We should not hit each other over the head with such biases during the everyday efforts we put into building a scientific discipline. . . . We unify through an appreciation of the complementary diversity of our groundings" (Rychlak, 1993, p. 939). Rychlak makes room for diverse psychological explanations, such as theories of meaning, but not for methods—all psychological research should be tested by the same scientific, in other words, reductionist, methods of study.

Proposals such as those of Henriques and Rychlak do provide the terms for an overarching theoretical topography for psychology, but they do not provide the terms for integration at the conceptual level. They would leave psychology as separate discourse communities, each working on their distinct piece of the problem, connected through joint points (Henriques) or respectful complementarity (Rychlak).

Other approaches are concerned with integration on the local, conceptual level, in order to set the stage for a more comprehensive unity to emerge. According to Staats (2004, 2005), there is a great deal of redundancy and imprecision in the system, which has a structural incentive for novelty; in order to enhance their distinctive contributions, psychologists are constantly producing new concepts and new theories. Staats argues for a "unified positivism" that seeks to find commonalities across perspectives and research traditions. Psychologists should specify in clear terms the language and concepts used across the discipline in order to develop a commonly accepted terminology. As Staats (2005) argues, the terminology in other sciences, such as physics, is very precise,: "A quark is a quark is a quark." But "[t]he existence of a large number of redundant terms in psychology within the many different and usually competitive theory languages is a huge handicap" (p. 171). Likewise, for theory, "there is no systematic attempt to interrelate various theories" (p. 171). For Staats, the disciplinary structure of incentives needs to change in order to value the difficult work of bridging concepts and theories.

Sternberg and colleagues (Sternberg & Grigorenko, 2001, 2005) offer another solution to fragmentation, which they call "unified psychology," asking psychologists to coordinate their inquiry around phenomena of interest, rather than remaining committed to vested theoretical or methodological interests. In other words, psychologists should be generalists, not encamped in a particular perspective, but in an approach that they call "converging operations," recognizing that "any one operation is, in all likelihood, inadequate for the comprehensive study of any psychological phenomenon" (Sternberg & Grigorenko, 2001, p. 1071). Like mixed methods, converging operations advocates multiple approaches, but pools together research efforts on the same phenomenon from different studies into a constructive dialogue in order to lead to a more complex and multifaceted understanding of the phenomenon itself.

But is developing into one disciplinary psychology, united at least by some transversal theory, and perhaps a reductionist methodology, as most of the literature presupposes, even a desirable goal? Proposals to increase dialogue in the field, such as those by Henriques, Rychlak, Sternberg, and others, and to translate concepts and theories, such as that of Staats, make good common sense. And, although I have argued forcefully against variable-centered reductionism as the one and only methodological choice for exploring human psychology, I strongly believe in the value of dialogue between points of view in order to strive for more comprehensive, synthetic, theories about human beings. As psychologists, we should pay attention to what our colleagues have to say and try to see the value, and logic, in their theories and research and connections with our own.

Toward such a goal, dialogue is essential. However, I believe that we should be wary of proposals that claim to unify psychology as whole, which throw an arbitrary boundary line around what could be or should be considered inside the proper domain of psychology and exclude others as outside that arbitrary boundary. By consequence, "those who have ideas outside these boundaries will feel marginalized or rejected for no other reason than definitional fiat" (Slife, 2005, p. 108). The intention of efforts to unify psychology are, without a doubt, beyond reproach, but the end result could be, paradoxically, to curtail a conversation with emerging and innovative perspectives key to synthesis.

Likewise, Stam (2004) argues that "the unification of psychology is largely a disciplinary manoeuver and not primarily an epistemological act" (p. 1259). Although such definition might be interesting institutionally, to granting organizations or university administrations, Stam argues, this is "fundamentally different ... from the business of solving real problems that might be characterized as psychological." And, furthermore, "the problems seeking solutions should always be the primary impulse for any activity that seeks to call itself scientific" (p. 1260).

In regard to the idea of unity, I prefer descriptive indifference. In my opinion, psychological science should, formally, have no position on such metaphysical matters as consilience or unity. We can have faith in the practice, that we will learn something valuable from our research, but remain agnostic about more far-reaching goals or outcomes.

More comprehensive, penetrating, and enduring understandings of human psychology are possible. There is something to be said for integration and synthesis; it is a basic part of the scholarly, disciplinary, and interdisciplinary enterprise. But, in my view, putting together ideas to have a broader, more complete, view of persons is a far cry from the grand version of scientific consilience espoused by Wilson or the unified psychology advocated by Henriques, Staats, and others.

As Shweder (2001) argued in his address to the New York Academy of Sciences conference on Wilson's theory, "Unity of Knowledge," there are several reasons for questioning, if not outright resisting, efforts at unifying the physical and biological sciences with the human sciences. First, although sweeping generalizations about all human beings are sometimes possible, "universal generalizations are often brought at the price of describing the world of culture and mind at a level of abstraction so distanced from lived realities that they are devoid of sufficient content and meaning and have little predictive validity" (p. 222). In other words, we miss what is really essential to know and describe. Second, some truths may just *be* non-consilient:

> There *are* times when the supposed difference between two or more points of view are more illusory than real and at such times a limited "unification" may be possible, but not always or even often when it comes to the types of issues that arise when one examines the links between culture, mind, and biology. (p. 222)

Synthesis is more easily accomplished between related domains. Rychlak's *physikos* and *bios*, for example, fit nicely together. But once we begin to move further afield into more distantly related domains of inquiry, synthesis becomes more difficult and, perhaps, both unfeasible and undesirable.

Indeed, when we begin to introduce interpretation and meaning, phenomena so tightly bound to the sensibilities of our everyday experience, synthesis with the distant biological and physical realms becomes much less obvious. Can synthesis move beyond "a level of abstraction so distanced from lived realities" (Shweder, 2001, p. 222) to say something descriptive, nuanced, and pertinent about those persons whom we study? Certainly, interpretation and meaning making are capacities that are given to us through our genetic makeup and evolutionary heritage, but they are also developed and honed through our reflective engagement with others in a world already seeping with meaning. And what things mean changes everything.

In this light, Shweder (2001) discusses Benjamin Whorf's research on linguistic relativity, which argues for universal emotional reactions to sounds such as certain nonsense words, "queep," for example. According to Whorf, persons universally rate the sound "queep" as fast, sharp, light, and narrow. However, once semantic meaning is introduced, the situation changes. Persons who are unfamiliar with English have a similar reaction to "queep" as to the English word "deep." But, for English speakers the "meaning totally overrides its impact as pure physical sound . . . and completely reverses our nervous system response" (p. 230).

Shared social and cultural meanings change our stance toward the world, but so do the interpretations that persons make about life. As I have argued, life is always open to new interpretations. At any given moment, persons have the opportunity to revisit and revise previously held understandings about themselves, their past, the world. This active, back-and-forth process of construal, and re-construal, has the capacity to reset our life course, leading us to new, and unforeseeable, pathways, goals, and actions.

A synthetic psychology needs to account for the complexity of meaning making, not as some periphery element to be added onto a human mechanism, but throughout our deliberations about how persons think, feel, and act. Such a synthesis is not a metaphysical proposition to be imposed from the top down, or the collation of concepts and theories; rather, it should be meticulously studied and argued from the ground up. Synthesis is an act of innovation that comes from the hard work of observing and theorizing how multiple points of view come to bear on the phenomenon itself—as Stam (2004) argued, in the act of scientific inquiry. It rises out of our work. If there is to be some *intra*-disciplinary synthesis, between psychology's diverse perspectives, and *inter*-disciplinary synthesis, between psychology and the natural and social sciences *and* the humanities, it needs to be rooted, first and foremost, in the arduous theoretical and empirical work of understanding how persons interpret action and thought in their appropriate context.

The kind of synthesis that I envision is premised, first, upon a broadened definition of psychology that is able to more fully account for the context and complexity of human lives in theory and method (Clegg, 2013). As Sugarman and Martin (2005) argue in their call for a hermeneutic psychology,

> Psychological study, first and foremost, must be faithful to the particular nature of human existence, and consequently begins by attempting to interpret this nature and the conditions that make it possible. In other words, if we want to know how people think, act, and experience their lives, it is necessary first to have some notion of what it is that thinks, acts, and experiences. (p. 252)

Because ontologically, meaning making is at the core of human existence, it must also be at the center of the discipline. For me, "how do persons make sense of life?" "how do persons narrate experience?" and "how do persons interpret self, other and the world?" are fundamental psychological questions and deserve a serious and prominent place in the canon of psychological science. They are also synthetic questions. They necessitate that psychologists account for multiple influences and levels of analysis, simultaneously, and propose new models to account for, theoretically and empirically, the way that persons actually experience and interpret themselves and the world around them.

Although, on the one hand, we could view the narrative perspective as cordoned off outside of the mainstream, a marginal discourse community exploring the esoteric problem of meaning, this is not my view. Even, to make matters worse, what I am arguing could potentially be viewed as an even more fragmented psychology in which narrative is the latest splinter group. However, on the other hand, we could view the narrative perspective as a centralizing and synthetic force in order to wrestle with questions about how the multiple and various influences on human lives all come together. In my view, narrative allows us to synthesize ideas, concepts, and research, from within psychology as well as other disciplines, into one interpretive framework and to understand them together, as facets of a single thread, in the same research argument. Because, when all is said and done, experience doesn't come to us in a piecemeal fashion, but as one integrated whole, where the social is indistinguishable from the personal, the cognitive from the emotional, language from thought, action from attitude. Brockmeier (2015) writes:

> The idea of such synthesis is based on the argument that narrative is a ubiquitous social practice that combines linguistic, cognitive, and affective modes of human activity. Whereas these modes, as the argument goes, are often (and in psychology typically) investigated separately, my point is that everything depends on understanding how they operate together, forming one complex synthesis. (p. 168)

In my view, narrative offers a tremendous opportunity for a more integrated view of human beings and human psychology. This is the approach that I have outlined here. Narrative provides a center for psychological science by focusing on issues at the core of human existence—it provides a window for investigating the day in and day out, moment by moment, effort of human understanding.

Although the debate on unity exposes some of the major fault lines in the discipline, in the final analysis, the question of unity is more a question of the power of ideas to disclose and electrify, to motivate students and researchers, and to galvanize new lines of thinking and programs of research. Unity begins with our ability to make powerful arguments, beginning in the scientific activity of research, and to rally around those ideas. Sure, the argument matters, but so do the social groups who discuss and debate those arguments, form communities around them, and embody those ideas. In the final analysis, it is not knowledge that unifies people, but rather the opposite: people unify around ideas. The question is, can we bring psychologists together around a set of insights and theories?

Although we might question the idea that our research is building toward universal descriptions of humans or the universe, I believe that it is a mistake to give away our critical faculties to judge theories and research and say that all points of view are equal. There are better and worse arguments for or against particular theories and research. Part of the rationale for narrative rests on the fact that psychologists can account for more complexity, agency, and context in their observations and theories of persons. Narrative unveils the phenomenon and makes it available to understanding. Some psychologists have argued that it is, perhaps, more desirable and accurate to drop the self-description of "science" from our identity and rather think of the discipline as loosely affiliated "psychological studies" (Kirschner, 2006; Koch, 1981). However, I believe that we stand to lose the seriousness that we, and others, take in our project.

Although I am sure that some will not be convinced, I believe that a narrative perspective can serve as a positive centralizing force in the discipline. Narrative attempts to provide insight into what I take to be one of the fundamental ontological missions of psychology that has for too long been a bystander in the discipline. Human beings are interpreters—human beings are meaning makers. We are always and forever engaged in this incredible, wondrous, and confusing sense-making project. How persons come to understand self, other, and world is not a trivial problem, but wholly fundamental to scientific psychology. We can't ignore it. Or, rather, ignoring the problem only leads to an impoverished and incomplete psychology.

In my opinion, the project of psychology is to provide an integrative view of persons as actors and interpreters. Given their position in the social and cultural world, persons are engaged in the project of meaning making. There can be no doubt that persons are shaped by the world in ways that they cannot understand. But, equally, there should be no doubt of the creative invention of that very same world.

I have attempted to open a space for a narrative perspective in the tradition of psychological science. Narrative does tell the story of the capacity of human beings, in conversation with immediate social relationships and more distant cultural figures, to creatively and actively come to interpret what life is all about. But narrative can't do everything, nor should it be expected to. Narrative can only tell part of the story and should work in dialogue with other perspectives.

However, for far too long the story of psychology has been about the relationship between variables, rather than the substance of experience itself. For far too long we have pushed meaning to the side. Narrative is a game changer. It says that we can study exactly those phenomena central to human existence, those qualities that make us human, and that profoundly influence how we understand self and reality, and that we can do so in a way that both retains the complexity of life and is scientific. The challenge is huge, but so are the payoffs.

IMAGINING AN ALTERNATE PSYCHOLOGY

Imagine that psychology did turn narrative. Or, maybe not all of psychology, but a significant part, such as those branches most closely associated with the study of persons and thinking (personality, cognitive, and clinical) and social interaction (social and cultural). A large contingent of researchers put aside their questionnaires and experimental protocols and pick up voice recorders and video cameras to speak with people and observe how they talk, act, and make interpretations about the self, world, and others.

Imagine that there is a massive effort put into describing the processes and dynamics of interpretive actions. Mainstream journal editors open their pages to narrative research, granting organizations issue calls for funding, and universities open academic positions expressly intended for narrative psychologists. In short, it happens; there is a narrative revolution.

Sure, the scenario is optimistic—perhaps overly so. But it isn't wholly unfounded or, really, all that far-fetched. For many reasons, I believe that right now, at the beginning of the twenty-first century, there is a real opportunity, and a desperate need, to bring a critical and vibrant narrative perspective into the center of psychology.

The problems that a narrative perspective addresses are similar to those that every perceptive child, adolescent, or young adult wondered about at one time or another. They concern the very nature of human understanding, what we know and come to know, about ourselves, others, and the world. I also suspect that this basic curiosity about life and others was the driving force attracting many (if not all) psychologists into the field. We began our exploration of psychology with innocent inquisitiveness and wonderment about fundamental questions: What is the nature of reality? How do persons come into being and come to have something called a world? How can I know what other people think or how their minds work? Do I have control over my own thoughts and actions, or does the social world? Why do others act so strangely? Why do people appropriate particular identities or worldviews?

For those at the beginning of their studies, I hope that I have shown a possible way forward to pursue psychology and remain committed to those primeval motivating curiosities. For a variety of reasons, most abandon psychology as a course of study. Sometimes this choice is because of practical considerations on the kinds of careers open to us in the job market, or because we discover another more captivating interest. Of course, a career in psychology is not for everyone—that's not what I am advocating. But many choose another path after they realize that psychology is not really concerned with the questions that they always wondered about. At some point, they realize that the discipline has failed to live up to its potential to address the core questions about human beings. I think that I have convincingly argued that there is another path forward, that, conscientiously applied, can approach those basic curiosities through the careful study and observation of the lives and words of others.

For those who are psychologists, I hope that I have shown a way to recapture your initial wonderment about persons, how to think about them, and to study them. Somewhere, the spark remains, and I hope that I have reignited it. This is one of my reasons for optimism. At some level, the curiosity is still there and just needs to be rediscovered. I hope that my argument has shown that there are ways of recapturing these passions and researching the core problems about human beings systematically and scientifically. After all, I believe that there is power from a good argument to create a sea change.

As I have argued throughout this book, a narrative perspective is necessary in order to study those pressing basic, pure research problems on the very nature of human psychology—those problems that have to do with the fundamental human project of interpreting life experience. To state the matter boldly, we simply can't understand human psychology without narrative. Without narrative, we misunderstand both persons and psychological processes. I strongly believe that the narrative perspective is the most efficacious route to describing, understanding, and communicating insights into the fundamental questions about human beings.

Documenting and describing psychological phenomena, narrative psychology can provide creative and grounded insights into how persons interpret their actions, experiences, identities, feelings, and motivations. It provides our observations of human beings with the much "needed touchstone of reality" (Allport, 1942/1951, p. 143). Narrative allows us to observe how interpretations unfold in the context of a person's life, situated in time and space, and how persons, in their distinct voice and vocabulary, make interpretations and make connections between various aspects of their lives and experiences. We need narrative in order to have a more accurate accounting of human psychology.

As I have argued, the study of the process of mental life, inside the interpretations of persons and inside the contexts in which persons perpetually find themselves, is simply not possible using the dominant model of variable-centered research. In moving to narrative, psychology circumvents the ubiquitous and "fatal" problem (Lamiell, 2003) of mistaking group averages for individual psychological processes and mistaking the statistical relationship between two or more variables for what must be happening at the level of the person. Rather, narrative psychology has the very powerful virtue of, credibly, putting problem and method in communication with each other. Nuanced theories about the complex phenomena of human thought and action are grounded in our observations of what persons say and do, in their interpretive actions. Theory is explicitly and visibly tied to research observations. In turning to narrative, psychology can move beyond the trenchant conceptual imbroglio and on to the more serious matters of investigating and describing, directly, those pressing problems that so desperately require our attention and understanding.

Indeed, another important motivation for disciplinary change has to do with the need for psychology to address the persistent challenges of our current historical moment. At the beginning of the twenty-first century, we face enormous and pressing problems. As I am writing, the war in Syria continues to rage, with hundreds of thousands dead and millions of refugees trying to make their way to safety and security. The climate is changing rapidly, bringing higher average temperatures each year, the depletion of resources, and significant costs for human lives, security, and biodiversity. Right-wing political parties are on the rise in Europe and the world, and even in the United States. Some are in power. There is a resurgence throughout the world of anti-Semitism, hatred of Muslims, and a general fear of others. Prejudice and discrimination in race, ethnicity, gender, and sexual orientation are still painfully present. Terrorism, mass killings, and genocide continue to plague us. Glaring inequalities persist in wealth and opportunity.

Unfortunately, I could continue. This is not a historical moment of great hope and enthusiasm for the future. Thankfully, life is not all pain and misery. Also, it is debatable if there has ever truly been a period of stability and prosperity for all. But shouldn't we still be asking ourselves, what kind of world do we live in? And can't psychology do something about it for the better?

Right now and right before our eyes, the world is crying out for understanding, for innovative solutions to real-world problems, of which there are far too many to choose. Psychologists can not close their eyes and wish it all away. Often, psychological research is concerned with the most esoteric questions, far removed from everyday life and any kind of practical application. We need to ask, what use is our research to understanding the problems breaking apart the world and putting our future at risk? How can psychology participate in remaking and renewing the world?

This is not merely a matter of idealism—the political, social, ethical, relational, and personal problems of the world are too massive to stand aside and abdicate solutions to others. Psychology, in general, and a narrative psychology, in particular, are necessary players in such conversations because, when all is said and done, the problems that we face are not natural phenomena, but standing behind each and every one of our contemporary failures are human actors. Economic and social inequality, the environment, conflict and peace, and many many other forms of psychological and social distress are not physical, chemical, or biological problems; they are, first and foremost, human problems. There are human beings, alone and together, involved in the project of poetically making life and world. They are, indeed, human-made catastrophes and require disclosing in concrete detail the processes involved, careful analysis, and understanding before solutions can be offered.

How can we better understand hatred, racism, violence, and conflict? How can we better understand why people choose to ignore the environmental crisis? The answers that we are able to give to these critical applied questions will depend on our basic understanding of human actors in context and the ability of our methods and theories to provide a deeper understanding of these problems and the persons and contexts implicated. How can we propose effective solutions if at first we don't thoroughly understand the dynamics of the problem itself? Sometimes understanding is enough to create positive social change, and sometimes further actions are required.

Although the goal of understanding might sound somehow fanciful or romantic, it really isn't. As I have described, the work is difficult and painstaking, and the result is always tentative. But "understanding" is definitely the critical word. Narrative psychology seeks to understand how persons, alone and together, navigate their world and come to make sense of it. Through meticulous study and systematic questioning, we aspire to understand the reasons that persons use to interpret their lives in the way that they do. What meanings do persons arrive at? How are they articulated? Why this interpretation? What is its function? Narrative psychology invites creative approaches to understanding human psychology, not as an abstract and decontextualized variable, but as part of the life and experience of persons as embodied, contextual, and meaningful actions.

When narrative researchers talk to persons or observe their interactions, their interpretations are made present in their narratings and are interpretable by the researcher. But researchers can, in their turn, make their interpretations of others present for larger communities of researchers and the public. Whether we like it or not, the enterprise of research is a political action—there's no escaping it. In presenting the narratives of others, always with our interpretations layered over, their narratives are recast and refracted into other domains. We make their interpretations accessible and give their stories a voice.

Of course, this isn't the only purpose of narrative research, but it is an important one, and one of the reasons that narrative is so needed. The findings from narrative research have the potential to have large effects on public thinking and social policy. In this light, the often criticized literary quality of narrative research, presenting the researcher's interpretation of a life in natural language, has the advantage of allowing others to easily understand and empathize with the other, producing, one would hope, a larger impact than just numbers on a page.

It is time for psychology to return to the human world—to the world of human actors working alone and with others to make sense of life. It is a world in profound need of understanding. This is the most fundamental aim and purpose of narrative psychology, and it is my hope that, together, we can rise to the urgent challenges we face and, in so doing, restore psychology to its rightful place as a human science and as a force for understanding and progress.

If there is a sea change, and I hope there will be, this isn't the end of psychological science as we know it, but a new beginning. Certainly, a narrative revolution would bring with it a wealth of concrete and descriptive studies describing the process and dynamics of meaning making for researchers to sift through and evaluate. But chaos won't break out on the streets. Psychology will not turn into a branch of literary studies. Such pessimistic scenarios would mean completely abandoning our critical faculties, which, as I have argued, are so essential to the scientific enterprise of going after knowledge. Psychologists must have faith in their capacity to evaluate the trustworthiness and usefulness of the research before them.

Although narrative psychology has been around for at least 30 years, we are still at the very beginning and very far from seeing the full potential of this perspective realized. It is time to get to work. Simply put, a narrative perspective is vital and timely, both for a more complete accounting of persons in the social world and for achieving concrete change. This is a compelling argument for the necessity of a new narrative in and of psychology.

REFERENCES

Abbott, A. (2001). *Chaos of disciplines*. Chicago: University of Chicago Press.

Abbott, H. P. (2008). *The Cambridge introduction to narrative* (2nd ed.). New York: Cambridge University Press.

Abu-Lughod, (1985/2000). *Veiled sentiments: Honor and poetry in a Bedouin society*. Berkeley: University of California Press.

Adler, J. M. (2012). Living into the story: Agency and coherence in a longitudinal study of narrative identity development and mental health over the course of psychotherapy. *Journal of Personality and Social Psychology, 102*(2), 367–389. http://doi.org/10.1037/a0025289

Allport, G. W. (1942/1951). *The use of personal documents in psychological research*. New York: Social Science Research Council.

Allport, G. W. (1954). *The nature of prejudice*. Oxford: Addison-Wesley.

Allport, G. W. (1962). The general and the unique in psychological science. *Journal of Personality, 30*(3), 405–422.

Andrews, M. (2014). *Narrative imagination and everyday life*. New York: Oxford University Press.

Andrews, M., Squire, C., & Tamboukou, M. (Eds.). (2013). *Doing narrative research* (2nd ed.). Thousand Oaks, CA: Sage.

Ardelt, M. (2000). Still stable after all these years? Personality stability theory revisited. *Social Psychology Quarterly, 63*(4), 392–405.

Assmann, J. (1995). Collective memory and cultural identity. *New German Critique, 65*, 125–133.

Assmann, J. (1997). *Moses the Egyptian: The memory of Egypt in Western monotheism*. Cambridge, MA: Harvard University Press.

Association for Psychological Science (n.d.). About. Retrieved from http://www.psychologicalscience.org/index.php/about

Bakhtin, M. M. (1981). *The dialogic imagination: Four essays* (M. Holquist, Ed.; C. Emerson & M. Holquist, Trans.). Austin: University of Texas Press.

Bamberg, M. (2004). Form and functions of "slut bashing" in male identity constructions in 15-year-olds. *Human Development, 47*(6), 331–353.

Bamberg, M. (2006). Stories big or small: Why do we care? *Narrative Inquiry, 16*(1), 139–147.

Bamberg, M. G. W. (Ed.). (1997). Special issue: Oral versions of personal experience: Three decades of narrative analysis. *Journal of Narrative & Life History, 7*(1–4).

Bamberg, M., & Georgakopoulou, A. (2008). Small stories as a new perspective in narrative and identity analysis. *Text & Talk*, 28(3), 377–396.

Barthes, R. (1966/1975). Introduction to the structural analysis of narrative. *New Literary History*, 6(2), 237–272.

Bauer, J. J., McAdams, D. P., & Sakaeda, A. R. (2005). Interpreting the good life: Growth memories in the lives of mature, happy people. *Journal of Personality and Social Psychology*, 88(1), 203–217.

Bauman, R. (1986). *Story, performance, and event: Contextual studies of oral narrative*. New York: Cambridge University Press.

Bekerman, Z. (2009). The complexities of teaching historical conflictual narratives in integrated Palestinian-Jewish schools in Israel. *International Review of Education*, 55(2–3), 235–250. doi:10.1007/s11159-008-9123-y

Bekerman, Z., Habib, A., & Shhadi, N. (2011). Jewish–Palestinian integrated education in Israel and its potential influence on national and/or ethnic identities and intergroup relations. *Journal of Ethnic and Migration Studies*, 37(3), 389–405. doi:10.1080/1369183X.2011.526777

Bhatia, S., & Ram, A. (2009). Theorizing identity in transnational and diaspora cultures: A critical approach to acculturation. *International Journal of Intercultural Relations*, 33(2), 140–149. http://doi.org/10.1016/j.ijintrel.2008.12.009

Biesta, G. (2010). Pragmatism and the philosophical foundations of mixed methods research. In A. Tashakkori & C. Teddlie (Eds.), *SAGE handbook of mixed methods in social and behavioral research* (2nd ed., pp. 95–117). Thousand Oaks, CA: Sage.

Block, J. (1971/2014). *Lives through time*. New York: Psychology Press.

Block, J., & Robins, R. W. (1993). A longitudinal study of consistency and change in self-esteem from early adolescence to early adulthood. *Child Development*, 64(3), 909–923.

Blumer, H. (1939). *An appraisal of Thomas and Znaniecki's* The Polish Peasant in Europe and America. New York: Social Science Research Council.

Breuer, J., & Freud, S. (1893–1895/2000). *Studies in hysteria*. (J. Strachey, Ed. & Trans.) New York: Basic Books.

Brockmeier, J. (2012). Narrative scenarios: Toward a culturally thick notion of narrative. In Jaan Valsiner (Ed.), *The Oxford handbook of culture and psychology* (pp. 439–467). Oxford and New York: Oxford University Press.

Brockmeier, J. (2013). Fact and fiction: Exploring the narrative mind. In M. Hyvärinen, M. Hatavara & L.-C. Hydén (Eds.), *The travelling concepts of narrative* (pp. 121–140). Amsterdam: John Benjamins.

Brockmeier, J. (2015). *Beyond the archive: Memory, narrative, and the autobiographical process*. Oxford: Oxford University Press.

Brockmeier, J., & Harré, R. (2001). Narrative: Problems and promises of an alternative paradigm. In J. Brockmeier & D. Carbaugh (Eds.), *Narrative and identity: Studies in autobiography, self and culture* (pp. 39–58). Amsterdam: John Benjamins.

Brockmeier, J., & Meretoja, H. (2014). Understanding narrative hermeneutics. *Storyworlds*, 6(2), 1–27.

Bruner, J. (1983). *Child's talk: Learning to use language* (1st ed.). New York: W. W. Norton.

Bruner, J. (1986). *Actual minds, possible worlds.* Cambridge, MA: Harvard University Press.

Bruner, J. (1987). Life as narrative. *Social Research, 54*(1), 11–32.

Bruner, J. (1990). *Acts of meaning* Cambridge, MA: Harvard University Press.

Bruner, J. (1991). The narrative construction of reality. *Critical Inquiry, 18*, 1–21.

Butler, R. N. (1963). The life review: An interpretation of reminiscence in the aged. *Psychiatry, 26*, 65–76.

Cain, C. (1991). Personal stories: Identity acquisition and self-understanding in Alcoholics Anonymous. *Ethos, 19*, 210–253.

Campbell, D. T., & Fiske, D. W. (1959). Convergent and discriminant validation by the multitrait-multimethod matrix. *Psychological Bulletin, 56*(2), 81–105. doi:10.1037/h0046016

Campbell, R. S., & Pennebaker, J. W. (2003). The secret life of pronouns: Flexibility in writing style and physical health. *Psychological Science, 14*(1), 60–65.

Cantor, N. (1990). From thought to behavior: "Having" and "doing" in the study of personality and cognition. *American Psychologist, 45*(6), 735–750.

Cantor, N., Norem, J. K., Niedenthal, P. M., Langston, C. A., & Brower, A. M. (1987). Life tasks, self-concept ideals, and cognitive strategies in a life transition. *Journal of Personality and Social Psychology, 53*(6), 1178–1191.

Carlson, R. (1971). Where is the person in personality research? *Psychological Bulletin, 75*(3), 203–219.

Carr, D. (1991). *Time, narrative and history.* Bloomington: Indiana University Press.

Caspi, A., Roberts, B. W., & Shiner, R. L. (2005). Personality development: Stability and change. *Annual Review of Psychology, 56*, 453–484.

Chafe, W. (1998). Things we can learn from repeated tellings of the same experience. *Narrative Inquiry, 8*, 269–285.

Charmaz, K. (2006). *Constructing grounded theory: A practical guide through qualitative analysis.* Thousand Oaks, CA: Sage.

Charon, R. (2008). *Narrative medicine: Honoring the stories of illness* (1st paperback ed.). Oxford: Oxford University Press.

Chase, S. E. (2003). Learning to listen: Narrative principles in a qualitative research methods course. In R. Josselson, A. Lieblich, & D. P. McAdams (Eds.), *Up close and personal: The teaching and learning of narrative research* (pp. 79–100). Washington, DC: American Psychological Association Press.

Chauncey, G. (1994). *Gay New York: Gender, urban culture, and the makings of the gay male world, 1890–1940.* New York: Basic Books.

Clandinin, D. J. (Ed.). (2007). *Handbook of narrative inquiry: Mapping a methodology.* Thousand Oaks, CA: Sage.

Clegg, J. W. (2013). The fragmented object: Building disciplinary coherence through a contextual unit of analysis. *Review of General Psychology, 17*(2), 151–155. doi:10.1037/a0032926

Cohler, B. J. (1982). Personal narrative and life course. In P. Baltes & O. G. Brim (Eds.), *Life span development and behavior* (Vol. 4, pp. 205–241). New York: Academic Press.

Cohler, B. J. (2007). *Writing desire: Sixty years of gay autobiography.* Madison: University of Wisconsin Press.

Cohler, B. J. (2008). Two lives, two times: Life-writing after Shoah. *Narrative Inquiry, 18*(1), 1–28.

Cronbach, L. J. (1957). The two disciplines of scientific psychology. *American Psychologist, 12*(11), 671–684. doi:10.1037/h0043943

Cronbach, L. J. (1988). Five perspectives on the validity argument. In H. Wainer, &. H. I. Braun (Eds.). *Test validity* (pp. 3–17). Hillsdale, NJ: Lawrence Erlbaum.

Danziger, K. (1997). *Naming the mind: How psychology found its language*. Thousand Oaks, CA: Sage.

Davies, B., & Harré, R. (1990). Positioning: The discursive production of selves. *Journal for the Theory of Social Behaviour*, 20(1), 43–63.

De Fina, A., & Georgakopoulou, A. (2012). *Analyzing narrative: Discourse and sociolinguistic perspectives*. Cambridge and New York: Cambridge University Press.

Dennett, D. C. (1991). *Consciousness explained*. New York: Little, Brown.

Denzin, N. K. (2010). Moments, mixed methods, and paradigm dialogs. *Qualitative Inquiry*, 16(6), 419–427. doi:10.1177/1077800410364608

Denzin, N. K., & Lincoln, Y. S. (Eds.). (2008). *Collecting and interpreting qualitative materials* (3rd ed). Thousand Oaks, CA: Sage.

Dilthey, W. (1894/1976). *Selected writings*. (H. P. Rickman, Ed. & Trans.). New York: Cambridge University Press.

Dilthey, W. (1989). *Selected works, volume 1: Introduction to the human sciences*. R. A. Makkreel & F. Rodi, Eds. Princeton, NJ: Princeton University Press.

Driver-Linn, E. (2003). Where is the psychology going? Structural fault lines revealed by psychologists' use of Kuhn. *American Psychologist*, 58(4), 269–278. doi:10.1037/0003-066X.58.4.269

Elder, G. H., Jr. (1974/1999). *Children of the Great Depression: Social change in life experience* (25th anniversary ed.). Boulder, CO: Westview Press.

Engel, S. (1986). Learning to reminisce: A developmental study of how young children talk about the past. Unpublished doctoral dissertation, City University of New York.

Erikson, E. H. (1950). *Childhood and society*. New York: W. W. Norton.

Erikson, E. H. (1958). *Young man Luther: A study in psychoanalysis and history*. New York: W. W. Norton.

Erikson (1968/1994) *Identity: Youth and crisis*. New York: W. W. Norton.

Erikson, E. H. (1969). *Gandhi's truth: On the origins of militant nonviolence* New York: W. W. Norton.

Feyerabend, P. (1976). *Against method: Outline of an anarchistic theory of knowledge*. London: Verso.

Fivush, R., Bohanek, J. G., Zaman, W., & Grapin, S. (2012). Gender differences in adolescents' autobiographical narratives. *Journal of Cognition and Development*, 13(3), 295–319. http://doi.org/10.1080/15248372.2011.590787

Fivush, R., & Nelson, K. (2006). Parent-child reminiscing locates the self in the past. *British Journal of Developmental Psychology*, 24, 235–251.

Fludernik, M. (1996). *Towards a "natural" narratology*. London: Routledge.

Frank, A. W. (2010). *Letting stories breathe: A socio-narratology*. Chicago: University of Chicago Press.

Freeman, M. (1984). History, narrative, and life-span developmental knowledge. *Human Development*, 27(1), 1–19.

Freeman, M. (1993). *Rewriting the self: History, memory, narrative*. Florence, KY: Taylor & Frances/Routledge.

Freeman, M. (2006). Life "on holiday?": In defense of big stories. *Narrative Inquiry*, 16(1), 131–138.

Freeman, M. (2010). *Hindsight: The promise and peril of looking backward*. New York: Oxford University Press.

Freeman, M. (2011). Toward poetic science. *Integrative Psychological and Behavioral Science, 45*(4), 389–396. doi:10.1007/s12124-011-9171-x

Gadamer, H.-G. (1960/1993) *Truth and method* (2nd rev. ed.).(J. Weinsheimer & D. G. Marshall, Trans.). New York: Continuum.

Gardner, H. (2005). Scientific psychology: Should we bury it or praise it? In R. J. Sternberg (Ed.), (2005). *Unity in psychology: Possibility or pipedream?* Washington, DC: American Psychological Association.

Gazzaniga, M. S. (1998). *The mind's past.* Berkeley: University of California Press.

Gee, J. P. (1999). *Discourse analysis: Theory and method.* New York: Routledge.

Geertz, C. (1984). "From the native's point of view": On the nature of anthropological understanding. In R. A. Shweder & R. A. LeVine (Eds.), *Culture theory: Essays on mind, self, and emotion* (pp. 123–136). New York: Cambridge University Press.

Georgakopoulou, A. (2007). *Small stories, interaction and identities. Studies in narrative 8.* Amsterdam: John Benjamins.

Georgakopoulou, A. (2017). Narrative/life of the moment: From telling a story to taking a narrative stance. In B. Schiff, A. E. McKim & S. Patron (Eds.), *Life and narrative: The risks and responsibilities of storying experience* (pp. 29–54). New York: Oxford University Press.

Gergen, K. J. (1985). The social constructionist movement in modern psychology. *American Psychologist, 40*(3), 266–275.

Gergen, K. (1994). *Realities and relationships: Soundings in social construction.* Cambridge, MA: Harvard University Press.

Gergen, K. J. (2009). *Relational being: Beyond self and community.* New York: Oxford University Press.

Gergen, K. J. (2014). Pursuing excellence in qualitative inquiry. *Qualitative Psychology, 1*(1), 49–60. doi:10.1037/qup0000002

Gigerenzer, G. (2004). Mindless statistics. *The Journal of Socio-Economics, 33*(5), 587–606. doi:10.1016/j.socec.2004.09.033

Goffman, E. (1959). *The presentation of self in everyday life* (pp. 1–21). New York: Doubleday.

Goffman, E. (1981). *Forms of talk.* Philadelphia: University of Pennsylvania Press.

Gottschalk, L., Kluckhohn, C., & Angell, R. (1945). *The use of personal documents in history, anthropology and sociology.* New York: Social Science Research Council.

Gough, B., & Madill, A. (2012). Subjectivity in psychological science: From problem to prospect. *Psychological Methods, 17*(3), 374–384. doi:10.1037/a0029313

Greenhoot, A. F., Sun, S., Bunnell, S. L., & Lindboe, K. (2013). Making sense of traumatic memories: Memory qualities and psychological symptoms in emerging adults with and without abuse histories. *Memory, 21*(1), 125–142. http://doi.org/10.1080/09658211.2012.712975

Gubrium, J. F., & Holstein J. A. (2009) *Analyzing narrative reality.* Thousands Oaks, CA: Sage.

Haan, N., Millsap, R. & Hartka, E. (1986). As time goes by: Change and stability in personality over fifty years. *Psychology and Aging, 1*(3), 220–232.

Habermas, T. & Bluck, S. (2000). Getting a life: The emergence of the life story in adolescence. *Psychological Bulletin, 126*(5), 748–769.

Habermas, T., & Hatiboğlu, N. (2014). Contextualizing the self: The emergence of a biographical understanding in adolescence. In B. Schiff (Ed.), Special issue: Rereading personal narrative and life course. *New Directions for Child and Adolescent Development, 2014*(145), 29–41. doi:10.1002/cad.20065

Haden, C. A., & Hoffman, P. C. (2013). Cracking the code: Using personal narratives in research. *Journal of Cognition and Development, 14*(3), 361–375. http://doi.org/10.1080/15248372.2013.805135

Halbwachs, M. (1980). *The collective memory*. (F. J. Ditter, Jr. & V. Y. Ditter, Trans.). New York: Harper & Row. (Original work published 1950) New York: Harper & Row.

Hammack, P. L. (2008). Narrative and the cultural psychology of identity. *Personality and Social Psychology Review, 12*(3), 222–247.

Hammack, P. L. (2011). *Narrative and the politics of identity: The cultural psychology of Israeli and Palestinian youth*. New York: Oxford University Press.

Hammack, P. L., & Cohler, B. J. (2009). Narrative engagement and sexual identity: An interdisciplinary approach to the study of sexual lives. In P. L. Hammack & B. J. Cohler (Eds.), *The story of sexual identity: Narrative perspectives on the gay and lesbian life course* (pp. 3–22). New York: Oxford University Press.

Hammack, P. L., & Toolis, E. (2014). Narrative and the social construction of adulthood. In B. Schiff (Ed.), Special issue: Rereading personal narrative and life course. *New Directions for Child and Adolescent Development, 2014*(145), 43–56. doi:10.1002/cad.20066

Harré, R. (1983). *Personal being: A theory for individual psychology*. Oxford: Blackwell.

Haugeland, J. (2013). *Dasein disclosed: John Haugeland's Heidegger*. Cambridge, MA: Harvard University Press.

Heavey, E. (2017). The body as biography. In B. Schiff, A. E. McKim & S. Patron (Eds.), *Life and narrative: The risks and responsibilities of storying experience* (pp. 139–160) New York: Oxford University Press.

Heidegger, M. (1926/1962). *Being and time*. (J. Macquarrie & E. Robinson, Trans.). New York: Harper & Row.

Helmreich, W. B. (1992). *Against all odds: Holocaust survivors and the successful lives they made in America*. New Brunswick, NJ: Transaction.

Hempel, C. (1962). Explanation in science and in history. In R. G. Colodney (Ed.), *Frontiers of science and philosophy* (pp. 9–33). Pittsburgh: University of Pittsburgh Press.

Henrich, J., Heine, S. J., & Norenzayan, A. (2010). The weirdest people in the world? *Behavioral and Brain Sciences, 33*(2–3), 61–83. doi:10.1017/S0140525X0999152X

Henriques, G. R. (2004). Psychology defined. *Journal of Clinical Psychology, 60*(12), 1207–1221. doi:10.1002/jclp.20061

Henriques, G. R. (2008). The problem of psychology and the integration of human knowledge: Contrasting Wilson's consilience with the Tree of Knowledge system. *Theory & Psychology, 18*(6), 731–755. doi:10.1177/0959354308097255

Henriques, G. (2013). Evolving from methodological to conceptual unification. *Review of General Psychology, 17*(2), 168–173. doi:10.1037/a0032929

Herman, D. (2002). *Story logic: Problems and possibilities of narrative*. Lincoln: University of Nebraska Press.

Herman, D. (2009). *Basic elements of narrative*. West Sussex, UK: Wiley Blackwell.

Hermans, H. J. M., & Dimaggio, G. (2007). Self, identity, and globalization in times of uncertainty: A dialogical analysis. *Review of General Psychology, 11*(1), 31–61. doi:10.1037/1089-2680.11.1.31

Hobsbawm, E. J., & Ranger, T. O. (Eds.). (1983). *The invention of tradition*. New York: Cambridge University Press.

Holland, D., Lachicotte, W., Jr., Skinner, D., & Cain, C. (1998). *Identity and agency in cultural worlds*. Cambridge, MA: Harvard University Press.

Holstein, J. A., & Gubrium, J. F. (2004). Context: Working it up, down and across. In C. Seale (Ed.), *Qualitative research practice*. London and Thousand Oaks, CA: Sage.

Holstein, J. A., & Gubrium, J. F. (Eds.). (2012). *Varieties of narrative analysis*. Los Angeles: Sage.

Husserl, E. (1954/1970). *The crisis of European sciences and transcendental phenomenology*. (D. Carr, Trans.). Evanston, IL: Northwestern University Press.

Hutto, D. D. (2008). *Folk psychological narratives: The sociocultural basis of understanding reasons*. Cambridge, MA: MIT Press.

Hydén, L.-C. (2011). Narrative collaboration and scaffolding in dementia. *Journal of Aging Studies, 25*(4), 339–347. doi:10.1016/j.jaging.2011.04.002

Hyvärinen, M. (2006). Towards a conceptual history of narrative. In M. Hyvärinen, A. Korhonen, & J. Mykkänen (Eds.), *The travelling concept of narrative*. Retrieved from http://www.helsinki.fi/collegium/e-series/volumes/volume_1/001_04_hyvarinen.pdf

Hyvärinen, M. (2010). Revisiting the narrative turns. *Life Writing, 7*(1), 69—82.

Hyvärinen M. (2013). Travelling metaphors, transforming concepts. In M. Hyvärinen, M. Hatavara & L.-C. Hydén (Eds.), *The travelling concepts of narrative* (pp. 13–41). Amsterdam: John Benjamins.

Hyvärinen, M., Hyden, L., Saarenheimo M., & Tamboukou, M. (Eds.) (2010). *Beyond narrative coherence*. Amsterdam: John Benjamins.

James, W. (1890). *The principles of psychology*, Vol 1. New York: Henry Holt.

Johnson, R. B., & Onwuegbuzie, A. J. (2004). Mixed methods research: A research paradigm whose time has come. *Educational Researcher, 33*(7) 14–26.

Johnson, R. B., Onwuegbuzie, A. J., & Turner, L. A. (2007). Toward a definition of mixed methods research. *Journal of Mixed Methods Research, 1*(2), 112–133. doi:10.1177/1558689806298224

Johnstone, B. (1996). *The linguistic individual: Self-expression in language and linguistics*. Oxford: Oxford University Press.

Josselson, R. (1994). Identity and relatedness in the life cycle. In H. A. Bosma, T. L. G. Graafsma, H. D. Grotevant, & D. J. de Levita (Eds.), *Identity and development: An interdisciplinary approach* (pp. 81–102). Thousand Oaks, CA: Sage.

Josselson, R. (2004). The hermeneutics of faith and the hermeneutics of suspicion. *Narrative Inquiry, 14*(1), 1–28.

Josselson, R. (2006). Narrative research and the challenge of accumulating knowledge. *Narrative Inquiry, 16*(1), 3–10. doi:10.1075/ni.16.1.03jos

Josselson, R. (2007). *Playing Pygmalion: How people create one another*. Lanham, MD: Jason Aronson.

Josselson, R. (2009). The present of the past: Dialogues with memory over time. *Journal of Personality, 77*(3), 647–668. http://doi.org/10.1111/j.1467-6494.2009.00560.x

Josselson, R. (2013). *Interviewing for qualitative inquiry: A relational approach* (1st ed.). New York: Guilford Press.

Josselson, R., & Lieblich, A. (Eds.). (1993). *The narrative study of lives*, vol. 1. Thousand Oaks, CA: Sage.

Josselson, R., & Lieblich, A. (2009). Reflections on *The Narrative Study of Lives*. *Narrative Inquiry, 19*(1), 183–198. http://doi.org/10.1075/ni.19.1.10jos

Jung, C. J. (1930/1960). The stages of life. In H. Read, M. Fordham, & G. Alder (Eds.), R. F. C. Hull (Trans.), *The structure and dynamics of the psyche: The collected works of C. G. Jung* (Vol. 8, pp. 387–403). New York: Pantheon Books.

Keneally, T. (1982). *Schindler's ark*. London: Hodder & Stoughton.

Kenyon, G. M., Bohlmeijer, E., & Randall, W. L. (Eds.). (2011). *Storying later life: Issues, investigations, and interventions in narrative gerontology*. New York: Oxford University Press.

Kenyon, G., & Randall, W. (1997). *Restorying our lives: Careful growth through autobiographical reflection*. Westport, CT: Praeger.

Kenyon, G. M., Clark, P. G., & De Vries, B. (Eds.). (2001). *Narrative gerontology: Theory, research, and practice*. New York: Springer.

Kirschner, S. R. (2006). Psychology and pluralism: Toward the psychological studies. *Journal of Theoretical and Philosophical Psychology, 26*(1–2), 1–17.

Klohnen, E. C., Vandewater, E. A., & Young, A. (1996). Negotiating the middle years: Ego-resiliency and successful midlife adjustment in women. *Psychology and Aging, 11*(3), 431–442.

Köber, C., Schmiedek, F., & Habermas, T. (2015). Characterizing lifespan development of three aspects of coherence in life narratives: A cohort-sequential study. *Developmental Psychology, 51*(2), 260–275. http://doi.org/10.1037/a0038668

Koch, S. (1981). The nature and limits of psychological knowledge: Lessons of a century qua "science." *American Psychologist, 36*(3), 257–269.

Koven, M. (2012). Speaker roles in personal narratives. In J. A. Holstein & J. F. Gubrium (Eds.), *Varieties of narrative analysis* (pp. 151–180). Thousand Oaks, CA: Sage.

Kuhn, T. S. (1962/1970). *The structure of scientific revolutions* (2nd ed.). Chicago: University of Chicago Press.

Kvale, S. (1994). Ten standard objections to qualitative research interviews. *Journal of Phenomenological Psychology, 25*(2), 147–173. doi:10.1163/156916294X00016

Labov, W. (1972). The transformation of experience in narrative syntax. In W. Labov, *Language in the inner city* (pp. 354–405). Philadelphia: University of Pennsylvania Press.

Labov, W., & Waletzky, J. (1967/1997). Narrative analysis: Oral versions of personal experience. *Journal of Narrative & Life History, 7*(1–4), 3–38.

Lamiell, J. T. (2003). *Beyond individual and group differences: Human individuality, scientific psychology, and William Stern's critical personalism*. Thousand Oaks, CA: Sage.

Lamiell, J. T. (2013). Statisticism in personality psychologists' use of trait constructs: What is it? How was it contracted? Is there a cure? *New Ideas in Psychology, 31*(1), 65–71. doi:10.1016/j.newideapsych.2011.02.009

Langellier, K. M. (2001). "You're marked": Breast cancer, tattoo, and the narrative performance of identity. In J. Brockmeier & D. Carbaugh (Eds.), *Narrative and identity: Studies in autobiography, self and culture*. (pp. 145–184). Amsterdam: John Benjamins.

László, J. (2008). *The science of stories: An introduction to narrative psychology* New York: Routledge/Taylor & Francis Group.

Levi, P. (1947/1993). *Survival in Auschwitz*. New York: Macmillan.

Lieblich, A. (1993). Looking at change. Natasha, 21: New immigrant from Russia to Israel. In R. Josselson & A. Lieblich (Eds.), *The narrative study of lives* (Vol. 1, pp. 92–129). Newbury Park, CA: Sage.

Lieblich, A. (2014). Narrating your life after 65 (or: To tell or not to tell, that is the question). In B. Schiff (Ed.), Special issue: Rereading personal narrative and life course. *New Directions for Child and Adolescent Development, 2014*(145), 71–83. doi:10.1002/cad.20068

Lieblich, A., Tuval-Mashiach, R., & Zilber, T. (1998). *Narrative research: Reading, analysis and interpretation.* Thousand Oak, CA: Sage.

Lieblich, A., Zilber, T. B., & Tuval-Mashiach, R. (2008) Narrating human action: The subjective experience of agency, structure, communion and serendipity. *Qualitative Inquiry, 14*(4) 613–631.

Little, B. R. (2000). Persons, contexts and personal projects: Assumptive themes of a methodological transactionalism. In S. Wapner et al. (Eds.), *Theoretical perspectives in environment-behavior research: Underlying assumptions, research problems, and methodologies* (pp. 79–88). Dordrecht: Kluwer Academic.

Lodi-Smith, J., Geise, A. C., Roberts, B. W., & Robins, R. W. (2009). Narrating personality change. *Journal of Personality and Social Psychology, 96*(3), 679–689. http://doi.org/10.1037/a0014611

MacIntyre, A. C. (1981). *After virtue: A study in moral theory.* Notre Dame, IN: University of Notre Dame Press.

Madigan, S. (2011). *Narrative therapy.* Washington, DC: American Psychological Association.

Magnusson, D. (1999). Holistic interactionism: A perspective for research on personality development. In L. A. Pervin & O. P. John (Eds.), *Handbook of personality: Theory and research* (2nd ed., pp. 219–247). New York: Guilford Press.

Maoz, I. (2004). Coexistence is in the eye of the beholder: Evaluating intergroup encounter interventions between Jews and Arabs in Israel. *Journal of Social Issues, 60*(2) 437–452.

Maoz, I., Steinberg, S., Bar-On, D., & Fakhereldeen, M. (2002). The dialogue between the "self" and the "other": A process analysis of Palestinian-Jewish encounters in Israel. *Human Relations, 55*(8), 931–962. doi:10.1177/0018726702055008178

McAdams, D. P. (1985). *Power, intimacy, and the life story: Personological inquiries into identity.* Homewood, IL: Dorsey Press.

McAdams, D. P. (1996). Personality, modernity and the storied self: A contemporary framework for studying persons. *Psychological Inquiry, 7*(4), 295–321.

McAdams, D. P. (2001). The psychology of life stories. *Review of General Psychology, 5*(2), 100–122.

McAdams, D. P. (2006). *The redemptive self: Stories Americans live by.* New York: Oxford University Press.

McAdams, D. P. (2008). Foreword. In H. A. Murray (reissue of 1938), *Explorations in personality: 70th anniversary edition* (pp. vii–xxxvi). New York: Oxford University Press.

McAdams, D. P. (2011). *George W. Bush and the redemptive dream: A psychological portrait.* New York: Oxford University Press.

McAdams, D. P. (2014). The Life narrative at midlife. In B. Schiff (Ed.), Special issue: Rereading personal narrative and life course. *New Directions for Child and Adolescent Development, 2014*(145), 57–69. doi:10.1002/cad.20067

McAdams, D. P., Anyidoho, N. A., Brown, C., Huang, Y. T., Kaplan, B., & Machado, M. A. (2004). Traits and stories: Links between dispositional and narrative features of personality. *Journal of Personality, 72*(4), 761–784.

McAdams, D. P., Reynolds, J., Lewis, M., Pattern, A. H., & Bowman, P. J. (2001). When bad things turn good and good things turn bad: Sequences of redemption and contamination in life narrative and their relation to psychosocial adaptation in midlife adults and in students. *Personality and Social Psychology Bulletin*, 27(4), 474–485.

McCrae, R. R., & Costa, P. T., Jr. (2008). The five-factor theory of personality. In O. P. John, R. W. Robins, & L. A. Pervin (Eds.), *Handbook of personality: Theory and research* (3rd ed., pp. 159–181). New York: Guilford Press.

McLean, K. C., & Breen, A. V. (2009). Process and content of narrative identity development in adolescence: Gender and well-being. *Developmental Psychology*, 45(3), 702–710.

Medved, M. I. (2007). Remembering without a past: Individuals with anterograde memory impairment talk about their lives. *Psychology, Health & Medicine*, 12(5), 603–616. doi:10.1080/13548500601164404

Meehl, P. E. (1985). What social scientists don't understand. In D. W. Fiske & R. A. Shweder (Eds.), *Metatheory in social science: Pluralisms and subjectivities* (pp. 315–338). Chicago: University of Chicago Press.

Meretoja, H. (2014a). *The narrative turn in fiction and theory: The crisis and return of storytelling from Robbe-Grillet to Tournier*. New York: Palgrave Macmillan.

Meretoja, H. (2014b). Narrative and human existence: Ontology, epistemology, and ethics. *New Literary History*, 45(1), 89–109.

Miller, P. J., Chen, E. C.-H., & Olivarez, M. (2014). Narrative making and remaking in the early years: Prelude to the personal narrative. In B. Schiff (Ed.), Special issue: Rereading personal narrative and life course. *New Directions for Child and Adolescent Development*, 2014(145), 15–27. doi:10.1002/cad.20064

Miller, P. J., Fung, H., & Koven, M. (2007). Narrative reverberations: *How* participation *in* narrative practices co-creates persons *and* cultures. In S. Kitayama & D. Cohen (Eds.), *Handbook* of *cultural psychology* (pp. 595–614). New York: Guilford Press.

Miller, P. J., Fung, H., & Mintz, J. (1996). Self-construction through narrative practices: A Chinese and American comparison of early socialization. *Ethos*, 24(2), 237–280.

Mishler, E. G. (1986). *Research interviewing: Context and narrative*. Cambridge, MA: Harvard University Press.

Mishler, E. G. (1990). Validation in inquiry-guided research: The role of exemplars in narrative studies. *Harvard Educational Review*, 60(4), 415–442.

Mishler, E. G. (1996). Missing persons: Recovering developmental stories/histories. In R. Jessor, A. Colby, & R. A. Shweder (Eds.), *Ethnography and human development: Context and meaning in social inquiry* (pp. 73–99). Chicago: University of Chicago Press.

Mishler, E. G. (1999). *Storylines: Craftartists' narratives of identity*. Cambridge, MA: Harvard University Press.

Mishler, E. G. (2006). Narrative and identity: The double arrow of time. In A. De Fina, D. Schiffrin, & M. Bamberg (Ed.), *Discourse and identity* (p. 30–47). Cambridge: Cambridge University Press.

Mitchell, W. T. J. (Ed.). (1981). *On narrative*. Chicago: University of Chicago Press.

Murray, H. A. (1943). *Thematic apperception test*. Cambridge, MA: Harvard University Press.

Nagel, T. (1986). *The view from nowhere*. New York: Oxford University Press.

Nelson, H. L. (2014). *Holding and letting go: The social practice of personal identities.* Oxford: Oxford University Press.

Nelson, K. (Ed.). (1989). *Narratives from the crib.* Cambridge, MA: Harvard University Press.

Neugarten, B. L. (1979/1996). Time, age and the life cycle. In D. A. Neugarten (Ed.), *The meanings of age: Selected papers of Bernice L. Neugarten* (pp. 114–127). Chicago: University of Chicago Press.

Nicolopoulou, A., & Richner, E. S. (2007). From actors to agents to persons: The development of character representation in young children's narratives. *Child Development, 78*(2), 412–429.

Nisbett, R. E., & Wilson, T. D. (1977). Telling more than we can know: Verbal reports on mental processes. *Psychological Review, 84*(3), 231–259.

Norem, J. (2001). *The positive power of negative thinking.* New York: Basic Books.

Norrick, N. R. (1998). Retelling stories in spontaneous conversation. *Discourse Processes, 25*(1), 75–97.

Norrick, N. R. (2007). Conversational storytelling. In D. Herman (Ed.), *The Cambridge companion to narrative* (pp. 127–141). New York: Cambridge University Press.

Nosek, B. A., Alter, G., Banks, G. C., Borsboom, D., Bowman, S. D., Breckler, S. J., . . . Yarkoni, T. (2015). Promoting an open research culture. *Science, 348*(6242), 1422–1425. http://doi.org/10.1126/science.aab2374

Novick, P. (1999). *The Holocaust in American life.* New York: Houghton Mifflin.

Noy, C. (2002). "You must go trek there": The persuasive genre of narration among Israeli backpackers. *Narrative Inquiry, 12*(2), 261–290.

Ochs, E., & Capps, L. (2001). *Living narrative: Creating lives in everyday storytelling.* Cambridge, MA: Harvard University Press.

Open Science Collaboration. (2015). Estimating the reproducibility of psychological science. *Science, 349*(6251), aac4716–aac4716. http://doi.org/10.1126/science.aac4716

Orne, M. T. (1962). On the social psychology of the psychological experiment: With particular reference to demand characteristics and their implications. *American Psychologist, 17*(11), 776–783. doi:10.1037/h0043424

Palmer, R. E. (1969). *Hermeneutics: Interpretation theory in Schleiermacher, Dilthey, Heidegger, and Gadamer.* Evanston, IL: Northwestern University Press.

Pasupathi, M., & Wainryb, C. (2010). On telling the whole story: Facts and interpretations in autobiographical memory narratives from childhood through midadolescence. *Developmental Psychology, 46*(3), 735–746.

Pennebaker, J. W., & Seagal, J. D. (1999). Forming a story: The health benefits of narrative. *Journal of Clinical Psychology, 55*(10), 1243–1254.

Pettigrew, T. F., & Tropp, L. R. (2006). A meta-analytic test of intergroup contact theory. *Journal of Personality and Social Psychology, 90*(5), 751–783.

Pettigrew, T. F., & Tropp, L. R. (2008). How does intergroup contact reduce prejudice? Meta-analytical tests of three mediators. *European Journal of Social Psychology, 38*, 922–934.

Phelan, J., & Rabinowitz, P. J. (2012). Narrative as rhetoric. In D. Herman, J. Phelan, P. J. Rabinowitz, B. Richardson, & R. Warhol (Eds.), *Narrative theory core concepts and critical debates* (pp. 3–8). Columbus: Ohio State University Press.

Phoenix, A. (2013). Analyzing narrative contexts. In M. Andrews, C. Squire, & M. Tamboukou (Eds.), *Doing narrative research* (2nd ed., pp. 72–87). Thousand Oaks, CA: Sage.

Phoenix, C. (2011). Young bodies, old bodies, and stories of the athletic self. In
    G. Kenyon, E. Bohlmeijer, & W. L. Randall (Eds.), *Storying later life: Issues,
    investigations, and interventions in narrative gerotontology* (pp. 111–125).
    New York: Oxford University Press.
Piaget, J. (1952). *The origins of intelligence in children*. M. Cook (trans.).
    New York: International Universities Press.
Pinker, S. (2002). *The blank slate: The modern denial of human nature*. New York: Viking.
Polkinghorne, D. (1983). *Methodology for the human sciences: Systems of inquiry*.
    Albany: State University of New York Press.
Polkinghorne, D. E. (1988). *Narrative knowing and the human sciences* Albany: State
    University of New York Press.
Prince, G. (2008). Narrativehood, narrativeness, narrativity, narratability. In J. Pier
    and J. A. Garcia-Landa (Eds.), *Theorizing narrativity* (pp. 19–27). Berlin: Walter
    de Gruyter.
Prince, G. (2012). Récit minimal et narrativité. In S. Bedrane, F. Revaz, & M. Viegnes
    (Eds.), *Le récit minimal* (pp. 23–32). Paris: Presses Universitaires de la Sorbonne
    Nouvelle.
Propp, V. (1928/1968). *Morphology of the folktale* (2nd ed.). Austin: University of
    Texas Press.
Ramírez-Esparza, N., & Pennebaker, J. W. (2006). Do good stories produce good
    health? Exploring words, language, and culture. *Narrative Inquiry*, *16*(1),
    211–219.
Reese, E., & Fivush, R. (1993). Parental styles of talking about the past. *Developmental
    Psychology*, *29*, 596–606.
Ricoeur, P. (1970). *Freud and philosophy: An essay on interpretation*. (D. Savage, Trans.).
    New Haven, CT: Yale University Press.
Ricoeur, P. (1980). Narrative time. *Critical Inquiry*, *7*(1), 169–190.
Ricoeur, P. (1981). *Hermeneutics and the human sciences*. (J. B. Thompson, Ed. & Trans.)
    Cambridge: Cambridge University Press.
Ricoeur, P. (1984). *Time and narrative*, Vol. 1. (K. McLaughlin & D. Pellauer, Trans.).
    Chicago: University of Chicago Press.
Riessman, C. K. (2008). *Narrative methods for the human sciences*. Thousand Oaks,
    CA: Sage.
Riessman, C. K. (2015). Entering the hall of mirrors: Reflexivity and narrative
    research. In A. De Fina, & A. Georgakopoulou (Eds.), *The handbook of narrative
    analysis* (pp. 219–238). Chichester, West Sussex, UK: John Wiley & Sons.
Roberts, B. W., & Mroczek, D. (2008). Personality trait change in adulthood. *Current
    Directions in Psychological Science*, *17*(1), 31–35.
Rosenthal, R. (1976). *Experimenter effects in behavioral research*. New York: Irvington.
Rosenwald, G. C. (1988). A theory of multiple-case research. *Journal of Personality*,
    56(1), 239–264. doi:10.1111/j.1467-6494.1988.tb00468.x
Rosenwald, G. C., & Ochberg, R. L. (Eds.) (1992). *Storied lives: The cultural politics of
    self-understanding*. New Haven, CT: Yale University Press.
Rouhana, N. (1997). *Palestinian citizens in an ethnic Jewish state: Identities in conflict*.
    New Haven, CT: Yale University Press.
Rudrum, D. (2005). From narrative representation to narrative use: Towards the
    limits of dentition. *Narrative*, *13*(2), 195–204.
Runyan, W. M. (1982). *Life histories and psychobiography: Explorations in theory and
    method*. New York: Oxford University Press.

Runyan, W. M. (2005). Evolving conceptions of psychobiography and the study of lives: Encounters with psychoanalysis, personality psychology, and historical science. In T. Schultz (Ed.), *Handbook of psychobiography* (pp. 19–41). New York: Oxford University Press.

Ryan, M.-L. (2005). Narrative. In D. Herman, M. Jahn, & M.-L. Ryan (Eds.), *Routledge encyclopedia of narrative theory* (pp. 344–348). New York: Routledge.

Ryan, M.-L. (2007). Toward a definition of narrative. In D. Herman (Ed.), *The Cambridge companion to narrative* (pp. 22–35). Cambridge: Cambridge University Press.

Rychlak, J. F. (1993). A suggested principle of complementarity for psychology: In theory, not method. *American Psychologist, 48*(9), 933–942. doi:10.1037/0003-066X.48.9.933

Sacks, H., Schegloff, E. A., & Jefferson, G. (1974) A simplest systematics for the organization of turn-taking for conversation. *Language, 50*(4), 696–735.

Sahlins, M. D. (1985). *Islands of history*. Chicago: University of Chicago Press.

Sarbin, T. R. (1986). The narrative as a root metaphor for psychology. In T. R. Sarbin (Ed.), *Narrative psychology: The storied nature of human conduct* (pp. 3–21). New York: Praeger.

Sarbin, T. R. (1998). Believed-in imaginings: A narrative approach. In J. de Rivera & T. R. Sarbin (Eds.), *Believed-in imaginings: The narrative construction of reality* (pp. 15–30). Washington, DC: American Psychological Association Press.

Schacter, D. L. (2001). *The seven sins of memory: How the mind forgets and remembers*. Boston: Houghton Mifflin.

Schafer, R. (1980). Narration in the psychoanalytic dialogue. *Critical Inquiry, 7*(1), 29–53.

Schafer, R. (1992). *Retelling a life: Narration and dialogue in psychoanalysis*. New York: Basic Books.

Schiff, B. N. (1998). *Telling survival and the Holocaust*. Dissertation. Dissertation Abstracts International: Section B: The Sciences and Engineering, Vol. 58(10-B), Apr. 1998, 5667.

Schiff, B. (2002). Talking about identity: Arab students at the Hebrew University of Jerusalem. *Ethos, 30*(3), 273–303. doi:10.1525/eth.2002.30.3.273

Schiff, B. (2006). The promise (and challenge) of an innovative narrative psychology. *Narrative Inquiry, 16*(1), 19–27.

Schiff, B. (2012). The function of narrative: Toward a narrative psychology of meaning. *Narrative Works: Issues, Investigations & Interventions, 2*(1), 34–47.

Schiff, B. (2014). Introduction: Development's story in time and place. In B. Schiff (Ed.), Special issue: Rereading personal narrative and life course. *New Directions for Child and Adolescent Development, 2014*(145), 1–13. doi:10.1002/cad.20063

Schiff, B., & Cohler, B. (2001). Telling survival backward: Holocaust survivors narrate the past. In G. M. Kenyon, P. G. Clark, & B. de Vries (Eds.), *Narrative gerontology: Theory, research and practice* (pp. 113–136). New York: Springer.

Schiff, B., & Noy, C. (2006). Making it personal: Shared meanings in the narratives of Holocaust survivors. In A. De Fina, D. Schiffrin, & M. Bamberg (Eds.), *Discourse and identity* (pp. 398–425). New York: Cambridge University Press.

Schiff, B., & O'Neill, T. (2007). The relational emplotment of mixed race identity. In R. Josselson, A. Lieblich, & D. P. McAdams (Eds.), *The narrative study of lives: The meaning of others* (pp. 143–163). Washington, DC: American Psychological Association.

Schiff, B., Skillingstead, H., Archibald, O., Arasim, A., & Peterson, J. (2006). Consistency and change in the repeated narratives of Holocaust survivors. *Narrative Inquiry, 16*(2), 349–377.

Schiff, B., Toulemonde, M., & Porto, C. (2012). Identity in the first person plural: Muslim-Jewish couples in France. In R. Josselson & M. Haraway (Eds.), *Navigating multiple identities: Race, gender, culture, nationality, and roles* (pp. 167–186). New York: Oxford University Press.

Schindler's list. (1993) [Motion picture]. Universal Pictures/Globus United.

Schleiermacher, F. D. E. (1986). *Hermeneutics: The handwritten manuscripts* (H. Kimmerle, Ed.; J. Duke & J. Forstman, Trans.). (originally written 1805–1833). Atlanta: Scholars Press.

Schultz, W. T. (2005). Introducing psychobiography. In W. T. Schultz (Ed.), *Handbook of psychobiography* (pp. 3–18). New York: Oxford University Press.

Schutz, A., & Luckmann, T. (1973). *The structures of the life-world* (R. M. Zaner & H. T. Engelhardt, Jr., Trans.). Evanston, IL: Northwestern University Press.

Searle, J. R. (1995). *The construction of social reality.* New York: The Free Press.

Shweder, R. (2001). A polytheistic conception of the sciences and the virtues of deep variety. In A. Damasio et al. (Eds.), *Unity of knowledge: The convergence of natural and human science* (pp. 217–232). New York: New York Academy of Sciences.

Shweder, R. (2003). *Why do men barbecue? Recipes for cultural psychology.* Cambridge, MA: Harvard University Press.

Shotter, J. (1993). *Conversational realities: Constructing life through language.* London and Thousand Oaks, CA: Sage.

Singer, J. A. (2001). Living in the amber cloud: A life story analysis of a heroin addict. In D. P. McAdams, R. Josselson, & A. Lieblich (Eds.), *Turns in the road: Narrative studies of lives in transition* (pp. 253–277). Washington, DC: American Psychological Association.

Singer, J. A. (2004). Narrative identity and meaning making across the adult lifespan: An introduction. *Journal of Personality, 72*(3), 437–459.

Slife, B. (2005). Testing the limits of Henriques' proposal: Wittgensteinian lessons and hermeneutic dialogue. *Journal of Clinical Psychology, 61*(1), 107–120. doi:10.1002/jclp.20093

Slife, B. D., & Williams, R. N. (1995). *What's behind the research? Discovering hidden assumptions in the behavioral sciences.* Thousand Oaks, CA: Sage.

Smith, B., & Sparkes, A. (2008a). Contrasting perspectives on narrating selves and identities: An invitation to dialogue. *Qualitative Research, 8*(1) 5–35.

Smith, B., & Sparkes, A. C. (2008b). Changing bodies, changing narratives and the consequences of tellability: A case study of becoming disabled through sport. *Sociology of Health & Illness, 30*(2), 217–236. doi:10.1111/j.1467-9566.2007.01033.x

Smooha, S. (1999). The advances and limits of the Israelization of Israel's Palestinian citizens. In K. Abdel-Malek and D. C. Jacobson (Eds.), *Israeli and Palestinian identities in history and literature* (pp. 9–33). New York: St. Martin's Press.

Smooha, S. (2005). *Index of Arab-Jewish Relations in Israel 2004.* Haifa: The Jewish-Arab Center, University of Haifa.

Spence, D. P. (1982). *Narrative truth and historical truth: Meaning and interpretation in psychoanalysis.* New York: Norton.

Squire, C., Andrews, M., & Tamboukou, M. (2013). Introduction: What is narrative research? In M. Andrews, C. Squire, & M. Tamboukou (Eds.), *Doing narrative research* (2nd ed., pp. 1–26). Thousand Oaks, CA: Sage.

Staats, A. W. (2004). The disunity-unity dimension. *American Psychologist, 59*(4), 273.

Staats, A. W. (2005). A road to, and philosophy of, unification. In R. J. Sternberg (Ed.), *Unity in psychology: Possibility or pipedream?* (pp. 159–177). Washington, DC: American Psychological Association.

Stam, H. J. (2004). Unifying psychology: Epistemological act or disciplinary maneuver? *Journal of Clinical Psychology, 60*(12), 1259–1262. doi:10.1002/jclp.20069

Stanley, L. (2010). To the letter: Thomas and Znaniecki's *The Polish Peasant* and writing a life, sociologically. *Life Writing, 7*(2), 139–151. doi:10.1080/14484520903445271

Steinberg, S., & Bar-On, D. (2002). An analysis of the group process in encounters between Jews and Palestinians using a typology for discourse classification. *International Journal of Intercultural Relations, 26*(2), 199–214.

Sternberg, M. (1992). Telling in time (II): Chronology, teleology, narrativity. *Poetics Today, 13*(3) 463–541.

Sternberg, R. J. (Ed.). (2005). *Unity in psychology: Possibility or pipedream?* Washington, DC: American Psychological Association.

Sternberg, R. J., & Grigorenko, E. L. (2001). Unified psychology. *American Psychologist, 56*(12), 1069–1079

Sugarman, J. H., & Martin, J. (2005). Toward an alternative psychology. In B. Slife, J. Reber, & F. Richardson (Eds.), *Developing critical thinking in psychology* (pp. 251–266). Washington, DC: APA Books.

Taylor, C. (1985). *Human agency and language: Philosophical papers 1.* New York: Cambridge University Press.

Taylor, C. (1971). Interpretation and the Sciences of Man. *The Review of Metaphysics, 25*(1), 3–51.

Teddlie, C., & Tashakkori, A (2010). Overview of contemporary issues in mixed methods research. In A. Tashakkori & C. Teddlie (Eds.), *SAGE handbook of mixed methods in social and behavioral research* (2nd ed., pp. 1–41). Thousand Oaks, CA: Sage.

Terdiman, R. (1993). *Present past: Modernity and the memory crisis.* Ithaca, NY: Cornell University Press.

Toulmin, S. (1958/2008). *The uses of argument* (updated ed.). New York: Cambridge University Press.

Toulmin, S. (1982). The construal of reality: Criticism in modern and postmodern science. *Critical Inquiry, 9*(1) 93–111.

Toulmin, S. (1992). *Cosmopolis: The hidden agenda of modernity.* Chicago: University of Chicago Press.

Toulmin, S. (2001). *Return to reason.* Cambridge, MA: Harvard University Press.

Trabasso, T., & Wiley, J. (2005). Goal plans of action and inferences during comprehension of narratives. *Discourse Processes, 39*(2–3), 129–164.

von Wright, G. H. (1971). *Explanation and understanding.* Ithaca, NY: Cornell University Press.

Vygotsky, L. S. (1978). *Mind in society: The development of higher psychological processes.* Cambridge, MA: Harvard University Press.

Wang, L. L., Watts, A. S., Anderson, R. A., & Little, T. D. (2013). Common fallacies in quantitative research methodology. In T. D. Little (Ed.), *The Oxford handbook of quantitative methods* (Vol. 2): *Statistical analysis* (pp. 718–758). New York: Oxford University Press.

Webster, J. D. (1993). Construction and validation of the reminiscence functions
scale. *Journal of Gerontology, 48*(5), 256–262. doi:10.1093/geronj/48.5.P256
Weisel, E. (1960/1982). *Night*. New York: Bantam.
Wertsch, J. V. (1991). *Voices of the mind: A sociocultural approach to mediated action*.
Cambridge, MA: Harvard University Press.
Wertsch, J. V. (2002). *Voices of collective remembering*. New York: Cambridge
University Press.
White, M., & Epston, D. (1990). *Narrative means to therapeutic ends*. New York: W.
W. Norton.
White, R. W. (1952/1966). *Lives in progress* (2nd ed.). New York: Holt, Rinehart &
Winston.
Wieviorka, A. (1989). *Le procès Eichmann*. Bruxelles: Editions complexe.
Wiley, A. R., Rose, A. J., Burger, L. K., & Miller, P. J. (1998). Constructing autonomous
selves through narrative practices: A comparative study of working-class and
middle-class families. *Child Development, 69*(3), 833–847.
Wilson, E. O. (1998). *Consilience: The unity of knowledge*. New York: Random House.
Wink, P., & Schiff, B. (2002). To review or not to review? The role of personality and
life events in life review and adaptation to old age. In J. D. Webster & B. K.
Haight (Eds.), *Critical advances in reminiscence: From theory to application* (pp.
44–60). New York: Springer-Verlag.
Winter, D. G. (1998). "Toward a science of personality psychology": David
McClelland's development of empirically derived TAT measures. *History of
Psychology, 1*(2), 130–153.
Wittgenstein, L. (1953/1958). *Philosophical investigations* (3rd ed.) (G. E. M.
Anscombe, Trans.). New York: Macmillan.
Wortham, S. (2000). Interactional positioning and narrative self-construction.
Narrative Inquiry, 10(1), 157–184.
Yanchar, S. C., Gantt, E. E., & Clay, S. L. (2005). On the nature of a critical
methodology. *Theory & Psychology, 15*(1), 27–50. doi:10.1177/
0959354305049743
Yanchar, S. C., & Slife, B. D. (1997). Pursuing unity in a fragmented
psychology: Problems and prospects. *Review of General Psychology, 1*(3),
235–255.
Young, K. G. (1986). *Taleworlds and storyrealms: The phenomenology of narrative*
Dordrecht: Martinus Nijhoff.
Young, K. (2004). Frame and boundary in the phenomenology of narrative. In M.-L.
Ryan (Ed.), *Narrative across media: The languages of storytelling* (pp. 76–107).
Lincoln: University of Nebraska Press.
Zerubavel, E. (2004). *Time maps: Collective memory and the social shape of the past*.
Chicago: University of Chicago Press.

INDEX

autobiographical reasoning, 56–57
Awlad Ali Bedouins of Egypt, 75

Bakhtin, M. M., 89–91, 105–106
Bamberg, Michael, 54
    Lieblich's research similarities to,
        185–191
    masculine identity formation research,
        177, 185–191
    Narrative Inquiry (ed.), 54
    "small stories" of, 73, 178
Bar-On, D., 33–34, 37
behavioral investment theory (BIT), 224
behaviorism
    experimental tradition in, 9–10
    skepticism in, 30
    Skinnerian (mind from life), 224–225
    synthetic psychology and, 222
"being a narrative" *vs.* "possessing
    narrativity," 78–79
Being and Time (Heidegger), 14–15
Bekerman, Z., 35, 36, 37
"Believed-in Imaginings: A Narrative
    Approach" (Sarbin), 107
Ben, Holocaust survivor (interview),
    159–176
    background information, 87, 159–160
    being protective narrative, 168–169
    being religious narrative, 169
    contradictory interpretations, 166
    cultural context, 173
    evaluations, 161–165
    guiding research questions, 159–160
    insights of, 168, 175–176
    interpretation of survival by, 161–163,
        165–166, 174
    interpretation of the Holocaust by,
        165–166
    interview structure, 171
    making present and, 87–88
    meeting Keneally narrative, 167–168
    object of interview, 160–166
    prison camp years, 87
    reflections, 161, 165, 171, 174
    self-portrayal by, 167–170,
        172–173
    serial storytelling narratives, 163–166
    survival narratives, 161–163
    Survivors or the Shoah
        participation, 171

bias
    Gadamer's solution to, 134–135
    in interpretation, 46, 134
    retrospective bias, 204
Big Five personality traits, 17, 58
"Big Q" questions (Josselson), 148, 159
Block, J., 18
Blumer, H., 46
Breen, A. V., 60
Brockmeier, J.
    advocacy for "narrative
        hermeneutics," 76–77
    on narrative for capturing complex
        human action, 94
    on *poíēsis*, 74
    on synthesis of psychology, 230
    "twofold movement" of narrative
        hermeneutics, 77
    on well-elaborated narrative, 79
Bruner, Jerome
    Acts of Meaning, 53–54
    Actual Minds, Possible Worlds, 53
    on autobiographical narratives, 68
    call to study narratives by, 56
    "Life as Narrative" (essay), 66
Butler, R. N., 173

California Q-sort, 17
Campbell, D.T., 219
Cantor, N., 58
Carlson, R., 9
Caspi, A., 17
Chase, S. E., 148, 149
chronicle, as narrating, 75
chronotope, 89–91, 105–106
Clay, S. L., 197–198
Clement and Marine, couple story,
    111–119, 127–128
cognitive approaches to narrative,
    56–57
cognitive personality psychology, 14
cognitive psychology, 107
cognitive revolution (late 20th
    century), 50, 53
cognitive-personality approaches to
    narrative, 59–60
Cohler, B. J., 50–51, 52, 144
Collardeau, Fanie, 111,
    113–114, 116
collective identity, 35, 84, 110–111

correspondence theory of, 107
definition, 91
failures of, 107
imagination *vs.*, 106–107
Meretoja, H.
on narrative as *poíēsis*, 74
on narrative hermeneutics, 76, 142, 144, 193
methodological eclecticism, 219–220
methods (narrative methods). *See also* qualitative methods; quantitative methods; variable-centered approach
of analysis, 51, 64
analytical strategies of, 138–141
correlational, 24
diversity of, 138–139
experimental, 4, 24–25, 30
as "flexible set of research techniques," 197–198
Gadamer's wariness of, 135
of interpretation, 47
narrative as, 48–49, 135–138
person-centered, 19
prejudice in use of, 5–6
reductive methods, 50, 66
rethinking method and theory, 38–40
statistical, 26–27, 30
theory and, 38–40
as unifying factor in psychology, 5
whole-life method of analysis, 203
Miller, P. J., 80
Mills College, ego-resiliency study, 27–28
Millsap, R., 17
mimesis, Ricoeur's analysis of, 82–84, 96, 127–128
minimal narratives, 78, 187
Mishler, E. G.
critique of qualitative research examples, 200–201
Research Interviewing: Context and Narrative, 51
on validation of research arguments, 200
Morgan, Christiana, 47
movement in understanding, 141–147
Mroczek, D., 17
multi-trait, multi-method model (Campell and Fiske), 219–220
Munch, Edvard, 77–78, 80

Murray, Henry, 10, 45–47, 57
Muslim identity, in Steve and Salima narrative, 120, 125–126
muthos, 83

Nagel, T., 133
narrating
as an interpretive act, 95–97
contextuality of, 82
forms of, 75–76
as imagining, 107–108
innovation and, 106
as making present, 84–85
narrating functions, 71–98
Brockmeier/Meretoja on, 74
creating meaning, 79–81, 84–85, 102
creating narratives in families, 80–81
creating reverberations, 102
description, 74–75
forms of, 74–75
fusion in time and space, 89–90
giving form to divisions, disagreements, 93
interpretive actions, 76–82
life functions/life experiences, 65–69, 74–77, 82, 86, 91, 93–97
making it so function of, 102, 103
making present, 84–89, 94, 96–97, 103, 105
personal and social identity, 55–56
structure and, 93–95
text and context, 82–84
narrative
Bamberg's approach to study of, 185–191
"being a narrative" *vs.* "possesssing narrativity," 78–79
big stories, 37, 178–179, 189–190
Brockmeier on, 79, 94
Bruner on, 53–54
challenges in interpreting, 131–158
in the chronotope, 106
description, 101
dialogic perspective, 55–56
factors favoring, 39–40
filmic narratives, 79
folklore and, 71
Freeman on proper functions of, 90
as "historical act" (Sarbin), 52–53
historical conflictual (Israel), 35–36

quantitative methods. *See also* variable-
centered approach
Abbott on distinction with qualitative
methods, 64
commonalities with qualitative
methods, 199
feature of variables in, 10
fractal quantitative-narrative
methods, 65
hermeneutics and, 194
idiographic psychology and, 45
interpretation and, 4, 198
mixed-method parallel with, 220
narrative perspective and, 218
in Palestinian youth identity
studies, 210
qualitative methods used in, 219
qualitative *vs.* (Abbott), 64
research arguments in, 210
role in research arguments, 210
statistical analysis and, 97
subjectivity/objectivity and,
132–133
triangulation in, 219
quantitative psychology, 133
quantitative sociology, 64
quantitative-narrative research, 137
questions
arguing interpretations and, 194
"Big Q," 148, 159
"pocket questions" (Lieblich), 159–160
in research arguments, 194, 197–203
"what" and "how," 149–151
"where" or "when," 151
"who," 152
"who-when," 154–156
"who-where," 153–154
"why," 156–157

Rabinowitz, P. J., 71
Radcliff College, ego-resiliency
study, 27–28
Randall, W., 66
rank order stability, 17
reality
"brute facts" of, 38
co-telling and, 93
making present and, 88
nature of, 101–102, 232
social constructionism and, 37, 102

"touchstone of reality" (Allport), 46
Toulmin on, 132
reasoned interpretations, 193–215
Reese, E., 57
reflection, as narrating, 75
reminiscing, functions of, 84–85
research arguments. *See* arguments,
research-related
*Research Interviewing: Context and
Narrative* (Mishler), 51
researcher subjectivity, 132–133, 145,
190, 215
resonating (resonance)
as chronotopic, 109
in couple stories, 110–127
description, 105
imaginings and, 109
personal resonance, 119
social resonance, 111, 119
Return to Reason (Toulmin), 195
"rhetoric of chosenness" (McAdams), 173
Ricoeur, P., 51, 74
on act of recollection, 91
"hermeneutics of self-doubt," 160
"hermeneutics of suspicion," 160
on interpretation theory, 142
"making present" and, 85
three-fold mimesis of, 82–84, 96,
127–128
Riessman, C. K., 201
Roberts, B. W., 17
Robins, R. W., 18
Rosenwald, G. C., 66
Runyan, W. M., 20, 44, 146–147
rupture (crisis) experience, 50, 99–100
Ryan, M.-L., 72
Rychlak, J. F., 224–225, 227

Samuel and Leah (artists), Freeman's
interviews with, 61, 137
Sarbin, T. R., 52–53, 75, 107, 109
scene of talk, 92, 184, 185
Schafer, R., 52
Schiff, Brian (book's author), identity
stories of Palestinian students,
202–211
Schindler's Ark (Keneally), 167
Schindler's List (film), 87, 167
Schleiermacher, Frederick, 99, 105, 142
Schmiedek, F., 57

TAT. *See* Thematic Apperception Test
tattooing mastectomy scars, as
    narrating, 75
Taylor, C., 142
Teddlie, C., 220
tellings
    arguments made by, 85
    co-telling, 93
    couple's stories, 111–127
    inside other tellings, 103
    interpretive acts in, 118–119
    of life, narrative as, 59, 67–68, 71
    and making present, 85–89
    Phelan/Rabinowitz on, 71
    retelling/reimagining of, 116
    shaping of mental life by, 48–49
    situatedness of, 62
    in social, cultural contexts, 65
    varied mediums of, 103
    Young on where telling happens, 90
temporal aspect of making present, 85
Thematic Apperception Test (TAT), 47
Thorndike maneuver, 25
thought process, 30, 56, 152
Tolman, Charles, 9
Toulmin, S., 49, 132, 160, 194, 195
trait psychology, 58
traits
    Big Five, 17, 58
    connection to life story themes, 59
    McAdams on, 58
    in multi-trait, multi-method
        model, 219
    NEO traits, 17
    psychological phenomena and, 14
Tree of Knowledge (ToK) system
    (Henriques), 224
triangulation, 219
Tropp, L. R., 31
Tuval-Mashiach, R., 54, 138, 150

understanding
    bias/prejudice in, 134
    description of process of, 143
    Gadamer's solution to bias in, 134–135
    hermeneutic engagement in, 143–144
    movement aspect of, 141–147
    subjectivity of, 133–134
unity in psychology, 217–236
    argument in favor of, 6

dialogue's role in achieving, 226–227
    fragmentation *vs.*, 222–223, 226
    growing interest in, 5
    growth of literature on, 222
    Henriques support for, 224–225, 226
    imagining of methods in achieving,
        231–236
    implications of, 223–224
    issues in synthesis of perspectives,
        221–231
    Rychlak's support for, 224–225, 226
    Shweder's questioning of, 227
    Slife's questioning of, 226
    Staat's concerns, 225–226
    Stam's questioning of, 227
    Sternberg's support for, 226
    theoretical *vs.* methodological, 10
    Wilson's support for, 223–224
usefulness concern, in research
    arguments, 201–202, 212

validation concern, in research
    arguments, 200–201, 212
van Gogh, Vincent, 146
Vandewater, E. A., 27
variable-centered approach
    behaviorism and, 9
    description, 15, 18, 22, 39
    division with linguistic, whole life,
        thematic-content approaches, 65
    interpretation, meaning making,
        and, 135
    life experience inferences made
        in, 29–30
    limitations/weaknesses of, 5–7, 12–14,
        16, 37–40
    Mishler on, 21
    narrative psychology *vs.*, 39
    narrative research contribution to, 66
    personality psychology and, 30
    reductive analysis and, 137
    strengths of, 12, 38
variables
    contact and prejudice, 31–33
    co-occurrences of, in life, 32–33
    correlation between, 23–27
    defined/construction of, 10–11
    experimental, 24–25
    functioning of, 9
    measurement of, 10–11